Exploring C

How should we understand children's creativity?

This fascinating collection of international research offers fresh perspectives on children's creative processes and the expression of their creative imagination through dramatic play, stories, artwork, dance, music and conversation.

Drawing on a range of research evidence from innovative educational initiatives in a wide variety of countries, *Exploring Children's Creative Narratives* develops new theoretical and practical insights that challenge traditional thinking about children's creativity. The chapters, written by well-respected international contributors:

- offer new conceptual and interpretive frameworks for understanding children's creativity
- contest conventional discourses about the origins and nature of creativity
- challenge the view that young children's creativity can only be judged in terms of their creative output
- explore the significance children themselves attribute to their creative activity
- argue the need for a radical reappraisal of the influence of the sociocultural context on children's creative expression
- discuss the implications of this research in relation to teacher education and curriculum design.

This broad yet coherent compilation of research on creativity in childhood is essential reading for students, researchers and policy makers in early childhood as well as for Early Years professionals with a particular interest in creativity.

Dorothy Faulkner is a member of the Centre for Childhood, Development and Learning and Director of the Psychology undergraduate honours degree at the Open University, UK.

Elizabeth Coates is Director of the Early Childhood Studies undergraduate degree programme at the Institute of Education, University of Warwick, UK.

Cover Illustration by Andrew Coates

Based on translations of Images made by: Lucy (age 4:5) A Spotty Dog; Ellie (age 4:0) My Dad's Got Hair Like This; Alex (age 4:7) That's Me and That's My Baby Annabel; Jamie (age 4:0) Humpty Dumpty; Nicholas (age 5:9) A Cheetah and a Baby Cheetah; Caitlin (age 4:9) A Daddy Pig; Daniel (age 5:1) Three Clouds.

Exploring Children's Creative Narratives

Edited by Dorothy Faulkner and
Elizabeth Coates

Routledge
Taylor & Francis Group

LONDON AND NEW YORK

This first edition published 2011
by Routledge
2 Park Square, Milton Park, Abingdon, Oxon OX14 4RN

Simultaneously published in the USA and Canada
by Routledge
711 Third Avenue, New York, NY 10017

Routledge is an imprint of the Taylor & Francis Group, an informa
business

Typeset in Baskerville by
Saxon Graphics Ltd, Derby
Printed and bound in Great Britain by
TJ International Ltd, Padstow, Cornwall

British Library Cataloguing in Publication Data
A catalogue record for this book is available from the British Library

Library of Congress Cataloging-in-Publication Data
Exploring children's creative narratives / edited by Dorothy Faulkner
and Elizabeth Coates. -- 1st ed.
p. cm.
1. Creative ability in children. 2. Drawing ability in children. I.
Faulkner, Dorothy. II. Coates, Elizabeth.
BF723.C7.E97 2011
155.4'1335--dc22
2010042312

ISBN13: 978-0-415-56562-2 (hbk)
ISBN13: 978-0-415-56563-9 (pbk)
ISBN13: 978-0-203-81892-3 (ebk)

This book is dedicated to Jan Neavill Hersh, a gifted and talented music educator, and to all the children we have worked with over the years.

Contents

Figures, tables and plates

Figures

Tables

Plates

The plate section is located between pages 100 and 101 of the text.

Contributors

Kerry Chappell is a part-time research fellow in the University of Exeter Graduate School of Education. Her research focuses on investigating how we conceive of and work for creativity (specifically within dance education but also generically) and developing this within a meaningful conception of educational futures. At present this is centred on the AHRC-funded Dance Partners for Creativity Project (www.education. exeter.ac.uk/dpc). This project investigates creativity and partnership with and for dance education practitioners, but also extrapolates theorising into relevant areas of creativity and educational futures. Kerry is currently lead author on the DPC book *Close Encounters: Dance partners for creativity*, due for publication in 2011. Recently Kerry has also taken on the role of CREATE Research Group Research Fellow within the Graduate School, which involves extending her research into new areas with other colleagues. All of Kerry's research is informed by her practice as a dance artist and aikido practitioner (Ni-Dan).

Andrew Coates is a part-time lecturer at the University of Warwick, where he teaches child development in art to students reading for a BA (Hons) degree in Early Childhood Education Studies. He is a practising artist and member of the Royal Birmingham Society of Artists. He was Head of Art at Westhill College, Birmingham where he was leader of the Performing and Visual Arts course, which involved students in the study of art, dance, drama and music. He continued in this position when the college merged with the University of Birmingham. Together with Elizabeth Coates he has been involved since September 2003 in an action research project which focuses upon young children aged between three and seven years talking and drawing together. While much of the data collected has still to be analysed, this has already resulted in a number of conference papers and exhibitions. His recent one-person exhibitions include in 2008, 'A response to primitivism – particularly in relation to the drawings of young children' at the Alexandra Gallery, University of Cumbria, Lancaster Campus, and in 2007, 'Children also have artistic ability and there is wisdom in their having it (Paul Klee, 1912): an exhibition of constructions, constructed collages informed by the drawings of young children' at the Royal Birmingham Society of Artists Gallery, Birmingham, England.

Elizabeth Coates is Director of the Early Childhood Studies Undergraduate Programme at the Institute of Education, University of Warwick. Her teaching includes child development, education, and early years policy and practice. During her time at Warwick she organised and directed five triennial international early years conferences. Her background as an early years teacher has been a strong influence, and with Andrew Coates she is involved in a longitudinal action research project focusing on young children (from three to seven years) talking and drawing together. This has resulted in joint conference papers and publications, which include 'Young children talking and drawing', *International Journal of Early Years Education*, 2006, **14**(3) (with Andrew Coates) and 'A commentary on "I forgot the sky", a research project with young children', in V. Lewis, M. Kellet, C. Robinson, S. Fraser and S. Ding (eds), (2004) *The Reality of Research with Children and Young People*, Open University Press/Sage. Other recent publications are 'Trends and issues in early childhood education: an English perspective' in J. McConnell (ed.), *The Education of Young Children, Research and Public Policy* (Linton Atlantic, 2009), and a special issue, 'Creativity and cultural innovation in early years education', of the *International Journal of Early Years Education*, 2006, **14**(3) (with Dorothy Faulkner, Anna Craft and Bernadette Duffy).

Dorothy Faulkner is senior lecturer in child development in the Centre for Childhood, Development and Learning at the Open University. She is a developmental psychologist with expertise in cognitive development and the psychology of education. Her current research interests include the development of children's thinking and problem solving, the influence of peer relationships on collaborative learning, and creative teaching and learning in the early years.She has carried out a number of research projects in schools to evaluate the impact of creative professionals and creative practices on the educational and personal experiences of children and their teachers. Recently she has carried out several projects funded by Creative Partnerships and Arts Council England that have supported children and young people to undertake their own investigations of creative teaching and learning in their schools. Her publications include *Learning to Collaborate, Collaborating to Learn* (2004) (with Dorothy Miell and Karen Littleton), 'Creativity and cultural innovation in early years education', a special issue of the *International Journal of Early Years Education*, 2006, **14**(3) (with Elizabeth Coates, Anna Craft and Bernadette Duffy), and the report, *Youth Voice in the Work of Creative Partnerships*, (with Sara Bragg and Helen Manchester, 2009).

Marie Fulková, Ph.D. is an associate professor of art education at the Faculty of Education, Department of Art Education, Charles University in Prague, where she teaches and supervises Master's and doctoral students. Her research and publications explore the interdisciplinary intersections between scientific, artistic and cultural discourses as a polysemy across different social domains. She designs contemporary art programmes for galleries and museums. She is a researcher and national coordinator in the international research project of six European councils, 'Images and identity. improving citizenship education through digital Art' (Erasmus, 2008–10). She has received numerous awards and grants, and serves on several boards. Her publications include articles in international journals, chapters in books, and books on art education.

P. Mani Das Gupta is a senior lecturer in the psychology department at Staffordshire University, UK. Her current research interests centre on child development in general, with a particular focus on the development of children's reasoning, teaching and learning, and the relationships between early attachment and later cognitive and social development.

Jenny Hallam is a lecturer in psychology at the University of Derby, UK. Her research utilises qualitative, ethnographic methods to explore the educational contexts that shape children's artistic development and children's experiences of art in the classroom. She has published critical qualitative research which examines the English Primary Curriculum for art, teachers' understanding of the English Primary Curriculum for art, and how art is co-constructed between teachers and children in primary school art lessons

Marjaana Kangas is a researcher and teacher of education at University of Lapland in Rovaniemi, Finland. Her research focuses on issues of play, learning, creativity, playfulness and the use of technology in future play and learning environments. She has been involved in multidisciplinary research work for developing the pedagogical groundwork for a technology-enriched indoor–outdoor play and learning environment, Playful Learning Environment (PLE); and in developing the concept of the future school for the Finnish InnoSchool research consortium. In her doctoral dissertation, *The School of the Future: Theoretical and pedagogical approaches for creative and playful learning environments,* she introduces an approach for creative and playful learning that contributes to the current debate of the role of new technology, modes of acting, participating and creating knowledge in the twenty-first century.

Annakaisa Kultima works as a computer games researcher at the University of Tampere, Finland and is a faculty member of the Department of Information Studies and Interactive Media. Recently she has been involved in the organisation of several international conferences on game research. She served as a member of the review board for the Philosophy of Computer Games Conference in 2008, held at Potsdam, Germany (http://www.gamephilosophy.org/) and regularly presents papers at conferences and workshops. Recently she presented a paper: 'Casual game heuristics' at the GameSpace workshop VII 2008, Helsinki, Finland, and a paper entitled 'Creativity techniques in game design', at the Games Developers Conference (Mobile) 2008, San Francisco, USA. She was also a member of the organising committees for 'Breaking the Magic Circle', the annual international Game Research Lab, 2008 spring seminar, and 'Gamers in Society', the annual international Game Research Lab 2007 spring seminar, Tampere, Finland.

Helen Lee is a senior lecturer in psychology at Staffordshire University, UK. Her research is informed by arguments in critical and discursive psychology. She has published critical qualitative research including articles on knowledge construction and individualism in 'new forms' of spirituality, critical psychology and education, and more recently, participatory action research centred on reducing health risks and improving literacy and career aspirations for Cambodian women.

Heli Ruokamo is a professor of education, with a specialty in media education, at the University of Lapland in Rovaniemi, Finland. She is also a director of the Centre for Media Pedagogy in the Faculty of Education at the same university. She has published approximately eighty refereed scientific publications, more than fifty of them international.

R. Keith Sawyer is a professor of psychology and education at Washington University in St Louis, USA. His research focuses on improvisational creativity, everyday conversation, and emergence in collaborating groups. He has published widely in scholarly journals and edited volumes, and in addition is the author of nine books related to creativity and development, including *Pretend Play as Improvisation* (1997), *Creativity and Development* (2003), *Explaining Creativity* (2006), and most recently *Group Genius: The power of collaboration* (2008). Professor Sawyer can be reached via www.keithsawyer.com

Teresa M. Tipton, Ph.D. is a senior lecturer in the Department of Humanities and Social Sciences at the Anglo-American University, Prague, Czech Republic. Her research and publications include reflective practice in art education, curriculum design, and organizational development. She has travelled extensively and taught in the USA, Africa, China, and the Czech Republic. With the Department of Art Education at Charles University, Prague she served as external evaluator for a six-nation EU lifelong learning project, Images and Identity (2008–10). She worked in Seattle-area community colleges as a curriculum and assessment specialist revising vocational-technical programs for ten years. As educational consultant for King County Arts Commission's Cultural Education program, she facilitated arts-in-education projects and conducted her own residencies in the Seattle area (USA).

Sylvia M. Truman's is currently a lecturer in Information and Communications Technology at Regent's College, London. Her background is in information systems and the development of e-learning systems. She is especially interested in the design of educational technologies that facilitate creative learning in the classroom. She completed her Ph.D. in 2008 at the Open University Knowledge Media Institute (KMI). Her Ph.D. research (supervised by Paul Mulholland and Atta Badii) concerned the development of a generative framework for creative learning and a music composition program called SoundScape. She has also worked as an e-learning designer on the G-LEARN project, an electronic resource to assist with secondary education, human geography learning and teaching (http://kmi.open.ac.uk/projects/name/G-LEARN). Her current interests concern the study of comparative approaches to e-learning, in particular those that facilitate music learning and research on creativity. Recent publications include a paper in the *British Journal of Educational Technology* (2006, **37**(1), pp. 131–42), and 'G-LEARN: An exploratory learning environment for school geography level' (with M. Smid, P. Mulholland, Z. Zdrahal, and S. Crouch, 2009).

Susan Wright is a professor of education at the National Institute of Education at Nanyang Technological University in Singapore. She has undertaken numerous research projects which have focused on children's semiotic meaning-making and arts-based pedagogy and curriculum development. She has published widely in scholarly journals and is the author of five books, including *Children, Meaning-Making and the Arts* (2003) which will go to a second edition in 2011, *The Arts, Young Children and Learning* (2003) and *Understanding Creativity in Early Childhood* (2010).

Susan Young is a senior lecturer in early childhood studies and music education at the University of Exeter. She is also senior research fellow at the Centre for International Research in Learning and Creativity in Education (CIRCLE), University of Roehampton, London and senior research associate of the Centre for Research in Early Childhood, Birmingham. She combines university lecturing with a range of freelance research, evaluation and consultancy specialising in the arts, particularly music, dance and theatre, and early childhood. She spent her early career teaching music in secondary and primary schools and in a range of early years settings. She has published widely in professional and academic journals and is frequently invited to present at conferences, both nationally and internationally. She has written several books, including *Music with the Under Fours* and *Music 3–5*.

Foreword

Creativity, communication, collaboration and curriculum: a Vygotskian perspective

It really is remarkable that so little connection has been made between contemporary creativity theory and developmental theory (Sawyer et al. 2003). After all, the core insight of the constructivism of both Piaget and Vygotsky was that children participate in the creation of their own knowledge. We would argue that a good deal may be learned about the nature of children's creativity from research on child development and play. Play not only reflects the cognitive and affective processes that are important in creativity, it also supports the development of creative capability. Sandra Russ (2003) points out, however, that our understanding of the specific cognitive and/or affective abilities or dispositions involved remains unclear:

> There is a large body of studies that have found relations between play processes and creativity. Most of these studies either looked at play in a global fashion or investigated cognitive processes in play. A smaller body of studies, including my own, has found relations between affective processes in play and creativity as well.
>
> (Russ 2003: 300)

Historically, Sylva, Bruner and Jolly (1976) established that play facilitates problem solving. It has also been established that divergent thinking is central to both play and creativity. In addition several longitudinal studies have demonstrated that creativity in pretend play is predictive of divergent thinking over time (Russ, Robins and Christiano, 1999).

We would propose, therefore, that the most appropriate pedagogies for creativity might usefully be considered to be those that support varieties of play, but what would an appropriate curriculum for creativity look like? The English Early Years Foundation Stage framework defines creativity as being all about taking risks and making connections. Later, when children enter the more formal stages of education, creativity is described in the curriculum as involving: questioning and challenging; making connections and seeing relationships; envisaging what might be;

exploring ideas; keeping options open and reflecting critically on ideas, actions and outcomes.

Ultimately creativity is seen as supporting life-long learning and preparing pupils for life in the world of employment and specialised communities of practice. Curriculum progression here is all about developing breadth (of knowledge, skills and understanding) and later, a degree of specialisation as well.

In discussing creativity, it is really important to acknowledge the significance of these specialised 'communities of practice' that we all become members of as adults. In the United Kingdom, Craft (2003: 6) and colleagues emphasise the importance of promoting creativity in education with a little 'c'. This is considered to be a: 'life-wide resourcefulness which is effective in successfully enabling the individual to chart a course of action by seeing opportunities as well as overcoming obstacles' (2003: 6), as opposed to a big 'C' of 'creativity in the arts' (Craft 2003). The 'arts' represents many different specialist communities of practice. In the case of every specialist community of practice (including those such as science and technology), to be an active member one has first to 'master' and accept the necessity of drawing upon the body of knowledge, established practices and conventions that have been accumulated historically by past and present members of that community. In any event, the quality of the creativity of an individual's art, science or technology will be judged according to the current standards (or canon) of their community. This is not at all true of creativity with a little 'c': in this case, an individual can (quite originally) create something that has been created before many times. Similarly, as individual scientists we can 'discover' things that turn out to be false, and as technologists we can produce things that do not work very well. In terms of social value, we want to nurture creativity with a small 'c', as well as to introduce children to the established bodies of knowledge and practices that support the collaborative efforts of big 'C' communities of practice. This edited collection contains chapters by researchers and educators, such as Jenny Hallam, Helen Lee and Mani das Gupta, whose work provides evidence that supports these arguments and offers further theoretical justification for strengthening our focus on the curriculum for creativity.

The collection provides further theoretical elaboration of the relationship identified between creativity, narrativity and collaboration by R. Keith Sawyer, Dorothy Faulkner, Marjaana Kangas, Annakaisa Kultima and Heli Ruokamo, and Elizabeth and Andrew Coates. It draws strongly on the Vygotskian theoretical tradition. Vygotsky's writing about creativity has become available in the recently published paper, 'L. S. Vygotsky on children's imagination and creativity' (2004). Vygotsky conceptualised creative activity as combinational, syncretic activity, where the individual brings together recalled images, actions and/or experiences to envisage (or imagine) something new. These processes of imagination are present in all aspects of our day to day life and mental activity. All forms of learning, science and technology just as much as the arts, would be impossible without them:

> in the everyday life that surrounds us, creativity is an essential condition for existence and all that goes beyond the rut of routine and involves innovation, albeit only a tiny amount, owes its existence to the human creative process.
>
> (Vygotsky 2004: 11)

The chapters in this collection build on Vygotsky's notion of creativity as combinatorial syncretic activity, and draw attention to the combinatorial, multimodal representational systems children employ when engaged in creative activity. The chapters also accord with van Oers's (1998) view, that the creative process involved in learning and development may be characterised as one of 'progressive continuous re-contextualisation' (PC-R) where it seems that as soon as the individual recognises the potential of achieving a recalled (and motivating) object (or outcome), he or she is able to re-contextualise that object, transforming (or 'transferring') the (structure and meaning) of the activity. Van Oers's account of this process has a number of advantages over earlier accounts of the development of abstract thinking, such as 'decontextualisation' (Vygotsky 1987), and references to 'disembeddedness' (Donaldson 1978). One important advantage of accepting van Oers's argument is that it avoids applying a negative qualification: progressive continuous re-contextualisation (however much it is a mouthful) indicates a positive and ongoing process. Even more importantly, it acknowledges the importance of recognising that individual interpretations of the context are involved. Arguably, it will always be the 'affordances' of the perceived object that are most significant in the process of re-contextualisation. This is demonstrated convincingly by Kerry Chappell and Susan Young in their chapter on learning and creativity in early years dance education.

To see how the processes described above may also be applied in the case of the child's reasoning and conceptual development, we can borrow a short dialogue from Donaldson (1992), who uses it to illustrate what she refers to as children's 'spontaneous wonderings' (1992: 44). Apparently, Jamie (3 years 11 months) was standing in a lane beside a house in the English countryside. It was a warm and dry day, and a car was parked on a concrete drive nearby:

Jamie: 'Why is it [the car] on that metal thing?'
Adult: 'It's not metal, it's concrete.'
Jamie: 'Why is it on the concrete thing?'

Adult: 'Well, when it rains the ground gets soft and muddy, doesn't it?'
[Jamie nods, bends down and scratches the dry earth.]
Adult: 'So the wheels would sink into the mud.
But the concrete's hard, you see.'
Jamie [excitedly]: 'But the concrete's soft in the mix!
Why is it soft in the mix?'

(Donaldson 1992: 44)

To understand what is happening here, a strong clue may be in Jamie's use of the word 'mix'. At some point in the past he may have seen concrete being mixed with a shovel or concrete mixer. If so, he will have been left with an apparent contradiction when he was told at this point that this hard (metal) material was also 'concrete'. He had only ever seen it very soft and fluid like mud. Donaldson tells us that the adult was thrown into some confusion by the child's question and was not able to answer. So there may have been a missed opportunity here. Had the adult listened (or reasoned themselves) more carefully they might have been able to explain how concrete, after it is mixed, then sets, providing the opportunity for the child to engage in a 'progressive continuous re-contextualisation' of his understanding of concrete, its properties and affordances.

Many authors in this collection write compellingly of the insights that can be gained when adults listen carefully (or watch intently) children engaged in this process. The chapter by Elizabeth and Andrew Coates is particularly notable in this respect. Donaldson's example also illustrates the syncretic motivation to reconcile different experiences or stimulations, which Vygotsky (2004) identifies as important for the generation of creative ideas or thinking creatively. This provides further justification for educators to draw upon multi-modal metaphors and analogies in their teaching (as argued in chapters by Susan Wright, Marie Fulkova and Teresa Tipton, Sylvia Truman, and Dorothy Faulkner). Progressively, as children continue to communicate with adults and other children, the new meanings that they construct are mediated by all their previous historical moments of significant activity. Increasingly we can see that socio-dramatic play, music making and other interactions are improvisational, reciprocal and collaborative. Whenever play partners communicate they do so from their own historically constructed perspective, which includes their understanding of the perspective of themselves constructed by the other participant in the communication. The chapters by Keith Sawyer and Susan Young further elaborate these perspectives.

The development of sophisticated levels of abstraction (metaplay, metacommunication and metaconciousness), as initiated through symbolic play, improvised narratives and collaborative activity, through dance, drama and music, facilitates the development of a wider metacognition (the knowledge and awareness that children acquire about their own cognitive processes and learning dispositions). This is amply illustrated in the accounts of children working with professionals from the creative arts offered by Kerry Chappell and Susan Young. As well as being fundamental for learning to learn, metacognition is also important for the development of the children's creative imagination as it enables them to describe, explain and justify their thinking about different aspects of the world to others. Creating space in the curriculum for children to exercise their imagination through play and to discuss and reflect on their own and each other's ideas is of crucial importance to the development of little 'c' creativity.

We warmly welcome the publication of this book, which is distinctive in its thinking about the multi-modal nature of narrative and emphasises the importance of valuing children's creative expression in educational settings.

Professor Iram Siraj-Blatchford, Institute of Education,
University of London
Dr John Siraj-Blatchford, Visiting Professor, University of Swansea

References

Craft, A. (2003) 'The limits to creativity in education', *British Journal of Educational Studies*, 51(2).

Donaldson, M. (1978) *Children's Minds* Harmondsworth: Penguin.

Donaldson, M. (1992) *Human Minds: An Exploration* London: Allen Lane/Penguin Press.

Russ, S. W. (2003) 'Play and creativity: developmental issues', *Scandinavian Journal of Education Research*, 47(3), pp. 291–303.

Russ, S. W., Robins, A. L. and Christiano, B. A. (1999) 'Pretend play: longitudinal prediction of creativity and affect in fantasy in children', *Creativity Research Journal*, 12(2), Special Issue: Longitudinal Studies of Creativity, pp. 129–39.

Sawyer, K., John-Steiner, V., Moran, S., Sternberg, R., Feldman, D., Nakamura, J. and Csikszentmihalyi, M. (eds), (2003) *Creativity and Development* (Counterpoints: Cognition, Memory and Language), Oxford: Oxford University Press.

Sylva, K., Bruner, J. and Jolly, A. (1976) *Play, Its Role in Development and Evolution*, Harmondsworth: Penguin.

van Oers, B. (1998) 'The fallacy of decontextualisation', *Mind, Culture and Activity*, 5(2), pp. 135–42.

Vygotsky, L. S. (1987) *The Collected Works of L. S. Vygotsky*, trans. N. Minick, New York: Plenum.

Vygotsky, L. S. (2004) 'L .S. Vygotsky on children's imagination and creativity', *Journal of Russian and East European Psychology*, 42(1), pp. 4–84.

Acknowledgements

We wish to thank the following for their support in the production of this book: our editors Claire Westwood and Alison Foyle, the three anonymous reviewers who provided valuable feedback, the John Benjamin Publishing Company for granting permission to use the article 'Improvisation and narrative' by R. Keith Sawyer, originally in *Narrative Inquiry* 2002, 12 (2), pp. 319–49, and DACS and the Paul Klee Estate for granting permission to reproduce the two Paul Klee images: *Composition on Parallel Horizontals* (1920) and *The Boulevard of the Abnormal Ones* (1938).

Finally this book would not have happened without the outstanding organisational skills, expertise and unfailing good humour of Julie May, who prepared the manuscript.

Dorothy Faulkner
Elizabeth Coates
November 2010

Acknowledgements

Chapter 1

Exploring children's creative narratives: some theoretical, methodological and applied perspectives

Dorothy Faulkner and Elizabeth Coates

The principal aim of this edited collection is to offer fresh perspectives on children's creative narratives and to explore what these reveal about their imagination, their thought processes and how they understand the world. Accordingly, the contributors to the collection draw on detailed ethnographic case studies, naturalistic observations, conversations and playful interactions with children ranging in age from two to eleven years to develop theoretical insights that challenge traditional accounts of creativity and narrative. Our contributors include social scientists and postdoctoral researchers, educators and creative artists who are also academics and educators. A leitmotiv of the collection is that a proper understanding of creative narratives has to be an interdisciplinary endeavour if it is to do justice to the rich, complex, multi-modal and embodied nature of the children's thought processes as revealed through their drawing and story-telling, music making, dance, drama and imaginative play.

A second theme that unites many of the chapters is that the narratives that emerge during the course of imaginary play episodes and classroom dialogue come about through collaborative, improvisational processes. Interpretation and analyses of these processes draws on socio-cultural accounts of creativity and creative development. These challenge more traditional accounts of creativity as an attribute or talent that belongs only to certain gifted individuals and that leads to exceptional, innovatory performance in domains such as the creative arts, science, mathematics and literature. As Iram and John Siraj-Blatchford mention in the Foreword to this collection, it is customary for contemporary accounts to refer to the distinction between everyday creativity, or creativity with a little 'c', and big 'C' creativity. The latter represents those grand endeavours that give rise to historically significant scientific and artistic innovation, or to cultural and theoretical paradigm shifts. This collection is about creativity with a little 'c', although for the children themselves, the narratives, creative acts and artistic outputs described in various chapters may well have had much more personal and emotional significance than seems warranted by this notion.

Contributors to the collection comprehensively deconstruct historical accounts based on decontextual analyses of children's creative outputs. In the past, this approach gave rise to theories that described creative development as progressing through a sequence of age-related stages. A third, overarching theme that runs through the collection, therefore, is the argument that if we are to understand the situated nature of children's creative activity it is important to examine the social, affective and cognitive processes that take place when they are immersed in such activity. Many of the contributors to the collection use a case study approach to support this argument, and offer detailed and careful interpretive, phenomenological and/or conversational analyses of these processes that draw on observations of individual children, or pairs and groups of children. The case studies draw on recordings of the running narratives and self-talk of children engaged in self-directed, creative activity. These demonstrate that for the children concerned, the meanings and interpretation of their creative outputs changed and evolved from moment to moment, such that the end product of the activity underwent many transformations. Again, as Iram and John Siraj-Blatchford point out, van Oers's claim (1998) that the nature of children's creative activity can be described as progressive continuous re-contextualisation seems to capture the essence of many of these case studies. This also means that any 'after the event' interpretation or judgement of the end product itself is bound to be inaccurate as it will fail to take into account the sophisticated, transformational nature of the thought processes that contributed to its generation.

A final theme that many contributors comment on is the challenge to conventional educational practices implied by these re-conceptualisations of children's creativity, and the recognition of the role and influence of popular culture and the mass media on their imagination. These contributors argue that formal educational training programmes should offer teachers more sophisticated cultural discourses and experiences which will allow them to gain a more rounded understanding of children's creative narratives.

Although many chapters offer detailed accounts of theories of creativity and of narrative, the focus of this volume is on the children themselves and on understanding how teachers, researchers and creative professionals scaffold their creative activity. In part this focus reflects our own interests as editors. Dorothy Faulkner is a developmental psychologist whose interest lies in the relationship between creativity and learning and in narrative development, while Elizabeth Coates is an educator with a wide knowledge and experience of training teachers to work with young children. Both of us are active researchers, and in the next two sections we offer our own perspectives on the significance of the various chapters in this collection.

The developmental psychologist's viewpoint

As a developmental psychologist, I have long been interested in the development of children's story comprehension and production, and the development of thinking and reasoning in collaborative contexts. Originally, my own research drew principally on the paradigms of experimental, cognitive psychology and on quantitative analysis of video observations of children in classroom contexts. This approach is roundly criticised by many contributors to this volume, including Jenny Hallam, Helen Lee and Mani Das Gupta (Chapter 6), and Kerry Chappell and Susan Young (Chapter 11). Fortunately, in recent years I have been able to collaborate with social psychologists and educational researchers who have introduced me to the power and elegance of qualitative methods of data collection and analysis. Having seen the error of my 'experimental ways' (although I still argue that there is considerable merit in the quantitative analysis of systematic observation data to compare children's language and behaviour in different naturalistic contexts), as the chapters began to arrive, I became intensely interested in the many different qualitative, methodological approaches to the exploration of children's creative narratives taken by their various authors.

Given that many authors agree that children's creative narratives are improvisational in nature, evolve through processes of creative emergence and are contextually situated in time and place, this raises the question of what researchers should use as the unit of analysis. Keith Sawyer (Chapter 2) and Susan Wright (Chapter 8) both discuss this in their chapters on play and drawing respectively. In his chapter, Sawyer uses his discussion of the relationship between social pretend play and narrative to propose that the unit of analysis should be the discursive event, by which he means a single conversational turn or sequence of turns that together make up a play sequence. He argues that using conversational analysis to study the contingent, processual nature of children's improvised dialogue offers a more fruitful way forward than traditional, analyses of the structure and form of children's narratives.

My own chapter (3) and the chapter by Marjaana Kangas, Annakaisa Kultima and Heli Ruokamo (Chapter 4) offer accounts of children's creative and narrative thinking and conversation that use the discursive event as a unit of analysis. Kangas, Kultima and Ruokamo describe a research project designed to uncover what activities children would build into an ideal play environment. They did this by inviting groups of children to participate in playful co-design sessions where they drew and discussed their ideas for play environments. This research had a practical application, and was intended to inform the design of technology-enhanced play environments in Finland. In their chapter, Kangas, Kultima and Ruokamo identify key features of the shared, collective narrative thinking that emerged through playful activity. They go on to outline a new, multidimensional framework for the analysis of children's narratives that moves beyond the notion of the story (or verbal narrative) as the fundamental unit of narrative analysis.

In my chapter (3), I describe a research project that investigated the impact of creativity training on teaching and learning in an English primary school. I draw on an analysis of the conversations that took place between a teacher and her pupils, first to examine how the teacher used various organizational 'process' tools offered by the training programme to scaffold children's creative thinking, and second, to discuss the improvisational nature of the creative collaborative thinking that emerged. Relating the findings to published research on the development of children's communication and inferential thinking, my analysis raises questions concerning the perceived need in some educational quarters for children's thinking to be trained.

Drawing on research that has investigated children's mark-making and drawing, Susan Wright (Chapter 8) argues that as the activity of drawing emerges as a multimodal event, the semiotic unit of analysis should be the event rather than the marks children produce. She argues that when they draw, children depict the meaning and content of their drawings through body-based action, talk, discussion and free-form narrative. It makes no sense, therefore, to take the picture or marks on the paper as the unit of analysis. This view is elaborated further in the chapters written by Maria Fulkova and Theresa Tipton (Chapter 7) and by Elizabeth and Andrew Coates (Chapter 5). In their chapter, Fulkova and Tipton develop a distinctive interpretive framework that draws on discourse and semiotic analyses to understand the nature and quality of children's visual language. Both Coates and Coates, and Tipton and Fulkova, offer an account of how the analysis of children's drawing has changed and developed over the past century, and Fulkova and Tipton describe how postmodern analyses that conceptualise art as a social practice allow us to approach the topic of children's drawings as coded, interdisciplinary, intertextual discourses with their own narratives and interrelated sign systems. In their chapter Coates and Coates offer a contextual analysis of the discursive events and conversations that take place between pairs of children engaged in self-directed drawing activity. They use this account to discuss how the subject matter of the drawings draws on the immediate environment, significant people and objects in children's lives, as well as on rich metanarratives that draw on images and characters from popular culture.

Other chapters offer further evidence which confirms that children rarely confine themselves to a single form of creative expression even when ostensibly engaged in specific curricular activities such as art, drama or music. Contributors to the volume argue that explanations of children's creativity that fail to take this into account do not allow us to capture its true inventiveness and originality. Similarly, impoverished explanations of children as static consumers rather than active producers of creative products cannot inform the design of technology-enhanced instructional programmes that aim to harness children's creative potential, such as the Finnish SmartUs (described by Kangas, Kultima and Ruokamo), SoundScape (described by Truman) and the MIT KidStory project (described by Sawyer).

From the standpoint of one trained originally in cognitive developmental psychology, and later in socio-cultural accounts of development, what also struck me about the research reported in several chapters were the authors' accounts of the rich, affective nature of children's creative narratives. Emotion and affect are rarely taken into account in discussions of children's cognition and social development. Like other contributors, Susan Young (Chapter 9) argues that we need to understand creativity and creative processes in relation to the wider socio-cultural context. She also argues that the analysis and interpretation of children's creative activity is incomplete without due consideration of the intense emotional energy that fuels much of this activity. In her chapter she draws on accounts of turn-taking musical exchanges between very young children and adults to develop the argument that creativity is rooted in non-verbal, embodied forms of expressivity and that moreover, this expressivity is the fount of the temporal arts. She goes on to claim that the interpersonal dimension – that is, the desire to make and sustain sociable contact through non-verbal means such as sound and gesture – is an important source of very young children's musical ideas. Young also draws attention to the importance of the intimate and highly supportive nature of the relationships that develop when adults act as sympathetic, playful partners. She argues that during three-way interactions between children, adults and sound-making objects, various forms of turn-taking structure children's creative activity and reciprocal musical exchanges. She also reminds us, however, that many children are fearful of letting go and engaging fully in such exchanges, and that for other children, there may be cultural constraints and educational expectations on their behaviour that preclude their involvement. Even where children may not want to participate fully in creative activity, however, their body language and the quality of their watching and listening demonstrate absorbed engagement in the activity.

Jenny Hallam, Helen Lee and Mani Das Gupta (Chapter 6) and Kerry Chappell writing with Susan Young (Chapter 11) also address the issue of the nature of children's engagement in their chapters. Hallam, Lee and Das Gupta argue that the wider social and educational contexts that shape the reception and interpretation of children's art and creative activity act to constrain this activity, so much so that as children get older, this often deteriorates in quality and falls by the wayside. Sylvia Truman makes similar arguments in her chapter (10), where she discusses the inhibiting effect of the traditional music education curriculum in the United Kingdom. Hallam, Lee and Das Gupta point out, however, that many children adopt a position of resistance and refuse to produce artistic work that conforms to teacher expectations and direction. They adopt a postmodernist analytic framework to explore the gaps that appear between children's constructions of the meaning of their artistic creations and the interpretations and constructions offered by adults. By contrast, Chappell and Young describe a project that provided opportunities for disadvantaged children to develop positive learning dispositions by working with a range of creative artists. They argue that many children are inhibited and fearful of expressing themselves through movement. This means that they find it difficult to engage with the playful exploratory responses that allow children to express creative thinking and to develop narratives through movement and dance, and other rich kinaesthetic experiences. In their chapter they offer case studies of such children who, over the course of a number of weeks, eventually allowed themselves to participate in improvisational collaborations with other children through movement and drama. Two dancers, a film-maker and a clay artist who assumed the role of playful partners supported these improvisational collaborations. Some of the joyful emotions the children experienced through these collaborations are captured in the photographs that accompany Chappell and Young's chapter.

Finally, in one way or another, all contributors to this collection address the notion of the role of children's voice in research, and there is general agreement that postmodernist and socio-cultural approaches allow children's voices to be heard, and their views and opinions to be taken seriously. The chapters by Truman (10) and Kangas, Kultima and Ruokamo (4) demonstrate this by co-opting children as researchers to inform the development of design-led educational technology. As well as offering their own interpretations and theoretical accounts of children's creative and narrative thinking, for the most part, the authors present many rich and varied examples of children's creative activity in their chapters, either by reporting children's own interpretations of conversations, or through the photographs of children's art work and experiences that are reproduced as plates in the middle of the collection.

I recognize that in this section of the introductory chapter, I have not been able to capture many of the sophisticated theoretical arguments represented in other chapters. I have commented on those aspects that I found interesting from a methodological and conceptual point of view, and invite readers to explore the chapters from their own theoretical and conceptual viewpoints.

In the next section, Elizabeth Coates discusses the main themes and messages that are likely to resonate with readers interested in the educational implications of the research studies reported in the collection.

The educator's viewpoint

What do educators understand by 'creativity' and how do they interpret its role in early years settings? In this book each author approaches the concept of creativity in a different way, but all stress the importance of constructive collaboration between children and the role of rich imaginative narrative to the development of creative solutions when solving problems and conceptualising outcomes. It would seem that creativity can be expressed through multiple narrative forms such as socio-dramatic play, music, art and dance, although these are often regarded by educators as merely part of the 'creative arts'. However, in the early years children delight in problem solving in all aspects of the curriculum, seeing learning as holistic rather than divided into subject areas. This involves the use of the imagination and verbal and non-verbal narrative, suggesting that areas such as scientific investigation are equally valid as a focus for future research in this respect. In England, as in many countries, there have been attempts to recognise the value of creative thinking throughout the curriculum, but this has been hampered by the nature of the National Curriculum, which is too closely aligned to the achievement of standards by means of precise cognitive objectives. These have largely militated against the development of innovative and imaginative methods of teaching. The projects contained in this publication, however, aim to show what can be achieved if children are encouraged in imaginative thinking, enabled by teachers who participate through collaborative dialogues.

Throughout, there is an emphasis on pedagogy since much of the research is classroom based, often involving explorations of the context in which most education is located. The prescribed curriculum common to most early childhood settings suggests that the direction and outcome of a lesson should lead to a specified set of results, and as Hallam, Das Gupta and Lee (Chapter 6) suggest, it is teacher-led and teacher-dominated as the children are guided to produce work that accords with their perceived requirements of the curriculum. There is little opportunity here for imaginative thinking, and too often the child is assessed by the end product rather than by the process leading to it. It is often the case that teachers fail to pay attention to what children say, or observe what they are doing. Perhaps this is a result of the pressures of organising a busy schedule and the need to produce assessable outcomes, but one of the first lessons to be learned as a young teacher is that each child is a person in their own right. A class is not a homogeneous whole but is composed of individuals, each with their own thoughts, personality and culture. It is this sense of individuality that permeates all the chapters in this book, coupled with the importance of collaboration between peers, and between children and adults. The narratives show how strong this collaboration can be as boundaries are pushed and notions of communication are extended far beyond the verbal to include visual and non-verbal expression. The question most frequently addressed in this book is how we can understand children's narratives successfully if we only pay attention to the end product. Throughout there is an emphasis on communication, with teachers recognising the creativity underpinning children's imaginative discourses and building on them. In England as a result of the longitudinal Effective Provision of Pre-School Education project (EPPE) based in the Institute of Education, University of London, this extended dialogue between child and adult is described as 'sustained shared thinking'. Faulkner (Chapter 3) provides fascinating examples of this as she describes the ways that skilful adults draw out children's ideas, moving their thinking forward by valuing and responding to their contributions. This dialogue, sometimes between two people but often involving more, shows not only how it is possible to engage in imaginative thinking, but also that the ideas children contribute are often highly innovative.

There is a tendency in education circles to think of creative narrative purely as a verbal element, either spoken or written, but the variety of projects discussed in this book move beyond this. Three chapters, Wright (Chapter 8), Tipton and Fulkova (Chapter 7) and Coates and Coates (Chapter 5), focus on the visual narrative related to children's drawings, and emphasise the richness of the accompanying interaction as children tell or act out the underlying story. The whoops, shouts and singing are invisible in the end product, but to the observer they convey the excitement and intensity of the activity, and attention paid to the interaction often reveals how the content of the drawing has changed and evolved. Seeing such drawing activities as occasions where children reveal their interests, use their imagination, engage in a kind of creative role play and develop social skills moves them far beyond the mark-making being seen merely as the precursor to letter formation and formal writing which has been highlighted in recent curriculum documentation.

To anyone who has worked or is working with young children, play is regarded as central to all areas of development. While role-play offers an opportunity for children to examine their experiences of the world, such play often expands to include fantasy by drawing upon characters from popular culture and creating new adventures for favourite heroes. Such play episodes see children as story creators, often changing direction as fresh ideas emerge, but also as scriptwriters, since when play is interrupted they often return to the same scenario, carrying on where they left off. Creative/socio-dramatic play forms the basis of Young's chapter (9), since she discusses the links between theatre and play when working with the under-fives, although she sees the main theme of creativity as being rooted in non-verbal, embodied expressivity. This is echoed in Sawyer's work (Chapter 2), as he suggests that there is a place for scripts in children's play, not in the formal written sense but in the way that children improvise play discourses. The provision of objects may affect the initial direction of play, but Sawyer found that it was the children's interpretation of the situation, their references to the media, films in particular, as well as their personal experiences, that controlled the way the play script developed. The richness of the narratives illustrated in his chapter provided ample justification to me, as an educator, for the provision of creative play areas in early years settings. The project undertaken in Finland by Kangas, Kultima and Ruokamo (Chapter 4) suggested that creativity could be integrated with curriculum-based education, setting groups of children the task of designing play areas. What started out as a fairly formal activity took flight as the adult sensitively encouraged the children to look beyond the ordinary, and extended their thinking to the point where the ideas were flowing profusely, incorporating not only technological devices but also fantastical characters.

Globally the influence of media permeates all aspects of education, and teachers incorporate the latest technology into their planning on a regular basis. Since children seem to assimilate such technology with an ease not often emulated by adults, this does seem a natural progression, and one which may afford the opportunity to provide more creative and flexible approaches to learning. There is a danger that new technology in inexperienced adult hands might be used in an unimaginative way, for example with interactive whiteboards being used as electronic work sheets, but judging from the creative way that new technologies have been used in many of the projects in this book they can become an integral part of children's developing creativity.

However, what about the natural exuberance of young children, with their need to express themselves through physical activity and vocal manifestation, as opportunities for children to move, dance, sing and create music in early years settings seem to be diminishing since the introduction of curriculum requirements? The influence of the more formal compulsory stages of schooling is strong, and there is pressure placed on early years teachers to introduce children to literacy and numeracy as soon as possible. Both Young (Chapter 9) and Truman (Chapter 10) focus on music as part of their research, although Truman's work examines the creation of composition when the domination of black notes is removed, and Young looks at creating music with three and four year olds. Young's second project with Kerry Chappell (Chapter 11) provides some insights into the possibilities of dance education with five year olds, drawing on the expertise of dancers, a film-maker and an artist in clay. This combination offers support to teachers who often feel unskilled in this area, and the project suggests that building up children's ability to think creatively through dance may give them a confidence which will be beneficial to all aspects of their school performance. This use of outside professionals forms part of the discussion in Faulkner's chapter (3), as she describes the Creative Partnership scheme established in England in the past decade and the government documentation designed to promote creative thinking across the curriculum. More influential in many countries, however, is the work in Reggio Emilia, where teachers, children and the local community work together on multiple projects.

Throughout this discussion of the diverse narratives revealed in these research studies, several things stand out. There is a need to remember that children come to pre-school already established as creative thinkers, and one only has to eavesdrop to recognize this. Does what we do to them in an educational setting extend or stifle this thinking, as while we are encouraged to listen to children's voices the other forms of narratives, visual and non-verbal, displayed by children are often forgotten? These studies show how important it is for adults to widen their horizons and pay attention to the social interaction, collaboration, imagination and playfulness that are central to children's creative narratives.

Unlike practice-based accounts of creativity in schools, the contributors to this volume offer theoretical explanations and novel frameworks to account for the collaborative, meaning-making processes when young children enter narrative modes of thinking. The collection draws on the experiences of researchers and educators from several countries, and does not rely on any single national perspective. The central focus of most of the chapters is on describing and understanding what children do and what they talk about. Although some chapters offer accounts of the professional development of teachers and practitioners and the design of educational tools to support young children's creativity, this is not primarily a collection about curriculum design and how to develop creative pedagogy. It is primarily a text about how detailed observations by sympathetic adults can reveal insights into the creative processes that emerge spontaneously between children, and about how these processes reveal the multi-modal nature of children's creativity. We hope that, as we did, other interested researchers and professionals will enjoy getting to know and understand the creative narratives and works of art that the children have generously shared with us through their participation in the research projects described in this volume.

References

van Oers, B. (1998) 'The fallacy of decontextualisation', *Mind, Culture and Activity*, 5(2), pp. 135–42.

Chapter 2

Improvisation and narrative

R. Keith Sawyer

In recent years, several narrative researchers have questioned the notion of narrative in its traditional connotation of a solitary, individual performer telling a story. In contrast, these researchers have observed that in many verbal contexts, narratives are co-constructed by multiple speakers (Coates 1997; Falk 1980; Tannen 1989; Watson 1975) and that in some social groups and settings, these jointly constructed narratives may be more prevalent than solo narratives (Eder 1998; Tannock 1998). Even in situations where there is one primary speaker, in many genres of oral narrative the audience is expected to contribute through various forms of verbal and non-verbal backchannel talk (Duranti and Brenneis 1986; Goodwin 1981).

At the same time, a growing body of research has explored how collaboration with peers may contribute to development. For certain skills and knowledge, collaboration seems to provide uniquely effective benefits, and these benefits derive from the interaction among participants (Johnson and Johnson 1992; Slavin 1992; Webb 1991). Conversational collaboration with peers is thought to be one of the most developmentally valuable characteristics of sociodramatic play (Sawyer 1997). The contribution of social pretend play to narrative skill has been widely studied both by narrative researchers (Fein, Ardila-Rey, and Groth 2000; Galda 1984; Pellegrini 1985; Pellegrini and Galda 1982, 1993; Sachs, Goldman and Chaille 1984) and by researchers whose primary interest is 'emergent literacy' (Christie 1991; Roskos and Christie 2000, 2001; Yaden, Rowe, and MacGillivray 2000). These studies are motivated by the obvious similarities between play and narrative: both have fictional characters who operate in a temporarily created reality, both involve the production and comprehension of decontextualized language, and both have plot elements such as motivating events, tensions, and release.

Yet several important questions remain unanswered. Exactly how does the collaboration of sociodramatic play contribute to narrative literacy? What are its strengths and weaknesses relative to traditional classroom practices such as reading a text and being explicitly taught its narrative components? Such questions are of critical practical importance to educators; teachers are interested in how collaboration and play can be used in the classroom, and how they can best be integrated with other classroom narrative practices. Educational technologists, who are developing computer tools to support children's collaborative narrative practice, also need to understand how playful collaborations contribute to narrative literacy.

I explore these questions starting with the observation that both peer play and situated narrative practices are 'improvisational': they are unscripted, not planned in advance, and the outcome is unpredictable. Because they are collaborative, the outcome cannot be controlled by any single participant; rather, it emerges from the collective actions and contributions of each participant (Sawyer 2001a). In collaborative improvisation, each child's contribution has to be evaluated before it is accepted by the others, and each child's turns in interaction successively build on the prior turns of the other children, resulting in the step-by-step emergence of a narrative (Sawyer 1997). Because both social play and co-constructed narratives are group improvisations, and the outcome emerges from the discourse of the group, I argue that the developmental benefits of these forms of peer narrative practice can only be fully understood by closely focusing on the group's conversation. A few researchers have studied the conversational dynamics of children's narrative practice (e.g. Daiute 1989; Dyson 1991), and this chapter continues in this tradition.

I begin by first defining improvisation, using an example of an adult improvised theater performance; I then define narrative. Following these definitions, I analyze a range of play episodes to reveal the many ways that narratives emerge from children's improvisational play. These examples show that certain conversational techniques result in more elaborate plot structures, and that scripts can act as scaffolds that guide the process of collaborative emergence without removing its improvisationality altogether. I then present a theory of 'collaborative emergence' to conceptualize the processes whereby narrative structure emerges from improvisation. I conclude by drawing parallels with recent research on computer-supported collaborative storymaking environments.

Improvisation

The key characteristics of improvisation are:

1. Unpredictable outcome, rather than a scripted, known endpoint;
2. Moment-to-moment contingency: the next dialogue turn depends on the one just before;
3. Open to collaboration;
4. An oral performance, not a written product;
5. Embedded in the social context of the performance

(Sawyer 1995a)

To demonstrate some important characteristics of improvisation, I begin with an example of dialogue taken from a 1993 performance by Off-Off-Campus, a Chicago theater group (Example 1). This is the first few seconds of dialogue from a scene that the actors knew would last about five minutes. The audience was asked to suggest a proverb, and the suggestion given was 'Don't look a gift horse in the mouth.' (Note: '=' in the dialogue indicates a pause.)

Example I

Lights up. Dave is at stage right, Ellen at stage left. Dave begins gesturing to his right, talking to himself.

1. **Dave**
   'All the little glass figurines in my menagerie, The store of my dreams. Hundreds of thousands everywhere!'
   (Turns around to admire)
2. **Ellen**
   (Slowly walks toward Dave)
3. **Dave**
   (Turns and notices Ellen)
   'Yes, can I help you?'
4. **Ellen**
   'Um, I'm looking for uh, uh, a present?'
   (Ellen is looking down like a child, with her fingers in her mouth)
5. **Dave**
   'A gift?'
6. **Ellen**
   'Yeah.'
7. **Dave**
   'I have a little donkey?'
   (Dave mimes the action of handing Ellen a donkey from the shelf)
8. **Ellen**
   'Ah, that's= I was looking for something a little bigger.'
9. **Dave**
   'Oh.'
   (Returns item to shelf)
10. **Ellen**
    'It's for my Dad.'

(from Sawyer 2002b)

By turn 10, elements of the narrative are starting to emerge. We know that Dave is a storekeeper, and Ellen is a young girl. We know that Ellen is buying a present for her dad, and because she is so young, probably needs help from the storekeeper. These narrative elements have emerged from the creative contributions of both actors. Although each turn's incremental contributions to the narrative can be identified, none of these turns fully determines the subsequent dialogue, and the emergent narrative is not chosen, intended, or imposed by either of the actors.

The emergence of the narrative cannot be reduced to actors' intentions in individual turns, because in many cases an actor cannot know the meaning of her own turn until the other actors have responded. In turn 2, when Ellen walks toward Dave, her action has many potential meanings; for example, she could be a coworker, arriving late to work. Her action does not carry the meaning 'a customer entering the store' until after Dave's query in turn 3. In improvisation, many actions do not receive their full meaning until after the act has occurred; the complete meaning of a turn is dependent on the flow of the subsequent dialogue. In Section 3, I show that this sort of retrospective interpretation is also common in children's play.

This example demonstrates the moment-to-moment contingency of improvisation. Anything could have happened at any turn of this dialogue; the actors don't know what is going to follow an action, and they don't know how their actions will be interpreted and elaborated. Improvisation must be analyzed as a discursive process to capture the moment-by-moment moves of each speaker, and the interactional techniques used by participants to create the narrative.

Narrative

How do improvisations like Example 1 result in the emergence of narratives? First, I explore what researchers generally mean by 'narrative.' Following accepted usage, I define narrative as:

1. A genre of text, which
2. can be written or oral, but is canonically written, and is
3. defined by certain structural properties.
4. It does not have to be performed, and it
5. can be separated from its context of origin, or 'decontextualized'
                                              (Michaels 1981; Pellegrini 1985)

This list corresponds to a somewhat traditional conception of narrative; it emphasizes narrative structure rather than narrative practice. Nonetheless, this conception influences most empirical work on children's narrative practice. I give two examples of how researchers have operationally defined narrative that both share the above characteristics. Research in children's narrative typically focuses on identifying the structural elements of narrative form, often with the goal of understanding children's mental representations of narrative structure.

Tom Trabasso's coding scheme

Trabasso proposed the goal–action–outcome (GAO) narrative coding scheme as a way of analyzing children's developing ability to understand narrative structures (Trabasso et al. 1992). The GAO scheme allows an operational definition of two forms of coherence. 'Local narrative coherence' refers to a narrative connection between an action and its immediate causing goal or its subsequent outcome. 'Global narrative coherence' refers to a linking of such local coherent structures into hierarchies of goals, actions, and outcomes.

Trabasso found several developmental transitions in a child's ability to understand these narratives. For example, three and four year olds mainly describe isolated events or external actions, and do not refer to goals or other internal states (Figures 2.1 and 2.2). Five year olds begin to comprehend local coherence, associating actions with their motivating goals and with their resulting outcomes; however, they are not yet capable of comprehending the global coherence of hierarchically structured goals and subgoals. By age nine, children develop the ability to comprehend hierarchically structured narratives, and their performance on these tasks is indistinguishable from that of adults.

This coding scheme has several benefits. It allows for an operational definition of various conceptions of narrative, and it provides a quantitative measure of narrative competence. However, the scheme also has several weaknesses. It emphasizes plot structures and seems to neglect other

S11	Once there was a girl named Betty.
E11	One day, Betty found that her mother's birthday was coming soon.
G11	Betty really wanted to give her mother a present.
A11	Betty went to the department store.
O11	Betty found that everything was too expensive.
O12	Betty could not buy anything.
R11	Betty felt really sorry.
E21	Several days later, Betty saw her friend knitting.
S21	Betty was good at knitting.
A21	Betty selected a pattern from a magazine.
A22	Betty followed the instructions in the article.
O21	Finally, Betty finished a beautiful sweater.
A31	Betty pressed the sweater.
A31	Betty folded the sweater carefully.
O31	Betty gave the sweater to her mother.
R31	Her mother was excited when she saw the present.

S= Settings, E= Event, G= Goal, A=Attempt, O=Outcome, R=Reaction.
The first number after the letter indicates the episode; The second number indicates the cumulative number of times the code has occurred in this episode.

Figure 2.1 A hierarchical narrative with global coherence
Source: Suh and Trabasso (1993).

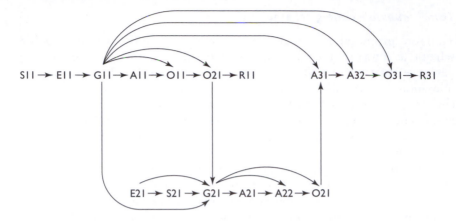

Figure 2.2 Trabasso's representation of the global coherence of the narrative in Figure
        2.1

potential forms of coherence, such as themes, morals, or trajectories
associated with character development. Many classic children's stories, for
example, are not driven by internal goals of characters, but by external
forces that act on characters, and how the character develops in response.

Colette Daiute's coding scheme

A second example of a narrative coding scheme is one used by Colette
Daiute (1999) to analyze friendship narratives (see Figure 2.3). The scheme
includes plot elements (items 2.3, 2.4, 3, and 4); however, plot elements are
subservient to character development and relationships. 'Complicating
actions' and 'conflict' are defined in terms of characters, not strictly in
terms of the plot's sequence of events.

   Although Daiute's coding scheme allows the identification of character-
based forms of coherence that are missing from Trabasso's scheme, Daiute's
scheme is weak in the area where Trabasso's is strong: this scheme does not
represent event sequences or their hierarchical structuring into a globally
coherent plot.

   Although the two narrative coding schemes emphasize different types of
coherence and trajectory in narrative, both schemes are designed to be
applied to entire narratives as completed fixed texts, and they are both
'structural' conceptions: they focus on the formal elements of narrative and
they conceive of a narrative as a decontextualizable product. Both
researchers use a methodology in which the narratives are elicited,
transcribed, and then analyzed and coded. As such, the complete narrative
is the unit of analysis (although Trabasso codes goals, actions, and outcomes
separately, he then aggregates these component entities to derive an overall

1. Narrative Elements
    1.1 Establishes focal character
    1.2 Action- sets story in motion or picks up on prompt
    1.3 Setting (place, time, condition)

2. Elaborate narrative
    2.1 Characters included
        2.1.1 Focal character/ Protagonist
        2.1.2 Other (multiple characters)
        2.1.3 Self included
    2.2 Character development
        2.2.1 physical description/ traits
        2.2.2 personality traits
        2.2.3 context (social, cultural info)
        2.2.4 character motivations
        2.2.5 other
    2.3 Event sequences (only)
    2.4 Secondary/ Compound plot line
    2.5 Literary devices used (dialogue, metaphor, suspense)

3. Interaction between character/ action
    3.1 Complicating actions (shaped sequences, builds; epic/ adventure, escalates, evaluative)
    3.2 Conflict established
        3.2.1 Conflict with environment
        3.2.2 Internal conflict (not expressed)
        3.2.3 Conflict with others (explicit)
    3.3 Turning point of climax

4   Resolution or enduring state
    4.1 Simple ending ('Goodnight'; 'The End'; other literary convention)
    4.2 Important character and/ or actions tied together/ literary resolution/ closure
    4.3 Conflict(s) resolved
        4.3.1 Simple or magical resolution
        4.3.2 Major issue addressed (but not in developed integrated way)
        4.3.3 Major issue resolved in developed/ integrated way
        4.3.4 Secondary issues resolved (as well)

5   Significance
    5.1 Explicit reflection about story
    5.2 Social significance of story
    5.3 Story set in cultural context

Figure 2.3 Daiute's friendship narrative coding sheet
Source: Daiute (1999).

rating of the narrative). Wolf and Hicks (1989) also noted that such theories of narrative focus on underlying schemas – or how the textual elements are bound together in a complex structure – and they neglect the ways that speakers combine voices to 'convey the texture of information and the author's fluctuating stance towards the information being shared' (1989:

333). I follow Wolf and Hicks in arguing that in studying improvisational dialogues such as Example 1, the unit of analysis cannot be the complete text; it must be the 'discursive event,' a single turn or a sequence of turns. A discourse focus allows one to study the contingent, processual nature of improvised dialogue.

Children's improvisational play

Children's sociodramatic play is improvisational, in the sense of Example 1, because it shares the key defining characteristics of improvisation. The outcome is unpredictable; there is moment-to-moment contingency from turn to turn; and the play is collaborative, with all children participating in the creation of the emergent narrative (Sawyer 1997). How does the improvisationality of children's collaborative play contribute to narrative development?

To address these questions, I analyze how narratives emerge in several different social pretend play episodes between five year olds. Five is the peak age for social pretend play (Pellegrini 1985) and is also the age at which children begin to frame their play narrative as distinct from everyday reality (Sachs, Goldman, and Chaille 1984; Scarlett and Wolf 1979). Example 2 is a transcript of a collaboratively improvised play narrative created among five year olds during naturally occurring play in a preschool classroom.

Example 2

Muhammed, Corinna, and Artie are playing with jungle animals in the block area (replica play). They switch between speaking as their plastic figurines and speaking out of character, as a narrator/director.[1]

1. **Corinna**
   'Guess what?
2. At the museum, someone is uh robbing us!
3. And they wanta take us to jail!'
4. **Muhammed**
   'That very bad.
5. How do you know a hippo, is robbing you?'
6. **Artie**
   'Uh, you saw them?'
7. **Corinna**
   'Yes, I saw him last night, was robbing my owner.
8. And I can't get him [a drip of] my favorite food,
9. mashed, mashed bugs.'
10. **Artie**
    '[ ] to get out of here.

11. The [ ] took it out
12. And I can get out, BOOM.
13. I blasted open the door.'
14. **Corinna**
    'Artie, you killed, you, uh
15. got killed, all right?'
16. **Artie**
    'And, we found him, OK?
17. He wasn't dead, he just in [jail]'
18. **Corinna**
    'OK.'
19. **Artie**
    '[ ] where were you? Now they're voicing what they planned.'
20. **Corinna**
    'I'm in jail.'
21. **Artie**
    'OK!
22. Boom
23. And here's the bad guys coming in [ ]'
24. **Corinna**
    'I wanna thank you.'
    Spoken in character
25. **Artie**
    'Let's pretend when you turned around,
26. the bad guys were [ ] in back of you, OK?'

The replica play in Example 2 is improvisational because the children are not follow a predetermined, shared script or routine, and it is collaborative because the flow of the play drama is collectively negotiated by all children; they negotiate in a give-and-take to create the resulting performance.

The dialogue of Example 2 does not result in the emergence of a coherent global narrative structure, in Trabasso's sense. Yet even though global coherence is not present, one can identify component elements of narratives that connect across multiple turns, forming pockets of local coherence (cf. Sachs, Goldman, and Chaille 1984). At line 2, Corinna introduces the threat of jail: 'Someone is robbing us, and they wanta take us to jail.' The 'jail' theme stays active through line 20, and after that, Artie introduces his 'bad guy attack/fight' theme, which Corinna readily accepts.

At line 5, in response to Corinna's proposal, 'Someone is robbing us,' Muhammed indirectly introduces an elaboration, that it is the hippo who is robbing: 'How do you know a hippo, is robbing you?' This is a retrospective interpretation (cf. Example 1), because although Corinna did not say it was a hippo, Muhammed's utterance assumes that that was what she meant. Artie extends this question at line 6, 'You saw them?' Like the talented adult improvisers in Example 1, Corinna accepts these retrospective interpretations at line 7. She answers, voicing as an animal, referencing her owner, and her favorite food, mashed bugs. At line 10, Artie jumps ahead with the jail theme, enacting as if Corinna is already in jail; yet Corinna had only proposed 'they wanta take us to jail.' Artie proposes that he rescues Corinna by exploding the door to the jail. Again, Corinna accepts the modification of her proposal and extends it, suggesting that Artie was killed in the explosion (line 14). Artie doesn't like the idea of his character being killed, so he responds with a modification (lines 16 to 17): We found him, but he wasn't dead, he was in jail. Corinna agrees, and after these seventeen lines of negotiation, the two begin enacting the scene they have just constructed.

At line 19, Artie speaks in character to Corinna's play character, 'Where were you?' She answers as they have planned, 'I'm in jail.' Artie enacts the explosion that will free Corinna's character. But then Artie introduces a new variant: the bad guys are coming in, not the good guys that would presumably rescue Corinna's character. At line 24, Corinna hasn't picked up on this shift. She responds as if Artie's character is rescuing her, saying 'I wanna thank you.' Artie realizes that Corinna has not understood his modification of the narrative, so he repeats his new idea more explicitly, saying 'Let's pretend' (line 25).

These children used a range of interactional strategies to negotiate this group improvisation. At times they shift to explicit, out-of-character talk to propose new ideas or to modify their playmates' suggestions (e.g., lines 23 and 25); this has been called 'metaplay.' Several researchers have shown that children's metaplay is related to measures of emergent literacy (Sachs, Goldman, and Chaille 1984; Trawick-Smith 1998, 2001; Williamson and Silvern 1991). Just as commonly, children propose or elaborate play ideas by speaking in character – an 'implicit metacommunication' (Sawyer 1997). In lines 1 through to 22, Artie and Corinna do not use the explicit metaplay that we find described in most of the research on play, yet they are negotiating nonetheless. In this negotiation the children combine a narrator's voice with their play character's voice using a 'dialogic' strategy (Bakhtin 1981; Wolf and Hicks 1989). Lines 12 through 17 are dialogic: the children speak within the play frame and use pronouns which resolve to play frame characters ('you got killed'), and they combine this voice with a narratological voice. These children often 'recast' information across voices: they propose a new development in the narrator voice, and then enact it with the replica character (Wolf and Hicks 1989: 342). Wolf and Hicks documented recasting in a single child's narrative; in Example 2, we see recasting across speakers – Artie in line 17, Corinna in line 20 – an important difference because it requires social negotiation and collaboration. Bakhtin developed the concept of dialogism to analyze how authors report dialogue in novels; of course, reported speech is a significant feature of oral storytelling as well (Lucy 1993). Bakhtin (1981: 314) used the term 'dialogism' to refer to the two-leveled nature of improvised dialogue; 'Behind the narrator's story we read a second story, the author's story .... We acutely sense two levels at each moment in the story; one, the level of the narrator ... and the other, the level of the author.'

Bakhtin's theory suggests how play dialogism might contribute to narrative ability. Yet because the narration is jointly negotiated, these dialogic processes are distributed across speakers (Sawyer 1995b).

In the following, I present additional examples of narratives emerging from the dialogic and metaplay strategies of five year old children's improvisational play discourse. The examples suggest that two features of improvised play are related to the emergence of well-formed narratives: the use of both metaplay and dialogic strategies, and the presence of scaffolding scripts.

Metaplay and narrative

What happens when children use neither metaplay nor dialogism? In Example 3, we see a play episode with very little explicit metaplay and very little dialogism.

Example 3

Kathy, Jennifer, and Rachel are playing in the doll corner, engaging in domestic and family themed play with a set of baby dolls.

1. **Kathy**
   'Ring ring!'
2. **Jennifer**
   'It's time for my babies to go sleepy-bye!'
3. **Kathy**
   'Hello?
4. Who are you?'
5. **Rachel**
   'Time for dinner, everyone!'
6. **Kathy**
   'You guys!' In an exasperated tone.
7. 'I'm on the='
8. **Rachel**
   '=Hang up that dumb phone.
9. Somebody's here.'

Unlike Example 2, in Example 3 there is no explicit metaplay and no dialogic negotiation; the girls are completely in-character and the narrator's voice is absent. Compared with Example 2, it is even more difficult to identify a coherent narrative theme. The three girls are each engaged in competing proposals for the narrative direction of the play, with Kathy on the phone, Jennifer putting babies to sleep, and Rachel initiating first a dinnertime theme, and then a 'guest' theme ('Somebody's here'). The lack of metaplay, combined with the lack of even local narrative coherence, is parallel to the findings of prior researchers of a link between metaplay and narrative.

A few minutes later, the same girls return to the dinnertime theme, but this time, their characters' voices begin to blend with a narrator's voice – a dialogic strategy (Example 4). The introduction of the narrator's voice allows the girls to begin to negotiate, although they do not come to an agreement on a shared play narrative.

Example 4

Kathy, Rachel, and Jennifer are playing in the doll corner. The following episode begins about nine minutes after Example 3.

1. **Kathy**
   'I think dinner's almost ready!'
2. **Rachel**
   'Dinner's ready!'
3. **Kathy**
   'I cooked the dinner.'
4. **Rachel**
   'Dinner's ready.'
5. **Kathy**
   'No it's not. Not yet!
6. I have to put a bit of eggs.
7. It's ready!'

This is a dialogic negotiation concerning who will occupy the role of 'mother,' a desired role in doll-corner play. Unlike Example 3, which was almost a Piagetian collective monologue, in Example 4 the girls negotiate a single shared issue. In line 3 Kathy announces, 'I cooked the dinner.' Although in-character, this is a claim to be the mother and a rejection of Rachel's competing claim to be the mother in Example 3. Rachel's shout 'Dinner's ready!' in line 2 is perceived by Kathy to be a competing dialogic proposal that Rachel is the mother. Up to this point, the role assignment of mother has not been explicitly discussed and the role remains ambiguous (perhaps intentionally, since girls typically argue about who gets to be the mother and no one wants to enact the lower-status 'child' role). In lines 5 and 6, Kathy voices another dialogic strategy in her bid to retain control of the mother role; using a within-frame justification, she says that dinner is not ready yet because the dish needs 'a bit of eggs' (cf. Sheldon 1990). The dialogic strategies of Example 4 are in contrast to the completely in-character voicings of Example 3, and this shift to dialogic strategy has allowed the girls to begin to negotiate a shared play narrative.

A few seconds after Example 4, Kathy attempts to gain Jennifer's support in her negotiation with Rachel. Her dialogism becomes less in-character and more narratological (Example 5).

Example 5

A few lines after Example 4.

1. **Kathy**
   'Jennifer, come on.
2. Jennifer,
3. I'll save you some tea.'
4. **Jennifer**
   'OK
5. But what about dinner for my baby?'
6. **Kathy**
   'I got dinner!'
7. **Jennifer**
   'Two babies!'
8. **Kathy**
   'All right.
9. Sit down.'

Although both Examples 4 and 5 are dialogic, the dialogism of Example 5 contains a stronger narrator voice. Kathy's tone of voice in lines 1 to 3 makes it clear that she is not speaking as her play character; she is asking the 'real' Jennifer to join her proposed narrative theme. Yet she combines in-frame material with this out-of-character request. Although she addresses Jennifer by name, her request is dialogic because in line three she refers to play frame activities and objects. The ensuing negotiation continues in this dialogic fashion, with Jennifer extracting a price for her cooperation: her own 'baby' theme must be incorporated into Kathy's dinner theme. Jennifer's counter-proposal in line 5 is dialogic because although it is negotiation about who will be participating in the play and what the play theme will be, Jennifer speaks as her play character in referring to 'my baby.'

At this point, Rachel gives in and accepts Kathy as the mother, and the three girls sit down. They enact a dinner narrative for the next 160 lines of dialogue, with Kathy bringing plates and utensils, and serving tea, stew, and a baby bottle for Jennifer's babies. After eating dinner, they clean up the plates and utensils and then Kathy serves ice cream. Throughout this enactment, Kathy acts as a narrative director, determining the timing of the narrative transitions without any input from Jennifer or Rachel; this enactment is thus not collaborative.

We see a progression from Example 3 through Example 5 from relatively in-character voice to an increasing integration of a narratological voice in dialogic strategies. In Example 3, the three girls enact competing play frames and engage in almost no negotiation focused on a common theme. In Example 4, with the shift to dialogic strategies, the girls begin negotiating with the intention of settling into a narrative enactment of a dinner theme, but they have not yet resolved the debate about who gets to be the mother. In Example 5, their dialogic talk takes on a stronger narratological voice, as Kathy addresses Jennifer by her real name.

In both the replica play of Example 2, and the doll-corner play of Examples 3 through 5, the improvisational, collaborative negotiation of the play results in a shared frame that has many narrative elements. However, in neither play group are the children explicitly attempting to create a story or to write a narrative, as defined in a coding scheme like Trabasso's or Daiute's; rather, they are simply engaging in the common negotiations of social pretend play. The narrative elements emerge from the group's improvisation, just as in the adult improvised dialogue of Example 1.

Scripts and improvisation in narrative

In the above examples, children's improvisational play rarely results in complex narrative structures with global coherence. When do children's play dialogues result in narratives with global coherence? Several researchers and educators have experimented with different 'scaffolds' in an attempt to enhance the developmental benefits of improvisational group play for narrative development. In 'thematic fantasy play' (Saltz, Dixon, and Johnson 1977), children hear a story read to them, select or are assigned roles from the story, and enact the story with teachers prompting, narrating, and at times taking roles and joining in the enactment. Vivian Paley encouraged her preschool students to share their stories with the class, and enact them with other children in a play-like fashion (Paley 1988; cf. Fein, Ardila-Rey and Groth 2000). Trawick-Smith (2001) recommended that teachers spontaneously scaffold children's play by interjecting appropriate leading questions related to character and plot development, although this must be done carefully; Pellegrini and Galda (1993) found that adult intervention may inhibit the sophistication of children's play language. Daiute (1989: 20) studied third through fifth graders' (eight to eleven year olds') collaboratively generated stories, and concluded that children were only able to generate effective collaboration and effective narratives because they had been provided with a 'general narrative structure,' instructions from the teacher such as 'Tell a story about a child who gets lost in Boston.'

An informal form of scaffolding is sometimes found in children's sociodramatic play, when children spontaneously enact scenes from popular children's books or movies. Such play is loosely scripted; each of the children in the group have seen the movie, but they sometimes collectively decide to modify the events of the movie and improvise an alternative plot line. These improvisations are loosely guided by the children's shared internalization of the movie's plot. In the following examples, I show how these shared scripts act as scaffolds, and I show that play remains improvisational even in the presence of a shared script.

Example 6

Improvisational embellishment of thematic elements from the movie *The Land Before Time*. Jennifer and Kathy are playing at the sand table. Jennifer has a plastic brontosaurus and tyrannosaurus, and Kathy also has a tyrannosaurus (replica play).

12 **Kathy**
    'And Cera's not mean in this one.'
13 **Jennifer**
    'OK.'
    …
18 **Kathy**
    'And know what?
19 It it do it has a earthquake in it but
20 this earthquake is
21 the earthquake will be right here, all right?'
22 **Jennifer**
    'OK, but pretend no one got hurt in this one, OK?'
    …
42 **Jennifer**
    'pretend they had to hunt to the Great Valley.' …
74 **Jennifer**
    'And then the Sharptooth saw them fighting
75 and he came over to meet them, right?
76 OK I'll get the Sharptooth!
77 And pretend as the Sharptooth came
78 Littlefoot hided under them
79 and the mother, um
80 the mother ran away
81 so did the Littlefoot
82 And pretend the poppa's standed up stronger
83 I'll get the Sharptooth.'

From extended narrative sequences such as Jennifer's, in lines 74 through 83, one can surmise that Jennifer has internalized many narrative elements from the movie; for example, Sharptooth and Littlefoot are characters from the movie. However, even though the two girls are enacting a movie that both of them have seen, they do not always follow the narrative of the movie; they often embellish or modify the narrative to fit the ephemeral demands of the emerging play frame. In line 12, Kathy proposes that 'Cera's not mean in this one' (Cera is snobby and bossy in the movie); in line 22 Jennifer proposes that 'no one got hurt in this one' (many of the dinosaurs die in the movie); and in lines 79 and 80 Jennifer proposes that 'the mother ran away' (the mother was killed by Sharptooth in the movie).

One might hypothesize that these differences result because the children do not remember accurately what happened in the movie. If so, one could attribute these modifications to failed memory rather than to improvisational creativity. However, at several points the children demonstrate that they are aware that these embellishments are not faithful to the movie. About ten minutes into this play episode, Corinna joins the two girls and they summarize their play up to this point. When their reported narrative diverges from the movie, Corinna notices and asks the girls to explain their embellishments (Example 7).

Example 7

Kathy and Jennifer summarize their play for Corinna.

296 **Kathy**
   'Pretend a long time ago, all the animals [ ]'
297 **Kathy**
   'all of the guys were [ ]'
298 **Corinna**
   'I don't believe you, that things there is Littlefoot?'
299 **Jennifer**
   'Well, we're playing Littlefoot Kathy.'
300 **Corinna**
   'All right'
301 **Kathy**
   'Yeah, that's how big the longnecks are
302 You know the longnecks lived here?
303 A longlonglong long long long time ago
304 Before anyone was born.'
305 **Corinna**
   'Yes I know.'
306 **Corinna**
   'But then the dinosaurs='

307 **Kathy**
   '=All died.
308 They all died.'
309 **Corinna**
   'I know.'
310 **Kathy**
   'But we're just pretending that they they they
311 they came to life
312 And they were statues.'

At line 298, Corinna objects that Jennifer's brontosaurus figurine should not be used for the character of Littlefoot, because it does not look like the one in the movie. Littlefoot is a baby brontosaurus – a 'longneck' – and Jennifer's toy is obviously a full-grown adult. Kathy and Jennifer realize this, as evidenced by their unison shout, 'Well, we're playing Littlefoot.' Again, at line 306, Corinna is about to object that the dinosaurs all died in the movie; Kathy anticipates her objection, even to the point of completing her utterance, and then says 'we're just pretending' that they came to life.

The embellishments on the movie script that are collaboratively made in Example 7 are evidence that these children have internalized the plot of the movie, are capable of creative modifications of the movie plot, and are aware they are doing so. These embellishments show that even when enacting familiar shared narratives, children cannot assume that the story will continue in the usual manner; one of the children may propose a modification to the narrative, and after appropriate negotiation, the modification may be incorporated into the shared play frame. These collaborative embellishments show that there is always improvisation, even in these apparently more scripted play episodes (also see Branscombe and Taylor 2000).

When Kathy and Jennifer anticipate Corinna's objections, and explain them by saying 'we're just pretending,' it is evidence that the girls are aware that they have modified the usual narrative, and they know that their jointly constructed narrative diverges from the canonical version of the movie. After Kathy's explanation in line 312, Corinna readily accepts the play modifications, and joins in the enactment. In fact, rather than dinosaurs, Corinna has brought a duck and a hippopotamus, even though all three girls realize that such animals do not appear in the movie (contemporary animals only evolved after the dinosaurs were extinct). Jennifer and Kathy agree to accept that animals and dinosaurs can coexist in their narrative, despite its inaccuracy.

Example 8

An earlier negotiation of what play figurines Corinna will be allowed to use.

273 **Jennifer**
   'Corinna don't wanna get dinosaurs, she wants to get animals'
274 'is that OK?'
275 **Kathy**
   'Well, we don't have animals in our game.'
276 'The animals come when they die.'
277 **Jennifer**
   'No, she wants to have animals.'

Although the girls embellish the scripted narrative of the movie, the movie's script nonetheless functions as a scaffold for the play improvisation. Because all three girls have seen the movie, they have many narrative elements already provided for them. Thus, they can focus their improvisational negotiation on embellishments to this basic narrative, rather than having to create everything from scratch.

Several scholars have noted that children's play is often an embellishment on a routine in a theme-and-variation pattern (Corsaro 1985; Fein 1987; Sawyer 1997; Sutton-Smith 1981). Children repeat and embellish routines; the routine provides a narrative structure, but children at play do not simply reproduce it but rather embellish and modify it through improvisational collaboration. Such play may be more effective at encouraging narrative development than the completely improvisational play of Examples 2 through 5. Not only might it result in more complex collaboratively constructed narratives; it also gives the children an opportunity to think explicitly about these embellishments, and how they are different from the original narrative.

The collaborative emergence of narrative from improvisation

How does play collaboration result in the emergence of a shared narrative? Examples 2 through 5 do not contain well-formed, elaborated narratives, measured on either Trabasso's or Daiute's narrative coding scheme. They are highly embedded in the social context and thus not decontextualizable; and they rely on shared background knowledge among the participants. Examples 6 through 8 contain narratives with a higher degree of global coherence, as a result of the presence of a shared script that acts as a scaffold.

A critical methodological question is how to determine whether an improvised dialogue has resulted in a narrative. A common approach is to transcribe the dialogue and then to analyze the transcript as a static structure, applying the tools of structural analysis to it. For example, the narrative coding schemes of Trabasso or Daiute could be applied to transcribed improvisational encounters such as Example 2, just as they are to composed stories. The problem with such a methodology was noted long ago by conversation analysts: it transforms an improvisation into a fixed text, thereby removing what is most essential to improvisation – its processual contingency and its social and collaborative nature (Sawyer 2001a; Wolf and Hicks 1989). The difficulty in connecting collaborative improvisation and narrative is that while collaborative improvisation is a social practice, a processual notion, narrative is a structural notion, a property of stories and texts. These concepts refer to different orders of social reality (see Figure 2.4).

Socio-cultural perspectives have the potential to provide a theoretical framework to connect improvisation and narrative, because they situate emergent literacy within social and cultural practices (cf. Yaden et al. 2000: 444). Researchers in socio-cultural psychology and situated cognition argue that knowledge and intelligence do not only reside in people's heads, but are distributed across situated social practices that involve multiple participants in complex social systems. 'Knowing' is reconceived as the ability to participate appropriately in these shared cultural practices. In the sociocultural perspective, mind is considered to be 'social, cultural, and embedded in the world' (Gee 2000: 195).

Similarly, I argue that the narratives that emerge from collaborative improvisation are collective social products. To understand the connections between narrative and improvisation, one must use methods that acknowledge the moment-to-moment, processual, contingent nature of improvisation, and its social and interactional nature. Structural methods of narrative analysis cannot easily do either, because they do not theorize the process whereby the narrative emerges from the dialogue – the key question from a socio-cultural perspective. To theorize this process, I use Sawyer's concept of 'collaborative emergence' (1999, 2002b).

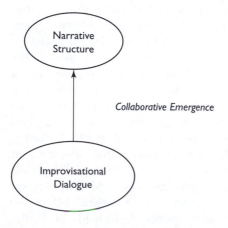

Figure 2.4 The collaborative emergence of narrative

Improvised narratives are created by the collaborative efforts of the entire group. No single speaker creates the narrative; it emerges from the give and take of conversation. The narrative is constructed turn by turn; one child proposes a new development for the play, and other children respond by modifying or embellishing that proposal. Each new proposal for a development in the narrative is the creative inspiration of one child, but that proposal does not become a part of the play until it is evaluated by the other children. In the subsequent flow of dialogue, the group collaborates to determine whether to accept the proposal, how to weave that proposal into the drama that has already been established, and then how to further elaborate on it.

Narratives are 'collaboratively emergent' from improvised dialogue for several reasons. First, they are unpredictable and contingent; their structures cannot be predicted in advance of the interaction. Second, the narrative emerges from the successive actions of all participants; it is not the conscious creation of any one person. For this reason, the social-interactional-discursive elements of dialogue are essential and defining features of the narratives that are generated. Third, because the narrative emerges out of an interactional, discursive process, no single child can drive its creation, and because it is a collective social product, it cannot be equated with any child's mental schema. Fourth, because improvisational discourse allows for retrospective interpretation, the emergent narrative cannot be analyzed solely in terms of a child's goal in an individual turn, because in many cases a child does not know the meaning of her own turn until the other children have responded. In improvisational play, narrative elements emerge that cannot be understood by focusing on individual children's mental representations and goals.

The emergent narrative is a collective social phenomenon. Drawing on theories of sociological emergentism (Sawyer 2001b), I argue that the emergent narrative is analytically irreducible to the actions, intentions, or mental states of participating children. Although the narrative is created by children through their collective action, it is analytically independent of their internal mental models and goals. This position is a version of what sociological theorists refer to as 'methodological collectivism': the position that although only individuals exist, there may be analytically irreducible phenomena that emerge from collective action. Arguments for analytic irreducibility have been accepted in a broad range of scientific fields, because irreducibility is a common feature of emergent phenomena (Sawyer 2002a). This approach is opposed to methodologically individualist approaches to the study of play narratives. Methodological individualism is the stance that all properties of group behavior can be reduced to, and ultimately derived from, properties of individuals. In the study of group narrative practice, methodological individualism corresponds to the view that the group's emergent narrative can be analyzed by analyzing the internal cognitive representations of it within a participating child's mind.

The reductionist thrust of methodological individualism remains implicit in many disciplines that study conversational interaction. For example, many cognitive psychologists assume that the emergent narrative is reducible to the participant's internal representations of it, as in Schank and Abelson's 'script' model and in 'event schemata' theories more generally (Mandler 1984; Tannen 1979). The theory of collaborative emergence associates the narrative with the emergent and negotiated social process, rather than with any mental representation of it. Emergent narratives cannot be fully explained by analyzing the actions or mental states of the participant individuals, and then by working 'upwards' to an explanation of the emergent narrative. This sort of analysis can partially explain the collaborative emergence of narratives, but cannot adequately represent the analytic independence of the narrative, or the conversational processes that generate them.

Collaborative emergence thus describes the connection between unstructured improvisation and the resulting narrative structure. Studying collaborative emergence requires a focus on the turn-by-turn symbolic processes that participants use to co-create their interactional frame. Conversation analysis can offer theory and methodology to study the emergence of narrative from improvisation; it is a commonplace among scholars of conversation that individuals work together to co-construct their social reality through interaction. Conversation analysts have noted that speakers co-construct the interactional frame, and that the frame, in turn, constrains the future actions of individuals. Conversation analysts have argued that higher-level structures (not only emergent narratives, but also social structures and institutions) are the product of the moment-to-moment unfolding emergence of collaborative, communicative interaction. Conversational dynamics produce and reproduce these higher-level structures. In turn, these emergent higher-level structures both constrain and enable future conversational actions (Giddens 1984; Sawyer 2002b).

Conversation analysts have argued that talk cannot be understood as a static transcript, but must be viewed as fundamentally in play during interaction (Schegloff 1990; Schegloff and Sacks 1973). In children's play dialogues, the narrative emerges from collective action. The emergent narrative is a dynamic structure; it changes with every turn. Until the play period is over or the group disbands, the analyst cannot stop the play at any one point and identify with certainty what the narrative's structure is. It is always subject to continuing negotiation, and because of its irreducible ambiguity, intersubjectivity must be continually negotiated and reproduced.

The theory of collaborative emergence suggests that the study of sociodramatic play and narrative must foundationally incorporate conversation-analytic methods that closely analyze the processual, turn-by-turn dynamics of pretend play dialogue. For example, conversation-analytic methods could be used to study metaplay and dialogic strategies in play conversation. How are such strategies combined in sequences of conversation? How does the presence or absence of these strategies affect the nature of the narratives that emerge? Answers to these questions will require a processual focus on the collaborative emergence of play conversation, as partially demonstrated in the examples of Section 3.

Conclusion

This chapter has explored the ways that narratives emerge from collaborative play improvisations, with the goal of better understanding how sociodramatic play might contribute developmentally to narrative literacy. I began by defining improvisation and narrative; I then analyzed several children's play episodes, organizing them to demonstrate two factors that influence the emergence of narrative from improvisation: the use of dialogic metaplay strategies, and the presence of scaffolding scripts. I followed these examples by proposing a theoretical approach to 'collaborative emergence' designed to help us understand how narratives emerge from improvised dialogue.

As with any other socially emergent phenomenon, in improvisational play we find that the emergent narratives cannot be reduced to the internal representations of any participant. As a result, analysis requires an empirical focus on the moment-to-moment interactional process of the group, and how the process leads to the emergence of the narrative. In conclusion I shall identify several implications for educators, drawing on the above examples and the theoretical approach.

First, I found that improvisational play rarely generates narratives with coherent global plot structures, but that the narratives that emerge are likely to be more well-formed if the children use metaplay and dialogic strategies. In fact, there is evidence from studies of adult improvisational theater that professional acting ensembles create more complex plot structures if they are allowed to use out-of-character techniques. Sawyer (2002b) compared two theater groups that perform 'long-form' improvisations, 30 to 60-minute plays that are fully improvised. One of the two groups, The Family, allowed their actors to step out-of-character and use a narrator's voice, whereas the other group, Jazz Freddy, required their actors to remain in-character for the entire 60 minutes. Sawyer found that the narratives that emerged from The Family's performances had much greater plot complexity, they had twice as many distinct plot lines, and the plot lines were integrated more fully by the end of the performance.

Second, I found that the skillful introduction of scaffolds, loose outlines of plots, or a shared memory of a fairy tale or movie, can help to guide children's natural collaborative improvisations into a narrative structure with global coherence. Again, there is evidence from Sawyer's (2002b) studies of long-form improvisational theater groups for the importance of scaffolds. Many of the groups that perform long-form improvisation have found it necessary to introduce some form of global outline or plot structure, because without it the performance wanders through pockets of local coherence but without generating a globally coherent narrative. For example, a group in Chicago used a format they called 'structured improvisation' to help them generate a 30-minute performance in the style of a television sitcom. The actors prepared a scenario in advance, complete with breaks for advertisements; the scenario specified how many distinct scenes would occur and what types of characters and relationships were appropriate to the genre. The scenario also specified a global structure to be followed: an initiating event, a conflict or misunderstanding, and a resolution. Such examples demonstrate that professional adult theater groups find it difficult to generate globally coherent narratives from group improvisation unless there is a scaffold; surely preschool children will find it even more difficult.

Educators could experiment with similar scaffolds. For example, children could collectively be given a general plot scenario, the scenario could be separated into three acts, and the children directed to accomplish a certain subset of the narrative within each of the three acts. Or teachers could scaffold children's narrative practice with well-timed prompts or queries about the unfolding story (cf. Saltz et al. 1977; Smilansky 1968). Baker-Sennett, Matusov, and Rogoff (1992) found that children's improvisational collaboration resulted in the generation of a globally coherent puppet play when the children were told to recreate a familiar fairy tale like Snow White.

Educational technologists have begun to experiment with using computer technology to provide scaffolds that help the improvisations of play result in the emergence of narrative. Two recent projects are of interest to narrative researchers, the MIT Media Lab's KidsRoom, and the European Union's KidStory project.

The KidsRoom project at the MIT Media Lab (Bobick et al. 1998) is an 'immersive environment,' a 'smart room' that creates a live fantasy environment for three or four children. The KidsRoom is equipped with several digital cameras with vision technology, and these cameras are programmed with the ability to detect the location and movement of the children in the room. Two walls of the KidsRoom are large screens with computer-generated images projected from outside the room, and these images are directed by the messages coming from the digital cameras, so that the children have the impression that the images on the walls are changing in response to their actions.

Because of the limitations of the technology, the KidsRoom designers decided to carefully limit the range of potential creative actions on the part of the children. The story line that children experience is largely scripted in advance, so that the number of wall images is manageable, and also so that the digital cameras know generally where to expect the children to be located. Within the script, there are places where the children have to collaboratively improvise to move the story forward, but the story has the same structure and the same conclusion every time. For example, at one point in the narrative, large monster figures are projected on the wall of the room, and the speakers play a loud roaring sound. The narrator's voice tells the children that if the kids yell, the monsters will quiet down. If the children shout loudly enough (as detected by microphones), the monsters stop roaring and the storyline progresses; if the children's shout is weak, the voice tells the children to shout louder. If the second shout is still weak, the KidsRoom is programmed to proceed with the narrative anyway, and the monsters become quiet after all.

In an attempt to encourage children's improvisational collaboration, the KidStory project (Simsarian 1999, 2000) started with the guiding assumption that the scaffolds should be less constraining than in the KidsRoom project. The researchers focused on developing intelligent toys that can enhance children's naturally occurring play activities by facilitating what they called 'storymaking.' For example, one toy developed by the KidStory team is the 'Story Dice,' a set of three large dice representing the Who, the What, and the Where of a story. The children first choose six characters, actions, and locations, and label the sides of the dice themselves. The dice are equipped with internal radio electronics so that a remote computer can detect which face of each dice lands up after a roll. The children then use authoring software to improvise a story that incorporates the Who, the What, and the Where that are rolled. The Story Dice thus provide a scaffold to guide children's improvisational play, but the scaffold is more open to improvisation and collaboration than the scripted narrative of the KidsRoom.

A third implication of this chapter is that emergent narratives may need new coding schemes, particularly if the researcher is interested in evaluating the developmental level of the participants. Trabasso's coding scheme uses plot structure to measure global coherence, whereas Daiute's coding scheme emphasizes characters and relationships. The play episodes in Examples 2 through 5 gain coherence from character enactments perhaps even more than from plot, but they do not score highly on either coding scheme. Eder suggested that collaborative narrations 'are more loosely structured than solo stories and tend to progress from one climax to another rather than build to a single high point' (1998: 84). Children's collaborative narrative practices may result in a different type of global coherence, one based more on processual organization, and thus might warrant a more processual conception of narrative.

In sum, I have explored the relationship between collaboratively improvised dialogues and narrative structure. Narratives emerge from improvisational play through a process of collaborative emergence, and I provided several examples of this process. These examples show that the use of metaplay and dialogic strategies can improve the coherence of the emergent narratives, and that scaffolds can guide the process of collaborative emergence without removing its improvisationality altogether. An awareness of these connections is important both to classroom teachers and to developers of software to support collaborative storymaking. Future research on this topic should be interdisciplinary, combining method and theory from the empirical study of conversation with developmental theory on narrative structure and competence.

Note

1 All play data are from Sawyer's dataset, gathered using methods described in Sawyer (1997).

References

Baker-Sennett, J., Matusov, E., and Rogoff, B. (1992) 'Sociocultural processes of creative planning in children's playcrafting,' pp. 93–114 in P. Light and G. Butterworth (eds), *Context and Cognition: Ways of learning and knowing*, Hillsdale, N.J.: Lawrence Erlbaum Associates.

Bakhtin, M. M. (1981) 'Discourse in the novel,' pp. 259–422 in *The Dialogic Imagination*, Austin, Tex.: University of Texas Press.

Bobick, A. F., Intille, S. S., Davis, J. W., Baird, F., Pinhanez, C. S., Campbell, L. W., Ivanov, Y. A., Schütte, A., and Wilson, A. (1998) *The KidsRoom: A perceptually-based interactive and immersive story environment*, Technical Report 398, Cambridge, Mass.: MIT Media Lab.

Branscombe, N. A. and Taylor, J. B. (2000) '"It would be as good as Snow White".: Play and prosody,' pp. 169–88 in K. A. Roskos and J. F. Christie (eds), *Play and Literacy in Early Childhood*, Mahwah, N.J.: Lawrence Erlbaum Associates.

Christie, J. F. (ed.) (1991) *Play and Early Literacy Development*, Albany, N.Y.: SUNY Press.

Coates, J. (1997) 'The construction of a collaborative floor in women's friendly talk,', pp. 55–89 in T. Givon (ed.), *Conversation: Cognitive, communicative and social perspectives*, Amsterdam: John Benjamins.

Corsaro, W. A. (1985) Friendship and peer culture in the early years, Norwood, N.J.: Ablex.

Daiute, C. (1989) 'Play as thought: thinking strategies of young writers,' *Harvard Educational Review*, **59**(1), pp. 1–23.

Daiute, C. (1999) *Understanding Conflict Narrative Coding Manual*, New York: Social Development and Literacy Group, CUNY Graduate School.

Duranti, A. and Brenneis, D. (eds) (1986) 'The audience as co-author,' *Text* **6**(3) Special issue.

Dyson, A. H. (1991) 'The roots of literacy development: play, pictures, and peers,' pp. 98–116 in B. Scales, M. Almy, A. Nicolopoulou, and S. Ervin-Tripp (eds), *Play and the Social Context of Development in Early Care and Education*, New York: Teacher's College Press.

Eder, D. (1998) 'Developing adolescent peer culture through collaborative narration,' pp. 82–94 in S. M. Hoyle and C. T. Adger (eds), *Strategic Language Use in Later Childhood*, New York: Oxford University Press.

Falk, J. (1980) 'The conversational duet,' pp. 507–14 in *Proceedings of the Sixth Annual Meeting of the Berkeley Linguistics Society*.

Fein, G. G. (1987) 'Pretend play: creativity and consciousness,' pp. 281–304 in D. Gorlitz and J. F. Wohlwill (eds), *Curiosity, Imagination, and Play: On the development of spontaneous cognitive and motivational processes*, Hillsdale, N.J.: Lawrence Erlbaum Associates.

Fein, G. G., Ardila-Rey, A. E., and Groth, L. A. (2000) 'The narrative connection: stories and literacy,' pp. 27–43 in K. A. Roskos and J. F. Christie (eds), *Play and Literacy in Early Childhood*, Mahwah, N.J.: Lawrence Erlbaum Associates.

Galda, L. (1984) 'Narrative competence: play, storytelling, and story comprehension,' pp. 105–17 in A. Pellegrini and T. Yaukey (eds), *The Development of Oral and Written Language in Social Contexts*, Norwood, N.J.: Ablex.

Gee, J. P. (2000) 'Discourse and sociocultural studies in reading,' pp. 195–207 in M. L. Kamil, P. B. Mosenthal, P. D. Pearson, and R. Barr (eds), *Handbook of Reading Research*, Vol. 3, Mahwah, N.J.: Lawrence Erlbaum Associates.

Giddens, A. (1984) *The Constitution of Society: Outline of the theory of structuration*, Berkeley, Calif.: University of California Press.

Goodwin, C. (1981) *Conversational Organization: Interaction between speakers and hearers*, New York: Academic Press.

Johnson, D. W. and Johnson, R. T. (1992) 'Positive interdependence: key to effective cooperation,' pp. 174–99 in R. Hertz-Lazarowitz and N. Miller (eds), *Interaction in Cooperative Groups: The theoretical anatomy of group learning*, New York: Cambridge University Press.

Lucy, J. A. (ed.) (1993) *Reflexive Language: Reported speech and metapragmatics*, New York: Cambridge University Press.

Mandler, J. M. (1984) *Stories, Scripts, and Scenes: Aspects of schema theory*, Hillsdale, N.J.: Lawrence Erlbaum Associates.

Michaels, S. (1981) '"Sharing time": children's narrative styles and differential access to literacy,' *Language in Society*, **10**, pp. 423–42.

Paley, V. G. (1988) *Bad Guys Don't Have Birthdays*, Chicago, Ill.: University of Chicago Press.

Pellegrini, A. D. (1985) 'The relations between symbolic play and literate behavior: a review and critique of the empirical literature,' *Review of Educational Research*, **55**(1), pp. 107–21.

Pellegrini, A. D. and Galda, L. (1982) 'The effects of thematic-fantasy play training on the development of children's story comprehension,' *American Educational Research Journal*, **19**(3), pp. 443–52.

Pellegrini, A. D. and Galda, L. (1993) 'Ten years after: a reexamination of symbolic play and literacy research,' *Reading Research Quarterly*, **28**, pp. 162–75.

Roskos, K. A. and Christie, J. F. (eds) (2000) *Play and Literacy in Early Childhood: research from multiple perspectives*, Mahwah, N.J.: Lawrence Erlbaum Associates.

Roskos, K. and Christie, J. (2001) 'Examining the play-literacy interface: a critical review and future directions,' *Journal of Early Childhood Literacy*, **1**(1), pp. 59–89.

Sachs, J., Goldman, J., and Chaille, C. (1984) 'Planning in pretend play: using language to coordinate narrative development,' pp. 119–28 in A. Pellegrini and

T. Yaukey (eds), *The Development of Oral and Written Language in Social Contexts*, Norwood, N.J.: Ablex.

Saltz, E., Dixon, D., and Johnson, J. (1977) 'Training disadvantaged preschoolers on various fantasy activities: effects on cognitive functioning and impulse control,' *Child Development*, **48**, pp. 367–80.

Sawyer, R. K. (1995a) 'Creativity as mediated action: a comparison of improvisational performance and product creativity,' *Mind, Culture, and Activity*, **2**, pp. 172–91.

Sawyer, R. K. (1995b) 'A developmental model of heteroglossic improvisation in children's fantasy play,' pp. 127–53 in A. Ambert (ed.), *Sociological Studies of Children*, Vol. 7, Greenwich, Conn.: JAI Press.

Sawyer, R. K. (1997) *Pretend Play as Improvisation: Conversation in the preschool classroom*, Norwood, N.J.: Lawrence Erlbaum Associates.

Sawyer, R. K. (1999) 'The emergence of creativity,' *Philosophical Psychology*, **12**(4), pp. 447–69.

Sawyer, R. K. (2001a) *Creating Conversations: Improvisation in everyday discourse*, Cresskill, N.J.: Hampton Press.

Sawyer, R. K. (2001b) 'Emergence in sociology: contemporary philosophy of mind and some implications for sociological theory,' *American Journal of Sociology*, **107**(3), pp. 551–85.

Sawyer, R. K. (2002a) 'Emergence in psychology: lessons from the history of non-reductionist science,' *Human Development*, **45**, pp. 2–28.

Sawyer, R. K. (2002b) *Improvised Dialogues: Emergence and creativity in conversation*, Westport, Conn.: Greenwood.

Scarlett, W. G. and Wolf, D. (1979) 'When it's only make-believe: the construction of a boundary between fantasy and reality in storytelling,' *New Directions for Child Development*, 6, repr. as pp. 29–40 in E. Winner and H. Gardner (eds), *Fact, Fiction, and Fantasy in Childhood*, San Francisco, Calif.: Jossey-Bass.

Schegloff, E. A. (1990) 'On the organization of sequences as a source of "coherence" in talk-in-interaction,' pp. 51–77 in B. Dorval (ed.), *Conversational Organization and its Development*, Norwood, N.J.: Ablex.

Schegloff, E. A. and Sacks, H. (1973) 'Opening up closings,' *Semiotica*, **8**, pp. 289–327.

Sheldon, A. (1990) 'Pickle fights: gendered talk in preschool disputes,' *Discourse Processes*, **13**, pp. 5–31.

Simsarian, K. T. (ed.) (1999) *Children and Narrative Workshop*, Barcelona, Spain: Swedish Institute of Computer Science.

Simsarian, K. T. (2000) *Developing Collaborative Storytelling Tools with Children in a Nascent Medium*, Stockholm, Sweden: Swedish Institute of Computer Science.

Slavin, R. E. (1992) 'When and why does cooperative learning increase achievement? Theoretical and empirical perspectives,' pp. 145–73 in R. Hertz-Lazarowitz and N. Miller (eds), *Interaction in Cooperative Groups: The theoretical anatomy of group learning*, New York: Cambridge University Press.

Smilansky, S. (1968) *The Effects of Sociodramatic Play on Disadvantaged Preschool Children*, New York: Wiley.

Suh, S and Trabasso, T. (1993) 'Inferences during on-line processing: converging evidence from discourse analysis, talk-aloud protocols, and recognition priming,' *Journal of Memory and Language*, **32**, pp. 279–301.

Sutton-Smith, B. (1981) *The Folkstories of Children*, Philadelphia: University of Pennsylvania Press.

Tannen, D. (1979) 'What's in a frame? Surface evidence for underlying expectations,' pp. 137–81 in R. O. Freedle (ed.), *New Directions in Discourse Processing*, Norwood, N.J.: Ablex,.

Tannen, D. (1989) 'Interpreting interruption in conversation,' in B. Music, R. Graczyk, and C. Wiltshire (eds), *Papers from the 25th annual Regional Meeting of the Chicago Linguistics Society*, Chicago: Chicago Linguistics Society.

Tannock, S. (1998) 'Noisy talk: conversation and collaboration in a youth writing group,' pp. 241–65 in S. M. Hoyle and C. T. Adger (eds), *Strategic Language Use in Later Childhood*, New York: Oxford University Press.

Trabasso, T., Stein, N. L., Rodkin, P. C., Munger, M. P., and Baughn, C. R. (1992) 'Knowledge of goals and plans in the on-line narration of events,' *Cognitive Development*, **7**, pp. 133–70.

Trawick-Smith, J. (1998) 'A qualitative analysis of metaplay in the preschool years,' *Early Childhood Research Quarterly*, **13**(3), pp. 433–52.

Trawick-Smith, J. (2001) 'The play frame and the "fictional dream": the bidirectional relationship between metaplay and story writing,' paper presented at the Annual Meeting of the American Educational Research Association, Seattle, Wa.

Watson, K. A. (1975) 'Transferable communicative routines: strategies and group identity in two speech events,' *Language in Society*, **4**, pp. 53–72.

Webb, N. M. (1991) 'Task-related verbal interaction and mathematics learning in small groups,' *Journal for Research in Mathematics Education*, **22**(5), pp. 366–89.

Williamson, P. A. and Silvern, S. B. (1991) 'Thematic-fantasy play and story comprehension,' pp. 69–90 in J. F. Christie (ed.), *Play and Early Literacy Development*, Albany, N.Y.: SUNY Press.

Wolf, D. and Hicks, D. (1989) 'The voices within narratives: the development of intertextuality in young children's stories,' *Discourse Processes*, **12**, pp. 329–51.

Yaden Jr., D. B., Rowe, D. W., and MacGillivray, L. (2000) 'Emergent literacy: a matter (polyphony) of perspectives,' pp. 425–54 in R. Barr, P. D. Pearson, and P. B. Mosenthal (eds), *Handbook of Reading Research*, Vol. 3, Mahwah, N.J.: Lawrence Erlbaum Associates.

Chapter 3

Angels, tooth fairies and ghosts: thinking creatively in an early years classroom

Dorothy Faulkner

Introduction to the educational environment and local context of the study

This chapter offers an account of the creative thinking and collaboration that took place in a class of five year olds in an English primary school during the academic year 2004–05. In terms of its location and size, there was nothing particularly remarkable about the school. It was a medium-sized school of about 350 pupils that served a semi-rural town in the east of England. Its pupils were local and most lived in the 1930s housing estate within walking distance of the school. What was special about this school, however, was its commitment to developing itself as a creative learning community by participating in a creativity training programme more usually employed in an adult business context. Moreover, it was willing to subject itself to the scrutiny of a university research team: the head teacher and senior management team had agreed to take part in a year-long case study to evaluate the impact of the training programme on teaching and learning in the school. This school was in no way unusual in wanting to develop its capacity for creative teaching and learning, but at the time its intention to embed creative thinking skills across all curriculum subjects was fairly uncommon. This intent was, however, very much in tune with national and international developments in education where strenuous efforts were being made to extend the reach of creative education which had for a long time been more or less exclusively associated with the arts. A very brief outline of these developments is offered to set the research in context and to explain the educational climate in which the school was working.

Over the past ten years, educational researchers have devoted a huge expenditure of effort to understanding creative teaching and learning, (e.g. Jeffrey 2006; Craft 2005). In developed and developing nations around the globe, this effort has been driven in part by the view that in the twenty-first century education must meet the needs of societies where, according to economists and policy makers, knowledge generation, creativity and innovation are key to the success of economic systems. As Sawyer (2006: 42) points out, 'If the core of the knowledge society is creativity, then the key task for educators is to prepare learners to be capable of participating creatively in an innovation economy.' A similar sentiment is voiced in the 1999 version of the *National Curriculum Handbook for Primary Teachers in England*:

> By providing rich and varied contexts for pupils to acquire, develop and apply a broad range of knowledge, understanding and skills, the curriculum should enable pupils to think creatively and critically, to solve problems and to make a difference for the better. It should give them the opportunity to become creative, innovative, enterprising and capable of leadership to equip them for their future lives as workers and citizens.
>
> (QCA 1999: 11)

In the United Kingdom, in response to this economic and cultural Zeitgeist, various influential reports and discussion papers on creativity and education were commissioned by government departments in the late 1990s and early years of the twenty-first century. The first of these, *All our Futures: Creativity culture and education* (NACCCE 1999), was commissioned jointly by the former Department for Education and Employment and the Department for Culture, Media and Sport. This was followed in 2000 by *Unlocking Creativity: A strategy for development* (DCAL et al. 2000), commissioned by Northern Ireland's Department of Culture, Arts and Leisure, and in 2001, *Creativity in Education* and *Creativity in Education – Case studies* (Learning and Teaching Scotland/IDES Network 2001a, 200ab). In turn, these reports gave rise to various curriculum development projects such as *Creativity: Find it, promote it* (QCA 2005) in England, and *Creativity Counts – Portraits of practice* (Learning and Teaching Scotland/IDES Network 2004). Similar curriculum development projects were initiated in Northern Ireland and Wales (SEED 2006).

Of these projects, in England the Creative Partnerships programme has been one of the most successful (Kendall et al. 2008; OfSTED 2006). This programme was set up in 2002 under the aegis of Arts Council England to serve schools and youth organisations in some of the most disadvantaged areas in England. The programme assisted schools to build sustainable relationships with creative professionals from fields such as the arts, cultural and media organisations, architecture and creative design industries. It achieved this through local delivery networks which assisted the establishment of working relationships between schools, creative professionals and organizations. Although Creative Partnerships came under the umbrella of a new organisation, Creativity, Culture and Education (CCE) in 2009, its core mission remained that of raising children's and young people's aspirations and helping them to develop the skills needed to perform well in the workplace and wider society (CCE 2010). The fundamental premises that informed Creative Partnerships vision of the nature of the partnerships between educational practitioners, schools and creative professionals are that:

> Teaching is fundamentally a creative profession and that teachers are well accustomed to finding creative solutions to complex challenges. By pairing the complementary skills of creative practitioners and teachers, Creative Partnerships helps liberate the creativity of everyone involved, so that fresh and engaging approaches to teaching and learning are developed through collaboration.
>
> (Creative Partnerships 2010)

The school where we carried out the research described in this chapter was a Creative Partnerships school. It was selected for a case study and second phase of an evaluation of a project called EXCITE! (Excellence, Creativity and Innovation in Teaching and Education). The evaluation was carried out by a team of researchers from the Open University and was framed by the government policy initiatives detailed above. The former Department for Education and Skills and Esmée Fairburn Foundation funded the project and the evaluation. At the time there was considerable interest in the question of whether creativity training programmes developed for business and industry could be adapted to develop creativity in schools (e.g. Fryer 2003). The EXCITE! project was designed to deliver a well-established, creativity-training programme, 'Synectics', to teachers from four English local education authorities. The training was delivered by 'creative facilitators' from Synectics Education Initiative (SEI),[1] an independent educational charity. These facilitators use experiential learning together with established tools and communication strategies to stimulate creative thinking and problem solving. One of the strengths of the SEI programme is that in addition to offering training in creative thinking techniques, it offers structures for collaborative group work. As genuine collaboration between pupils can be difficult to achieve during classroom group work sessions (Comber et al. 1999), this meant that the programme had additional potential benefits for teachers. The programme was modified for schools and colleges. The first phase of the Open University study investigated the impact of this modified programme on teachers' professional practice to determine whether it transferred successfully into the education sector.

Through its involvement with Creative Partnerships the primary school where the second phase of the Open University study took place was firmly committed to the view that teaching is a creative profession and that learning ought to be enjoyable. One of its teachers had participated in the initial phase of EXCITE! This teacher persuaded the head to bid for additional Creative Partnerships funding to secure the services of Mathilda

Joubert, a creative facilitator from SEI to work with the school.[2] 'Synectics' training sessions for the school's governors and all teaching and support staff took place at the end of the summer term (two days) and just before the start of the autumn term (two days). In consultation with the head teacher, Mathilda tailored the training to the school's needs, and continued to support the school throughout the year. She also contributed to the research study. The format and content of the creativity training over the first two days covered three themed areas: creative climates, creative thinking tools and creative process strategies.

On the first day, participants explored the current context, national educational climate and challenges to teaching for creativity, the language for creativity and were introduced to Synectics tools for creative thinking. The second day was devoted to problem solving, and covered the Synectics Problem Solving Diamond, creative excursions, planning input, backward/forward planning, best current thinking and agenda meetings. Working in small groups, members of staff from the school learned how to facilitate creative problem-solving sessions by working on real-life problems. They used video-based feedback to analyse their own performance. The training emphasised teamwork and strategies for creative collaboration.

The second two days of training took place immediately before the start of the autumn school term, and focused on developing innovative ways of working and remodelling the curriculum. These sessions allowed members of staff to practise using Synectics creative thinking tools and process strategies. The problems they worked on were 'How to teach for understanding', 'How to develop a secure and positive emotional climate for learning' and 'How to encourage creative learning and teaching for everyone'. The overarching goal for these two days was a workable action plan for curriculum change.

Two of the main aims of the research study were to examine the impact of this training on teaching and learning. We used questionnaires and semi-structured interviews with teachers and support staff to evaluate the impact of the programme on their teaching. To evaluate its impact on learning, we filmed the lessons and activities taking place in three classrooms at various points during the school year. This chapter draws on transcriptions of video observations of two lessons given by Sally, a year 1 teacher, and on her reflections on these lessons. A full account of the training programme, the research methodology and main findings of the EXCITE! evaluations are given in the main reports (details of how to access these are given at the end of the chapter).[3] Further details about Synectics tools can be found in Cesarani (2003) and Fryer (2003).

The next two sections discuss how Sally introduced some of the Synectics tools and techniques into her teaching. The first section draws on an extract from the transcript of a literacy lesson that was ostensibly about how to formulate different kinds of question. This lesson took place towards the middle of the autumn term. The following section uses extracts from a literacy lesson that took place during the spring term. As well as Sally's own reflections on these lessons, the chapter offers an interpretation informed by socio-cultural accounts of collaborative creativity (e.g. Moran and John-Steiner 2003; Sawyer 2003). It also draws on cognitive developmental explanations of how children construct intuitive and highly creative theories, stories and narratives to understand the world (e.g. Engel 2005; Gelman and Gottfried 2006).

Angels, tooth fairies and ghosts: creative excursions in year I

One of the founders of Synectics, George M. Prince describes the relationship between creative thinking and learning as follows:

> Underlying learning is the process of *thinking*. We go through the process of thinking to *create* meaning. We create meaning by making a connection between the new information and what we already know, so that the new information 'makes sense'. ... This description of the process of thinking to learn sounds surprisingly like that of 'creative thinking' to produce new ideas, concepts, products, etc. New ideas are the result of making connections between material that has not previously been connected. ... Learning and creativity are both, basically, the ability to make connections to create meaning or significance.
>
> (Prince and Logan 2005: 155)

He went on to say that instead of telling children they are wrong when they make novel, if unconventional connections:

> If we are respectful enough of all of a child's trial connection making, the chances are he will be a daring connection-maker. ... He will also be a very good learner.
>
> (Prince and Logan 2005: 158)

This section discusses how Sally used elements of her Synectics training to encourage her class of five and six year olds to make connections, and in doing so, revealed some of their intuitive theories about death and the supernatural. Encouraging people to generate novel and unusual connections using metaphor, analogy and visual imagery is key to a process Synectics trainers call 'excursion'. This process allows people to take a mental break from the problem they are working on to generate seemingly irrelevant ideas that they later connect back to the original problem or task. The excursion process allows people to generate alternative perspectives and new ways of thinking about a problem. In a classroom context, excursions can include drawing, story-telling, taking a walk, making collages, generating metaphors, analogies, paradoxes or anything the teacher decides to introduce.

On our first visit to the school in November, 2004 we filmed a 'philosophy' lesson with Sally's class of five and six year olds. In this lesson, Sally wanted to use excursion with the class. She also drew on her training in the use of a programme called Philosophy for Children (P4C) to structure the initial part of the lesson. Matthew Lipman (2003) developed P4C, a language-based programme, as a way of using dialogue and shared inquiry to develop children's deductive reasoning and critical thinking skills. Lipman's programme draws on the writings of Dewey (1910/1991) and Vygotsky (1978), who both emphasized the role of education in the teaching of thinking. Accordingly, teachers who use this programme are trained in discussion techniques that encourage disciplined practice in critical thinking. In a P4C 'community of inquiry', children are encouraged to discuss moral and ethical issues, usually presented through imaginative fiction. Lipman's paradigm emphasizes the importance of creative and moral thinking as well as critical thinking. Typically, these discussion sessions involve the whole class and their teacher sitting in a circle so that they can speak face-to-face with one another.

In both Synectics and P4C, the teacher adopts a facilitator role rather than a didactic role. As Synectics was originally developed in a business context, the role of the facilitator is related to how a team conducts a meeting. It includes making notes and keeping track of ideas and contributions from team members; making sure people's suggestions are listened to and developed before they are evaluated, introducing specific techniques such as excursions when appropriate, and generally making sure that team members understand what kind of contribution is required at each stage of the meeting. Sally employed all of these strategies with her class, and was careful to make sure that no one's contributions were overlooked, that ideas – however improbable – were accepted, and that children were given plenty of time to think. A central tenet of the Synectics philosophy is that all ideas are potentially valuable and should be accepted at least initially, and that no idea should be rejected until it has been given a fair hearing. This practice is designed to establish a positive emotional climate that is supportive of creativity.

With the children sitting on the floor in a big circle, Sally started off the lesson with a 'game' that encouraged children to formulate and progressively refine a philosophical question:

> We're going to play a game, just to start off with, with questions. It's a game that I haven't ever played before but it's just an idea I had last

night. Um, and what we need to is we need to start with a question. And it's like the um, stand up sit down, but instead we'll go round in a circle. And we're going to see how we can change a question. OK, so we're going to see how we can change it and what difference it makes to what the question means.

Thinking back to an earlier history lesson about Guy Fawkes,[4] one boy volunteered the first question: 'Why did he want to kill the whole world?' Another boy immediately jumped in with, 'But how do we know who he is?' and went on to explain, 'Yeah, cos how do we know, if you don't put "Guy Fawkes" instead of "he", cos how do you know who you mean?' Going round the circle, the children then took turns at making connections and changing words in the question to make its meaning clearer. Anyone who felt that they were not ready to contribute said 'Pass'. After about five minutes of intense discussion, the original question had been transformed into 'Why did Guy Fawkes want to blow up the king and the Houses of Parliament?' Each time a child suggested a change to the wording; Sally encouraged them to give a reason for their suggestion and also asked the other children whether they agreed to it. Once agreement had been reached she recorded the new question on a large sheet of paper so that children could see as well as listen to how its wording had changed. When she watched the video of the lesson later she commented:

> I think the uncovering what the question was really about relates to the Synectics training as well [as P4C] because it's really important, the Synectics training says it's really important … to have a clear understanding of what questions actually mean. I think getting children to stop and look at questions, and really understand what it means and make those connections around them; I think that really makes the kind of creativity that Synectics is all about.

Next, Sally introduced two excursions. The first excursion was a 'connections game' that she had invented. The children had played the game before, and enjoyed it as it involved a lot of activity and excitement. Sally reminded them of the rules by acting them out and modelling what the children were expected to do:

> I'm going to walk round the circle and we need to make the circle quite small, 'cos I'm going to walk round. I'm going to keep thinking of something connected with 'Parliament'. So we go round [walks round, touching children on head saying 'Parliament', when she reaches Josh, she says] 'King', now Josh is going to try and catch me. [Sally runs round the circle trying to beat Josh back to his space in the circle]. Josh, would you like to start at Joseph with 'King'. When you think of

something that connects with 'King' then you need to try and steal their place.

During the course of this game the chain of connections made by the children was 'king', 'government', 'queen',' princess', 'prince' and finally, back to 'government', at which point the game ended. After another excursion where children had to indicate whether they agreed or disagreed with a particular statement by moving to different areas of the room, they were ready for some more discussion. In this part of the lesson, Sally wanted to help her class to develop their dialogue skills. With the children again sitting in a circle, She started off by reminding them what dialogue means:

> [Last week] you were practising some skills, which are called dialogue skills and dialogue is about talking about your ideas. And you chose last week to do that for your homework, practise those things with mums and dads. So you must be quite good at that now, now you've had a practice so we could use those things that you were doing with mums and dads to talk about this question here that you've just changed.

The dialogue reported in Extract 1 took place towards the end of the lesson. It is worth reproducing in full as it shows in some detail how Sally skilfully used a series of open questions to draw out extended contributions from the children. For example in line 1 she asks 'What was your idea?' and in line 14 she asks 'Can you explain that a bit more?' She also used paraphrase to clarify children's connections, as in line 9 when she says, 'So the connections are the wings and looking after people', although she was careful to check that the children agreed with her understanding. She kept the discussion on track by prompting children to explain and give reasons for the connections that they made, as in line 6: 'So what's the connection between tooth fairies and angels?' In this way Sally helped the children to acquire important 'bridging skills' that, according to Perkins (1985), allow them to transfer learning and insights from one context to another, new context. She reinforced the concepts she wanted the children to understand by her careful use of language, as in line 12, 'OK so there are *similarities* and there are *differences*', and line 22, 'You've all got some very exciting, *connected ideas.*' She listened very carefully herself to what the children were saying, as in line 28 where Gary makes the surprising connection between 'poppies' and the discussion of skeletons, coffins and being buried. When Sally probed the children about this connection, boy 7 offered the explanation in line 27, 'They are for people who have died.' This led him and other children to make further connections between 'poppies' and soldiers being killed during wartime.

Extract 1

1. **Sally**[5] [...][6] I'm just interested in what Thomas just said because he said something about being rock solid. At the moment I feel quite rock solid. So I'm wondering how I go from being rock solid to being able to go up to heaven. I don't understand how that would work. What do you think Molly?

2. **Girl** Well ...

3. **Boy 1** Angels, angels bring you up.

4. **Sally** If we could just hold on cos I can see Molly's got an idea starting. You've got an idea about angels Thomas. Molly what was your idea? Do you have an idea you could tell us about or is it an idea you're still thinking about in your head? Do you want a bit more time to think about it? OK, just out of interest can you change places if you believe in angels? <Children swap>. Fantastic, fantastic. What did you just say Joseph?

5. **Boy 2** Tooth fairies are real.

6. **Sally** And what's the connection between tooth fairies and angels? [...]

7. **Boy 2** Tooth fairies take your tooth and they just (fly everywhere).

8. **Boy 3** They make sure people are OK in heaven. When they die (...).

9. **Sally** So the connections are the wings and looking after people?

10. **Boy 3** Yeah they look after people in heaven. Cos they only come down and they collect you in their ...

11. **Boy 1** And the angels, cos the angels, the other angels, not the tooth fairies, and the angels have, you know you'll be in heaven flying around but and they have a hoop but tooth fairies don't have a hoop round their head.

12. **Sally** [...] OK, so there are similarities and there are differences between the angels. So, about everything going to heaven then, there seems to be an idea that it's something to do with angels taking you. Does anyone disagree? Does anyone not think the same as Thomas, any one have a different idea how you get to heaven? (...)

13. **Boy 4** If you come down from heaven that means you be going to be buried.

14. **Sally** Can you explain a bit more?

15. **Boy 4** The ghosts come back for you, and you're staying down in the ground and you're in a coffin.

16. **Boy 5** Yeah.

17. **Sally** What's a ghost?

18. **Boy 5** A ghost is a spirit.

19. **Sally** A spirit?

20. **Boy 5** Ghosts are, ghosts are life coming out of you when you're a skeleton.

21. **Class** <Speaking over one another>

22. **Sally** Sorry guys, hang on a minute. Can you just wait one minute Gary? Cos we just want to, can you just make sure that you do this one at a time cos you've all got some very exciting, connected ideas. Sorry, so what were you going to say Gary? Um Thomas, we're missing people's ideas, OK. Sorry, James, what were you going to say?

23. **Boy 6** Um, if, if you come down from heaven, (…) ghosts come down and take all your skin off (…) and then you get buried cos you're skeletons, skeletons, but they don't break up your bones.

24. **Sally** So, does that mean you disagree with Kyle? You don't think it's angels who take you, you think it's ghosts.

25. **Boy 6** No, angels actually take you up to heaven, and when you come down ghosts actually take the skin off.

26. **Sally** Ah right. Sorry, can you let Callum finish his idea off.

27. **Boy 6** When you're in a coffin underground and if you're a skeleton then you're in a coffin buried, you'll have a (stake) and um, ghosts are your lives, ghosts are the lives and they come out of your body and help for you.

28. **Sally** Brilliant, so out of your body. Can I just ask Gary? Gary just suddenly just one word and you just said "poppies".

29. **Boy 7** They're for people who have died.

30. **Sally** Why? I wonder why people do that.

31. **Class** <All speaking over one another>

32. **Boy 2** One, two, three, four, five.

33. **Sally** Oh, thanks ever so much Joseph. I can hear lots of people talking about the same idea, but we seem to have lots of ideas at once at the moment. Right, Joseph would just like to tell us about his idea.

34. **Boy 2** I know why you have poppies. To put (onto) the soldiers who died in war.

35. **Boy 7** And they fighted for you.

36. **Sally** So you've made a connection there. I'm just going to draw a little bit of a chain here to show the connection between the poppies, and, and what were you saying about poppies?

37. **Boy 7** They fighted for you.

38. **Boy 2** Yeah, they fighted all the horrible people, so when we were born.

39. **Boy 3** In a different country.

40. **Sally** Could you just let him finish his idea Thomas is that all right? And then you can build on it if he's missed anything out. If you want to then.

41. **Boy 7** From different countries. Um, we fighted and some (war) soldiers got shot and killed and they sended poppies to (put on the soldiers.)

42. **Sally** Wow Joseph, that's a lot of information. Well done.

Line 22 offers an example of Sally's attention to the Synectics facilitation principle, namely the importance of trying to capture *all* ideas. Here she attempted to pace the children to make sure that everyone had a chance to contribute. Although this strategy may mean some children may forget their ideas because they have to wait their turn, Sally was reinforcing the principle that all ideas are valued by showing that she didn't want to miss out on any. Line 40 again shows Sally's skills as a facilitator. She 'credits' boy 7 as the owner of the explanation that poppies are for people who have died fighting for us, and reminded the other children that they could build on this contribution once he had finished. In Synectics parlance, crediting and building are important processes that encourage collaboration and create a sense of co-ownership of the ideas. Perhaps most importantly, however, this extract demonstrated that Sally did not attempt to correct the children's reasoning or challenge ideas that another adult might be tempted to correct. As she commented during the interview where she discussed this lesson, 'Creativity is not about being right or wrong.' Like Prince and Logan (2005), she believed that children's trial connection making should be respected and that their ideas should not be rejected: 'It's about seeing every idea as a stepping stone to another, potentially better idea.'

After she had watched the video of this lesson, one of the things that Sally said she was most impressed by was how the children's listening skills and concentration had developed in a few short weeks:

> It almost feels like a different class from September, actually [this is in early November]. I feel that their listening skills have improved immensely. They are calmer. They are more focused. We spend a lot of time talking about our learning, so that they really understand what's going on and they are quite quick to pick up on what they are learning now, to explain it to other people as well. I think they are far more respectful and tolerant of each other as well, when it comes to discussing things.

The way that Sally conducted this lesson shows that P4C and Synectics can be used to good effect with very young children. Asking genuinely open questions and giving children plenty of thinking time allows children to offer extended comments and explanations indicative of high-order thinking. The children in Sally's class lived up to her claim that:

> Children can work in the abstract ... learning is based on connections. Young children know their own thinking very clearly and if they are emotionally engaged they are going to find it very easy to tap into whatever is going on. We've got some community of enquiry going in the classroom as well.

Looked at from a developmental psychological perspective, this extract raises some interesting observations concerning the nature of young children's thinking. Based on studies of preschool children (two to four year olds), Susan Gellman and Gail Gottfried (2006) claim that four key features of young children's everyday thinking entail a considerable amount of creative thought. The features that demonstrate creative thinking in early childhood are the non-conventional and inventive use of language, pretence, theory construction and generalising from specifics. If this is the case, then one wonders whether young children need the kind of formal training in thinking skills offered by P4C and Synectics.

Many of the features of young children's thinking that Gellman and Gottfried identify as 'creative' appear in Extract 1. For example, in line 11, boy 1 uses the word 'hoop' to describe the halo that angels (but not tooth fairies) have round their heads. Gelman and Gottfried would class this as an example of an inventive use of language or 'overextension', where a child extends the use of an object's name to a different object that is perceptually similar but that she or she does not know the word for. Also, between lines 13 to 27 the children construct some very interesting theories about how people get to (and from) heaven when they die and about the relationship between angels, ghosts, spirits and skeletons. The construction of intuitive theories of the world helps both children and adults to organize their experiences, to make predictions and to arrive at causal explanations for events. Gellman and Gottfried argue that there are two reasons why these kinds of theories demonstrate creative thinking. First:

> Children's knowledge is not simply the accumulation of evidence from prior observations or facts imparted by others. Rather, young children build their own concepts and connections – they creatively form new connections on the basis of the available evidence.
>
> (Gellman and Gottfried 2006: 231)

Second:

> The constructs children come up with extend beyond directly observable entities. Young children's knowledge includes information about ontology, causation, function, intentions and other properties that are not directly observable.
>
> (Gellman and Gottfried 2006: 231)

Not everyone would accept that these arguments offer a convincing explanation as to how the children in Sally's class come up with the concepts and connections given in Extract 1. For example, Susan Engel (2005) might claim that the extract offers some compelling examples of story-telling and narrative thinking, particularly examples such as the extended contribution offered by boy 6 in lines 23, 25 and 27. She argues that when children tell a story, the narrative frame allows them to oscillate between different spheres of reality; their experience of the real world 'as is', and the world of their imagination, 'as if'.

> Each story offers the child a world in which, for instance, objects have personalities, time moves backward and forward, boundaries between domains are permeable, and the relationship between symbols and referents is shifting.
>
> (Engel 2005: 112)

Bruner (1986, 1990) proposed that there are two modes of thought, the narrative and the paradigmatic. He claims further that for both children and adults, the narrative mode for thinking is one of the main ways that people make sense of the everyday world. By contrast, the paradigmatic mode is used to think about scientific phenomena and employs more formal, rule-based mechanisms such as deductive inference. Children begin to use the narrative mode to construct stories and explanations at a very early age, and although some of their stories may seem 'unruly' and 'idiosyncratic' to use Engel's terms, 'they provide vital clues to the child's inner thoughts and fantasies' (Engel 2005: 115). Drawing on the pragmatic and semiotic theories of C. S. Pierce, Oatley (1996) claims that when people engage in narrative thinking they use abductive and inductive inferential reasoning processes to construct explanations. Abductive inferences are particularly useful for constructing informal hypotheses to explain how something might have come about. Oatley (1996: 126) explains that generally, abductive inferences are always best guesses based on observation and a relevant knowledge base, even though that knowledge base may be partial.

The notion that children's explanations are best guesses, or abductive inferences based on personal observation and partial knowledge, is an attractive one, given the evidence in Extract 1 above. For example, in the discussion about the relationship between angels, tooth fairies and ghosts (lines 1 to 27), the children identify and try to solve some difficult conundrums. First of all, Sally poses a problem, 'How do I go from being rock solid to being able to go to heaven?' The children propose the hypothesis that angels take people up to heaven, as like tooth fairies, angels are benevolent beings that have wings. As they have wings, therefore, they could take one up to heaven. The children know, however, that when someone dies it is customary to bury their body and that furthermore, they become skeletons. This poses a second problem: how can one be in heaven and at the same time be a skeleton buried in the ground? Again, the children propose an imaginative hypothesis: ghosts bring people back from heaven and take their skin off (but leave the bones). Leaving the skeletons in their coffins, the ghosts take the life that comes out of the body up to heaven again. The chain of inferences and the explanations that the children construct during this dialogue may seem creative and imaginative to an adult, but as Oatley suggests, to children they may well represent their best guesses based on their observations and knowledge. Fortunately, unlike adults, five to six year olds are not concerned with truth value in relation to their reasoning processes.

It is not possible to offer a conclusive interpretation of whether the children's contributions to the discussion in Extract 1 are examples of intuitive theories based on abduction or fantasy narratives. All three accounts seem plausible; to differentiate between them, one would need to go back in time and question the children further to ascertain the status of their beliefs. Nor is it possible to establish whether the children would have come up with these ideas without Sally's coaching in P4C and Synectics thinking skills. What does seem clear, however, is that in this lesson, Sally created a positive and supportive climate that allowed these five-year-old children to contribute to extended dialogues. In these dialogues they were able to share their knowledge and understanding of real cultural historical events: why Guy Fawkes wanted to kill the whole world and why people in England put poppies on soldiers' graves. This supportive climate also, however, allowed them to draw on their imagination to co-construct novel and unconventional connections between tooth fairies, angels and ghosts. By and large, the theories discussed so far offer accounts of intuitive theory construction and story-telling that do not quite capture this collaborative nature of children's creativity. The next section attempts to redress this.

History Mystery Investigators: improvisational creativity

Socio-cultural studies of creativity have established that everyday creative activity, more often than not, is social, and that even celebrated artists and scientists derive their inspiration from collaborating with other like-minded people. Vera John-Steiner's (2000: 3) analysis of the biographies of people who have enjoyed highly creative partnerships, such as the artists Pablo Picasso and George Braque and the scientists Marie and Pierre Curie, has confirmed that 'Generative ideas emerge from joint thinking, from significant conversations, and from sustained, shared struggles to achieve new insights by partners in thought.' Similarly Sawyer has rejected the view that creativity is the prerogative of the lone genius:

> A common but misleading myth is that the innovative economy is based on a few brilliant and creative inventors and entrepreneurs. ... Innovation is rarely a solitary individual creation. Instead, creativity is

deeply social; the most important creative insights typically emerge from collaborative teams and creative circles.

(Sawyer 2006: 42)

Synectics training is first and foremost a programme designed to facilitate creativity and innovation in team contexts. This section presents an extract from another lesson where Sally combined the use of dramatic role-play with a Synectics technique, the 'agenda meeting', to encourage her class to engage in a group thinking exercise.

The agenda meeting is one of the techniques Synectics facilitators use to support collaborative problem solving. Unlike conventional meetings where the agenda is determined in advance, usually by the chairperson, in a Synectics agenda meeting, the contributors volunteer agenda items during the meeting. Where a contributor has volunteered an item they become the 'problem owner' and must specify how other members of the group can help with the problem. So that everyone with an agenda item gets a chance to have their problem aired, a time limit is set for discussion of each item. The facilitator runs the meeting and keeps a written record of each agenda item, who contributed it, and any action points that emerge from the group discussion. The facilitator does not take part in the group discussion. The agenda meeting structure is tightly disciplined, in that a strict time limit is set for the discussion of each item, and problem owners are required to be very specific about why they raised the item so that the group understand what is needed and how they can help. At the same time it is fluid, as no one knows in advance what agenda items they will be asked to discuss.

Sally wanted to use the agenda meeting structure to help the children to come up with questions and problems that they could try to solve, by pretending that they were members of a company called the History Mystery Investigators. She hoped that the meeting structure would provide a framework that would encourage the children to come up with some well-defined questions and problems for the agenda as well as some creative solutions. In their role as History Mystery Investigators, the children had received the following invitation:

Dear History Mystery Investigators,

I'm writing in response to your newspaper advert. I feel that our church in town would be perfect for the programme you are making. Not only is our church made of flint but we also have many mysteries about the history of our church. Most of our records have been destroyed in a fire but I have enclosed copies of some that survive, which I have got here, to give you an idea of the history of the church. What is most interesting is that the tower of our church was partly destroyed in a storm (please see photos) and gravestones have all been

moved to the edge of the graveyard. We need help solving these mysteries. If you can help or if you have time please contact me at the above address.
Yours faithfully,
The Reverend D. E.

At the start of the lesson Sally reminded the children about how an agenda meeting was supposed to work and about their role as History Mystery Investigators. She told them that they needed to convene a meeting to plan their visit to the church and to decide which of its mysteries they would be interested in investigating. To help them get into role the children arranged their chairs as if they were sitting round a meeting table. Next Sally asked them to contribute two items for the agenda. Extract 2 is taken from the transcript of this part of the lesson at a point where the role-play had taken off in a direction that was not quite what she had anticipated.

Extract 2

1. **Sally** … I can tell you that the third thing on the agenda is a visit to [...] Church. Now I'm just wondering what the first two things might be, on the agenda, whether they're things to do with your office, whether they're things to do with the people who work in History Mystery Investigators. Whether they're to do with jobs to be done before, or jobs you might be doing in the future. I mean what might be the first thing that's on your agenda? What might it be?
2. **Boy 1** Um, that's there's been a rockslide. I heard it at nighttime. (...)
3. **Sally** Right, so why would History Mystery Investigators be told about a rockslide? What might be there that would be interesting to them?
4. **Boy 1** There could be skeleton bones and stuff. Cos I saw it, I climbed that mountain and it fell. And I was climbing up and I fell back down because that rockslide was there. And I tripped over a rock and the rockslide crumbled and I got covered but I managed to get out.
5. **Sally** [...] Right first of all, we've got, the first thing on our agenda then is that we've got a rockslide and some skeletons have been unearthed. Yeah? OK, what about, and we've just got to keep it really short, what about the second thing, just a headline that's on your agenda. Is it something about the office or people? What is it?
6. **Boy 2** There's people been complaining that the trains haven't been running for years now. Cos um, the tracks have been taken up

and put into roads and the people are now very tired of, getting tired of driving around.

7. **Boy 3** I can see that.

8. **Sally** Why would, one minute Luke, why would History Mystery Investigators be talking about (…).

9. **Boy 2** Cos people are talking, like now, I think there's big holes and (…) where trains keep getting stuck, people have to spend hours and hours on trains while people mend it.

10. **Sally** I don't quite, do you feel, one minute (…), do you feel that is a job for people who investigate things that happen in the past? No. Courtney what would you say was a job for people investigating the past?

11. **Boy 4** They wouldn't investigate that.

12. **Sally** You're not happy with that either Callum? History Mystery Investigators wouldn't do that? OK, what is, so the, we've got this first mystery is the rockslide and the skeletons which have been found, so what's this second mystery?

13. **Girl 1** I know what it really is. 'Cos the people in the office, it's getting worser and it's getting very, very, very tired and no one's getting any water out of their taps.

14. **Sally** So there's a problem with a water leak in the building, and it hasn't been fixed, and your building is now left without water.

15. **Girl 1** And, no water to drink.

16. **Sally** Ok, shhh, guys, it's very important that we listen to what Courtney's saying cos we're going to need to use Courtney's information.

17. **Girl 1** And, it's everyone else hasn't got any water.

18. **Sally** […] It looks like Hannah's already thought about it because Hannah's body language has changed quite a bit. I'm just wondering, if we were start talking about this in our meeting then, what kind of things might we be saying? Well, the pipe, we've done the skeletons already.

19. **Boy 4** The pipe is bursting underneath and water's coming up.

20. **Girl 2** What about our office?

21. **Boy 4** I know, but water's coming up and we'll all have to swim around.

22. **Sally** Um Ladies and Gentlemen, I have to ask you to go one at a time. I know this is an important issue and need to sort it out but we really, really do need to have clear ideas presented at these meetings.

23. **Boy 4** This water is coming up, so we'll all have to swim around.

24. **Sally** I don't know about you, but I'm not happy, I'm not working in conditions like this. The thing is, we need some action, we need to sort this out really quickly this is urgent.

25. **Boy 5** There might be a flood now.

26. **Sally**   Are you able to get something like that Joseph? [Joseph nods]
Cos we need it quite soon.

27. **Boy 5**   We could buy some Hoovers from a shop and suck all the water
up.

28. **Sally**   Just make a note of that. So Joseph, if you could sort out those
Hoovers for us (I'll put your name down for that). Um, would
you be able to sort that out this afternoon for us? OK. Ladies and
gentlemen I need to remind you again that we just need to have
one person speaking at a time at these meetings.

When Sally later reflected on the video that showed this part of the lesson,
she commented that she felt the lesson had not achieved its aims and
objectives in terms of the children's learning. Although the ideas the
children had come up with were creative and imaginative, she thought that
the children had not really understood the purpose of the role-play.

> When you are using excursion techniques like this, you've got to be so
> careful about role, because I've noticed that I wasn't very clear with the
> children about when I was in role, which role I was in, which role they
> were meant to be in, so for an excursion like that to be really successful,
> everybody has got to know where they are in terms of how they should
> be thinking at that moment. ... To their credit, they were fully engaged
> and really excited about everything that was happening but it was a bit
> too much and they couldn't manage that and I didn't manage it
> appropriately for them at the time.

Looked at from another perspective, however, it is possible to offer a more
positive interpretation of this extract. From the observations and analyses
he has carried out with jazz and improvisational theatre groups, Sawyer
(2003, 2006) has developed the concepts of 'improvisational creativity' and
'emergence' to describe how successful innovatory teams work. He claims
that there are a few simple rules that actors use to generate improvisational
dialogue. On of the most important of these is the 'Yes and ...' rule. He
explains this rule as follows:

> In every conversational turn, an actor should do two things:
> metaphorically say *yes*, by accepting the offer proposed in the prior
> turn, *and* add something new to the dramatic frame.
>
> (Sawyer 2006: 43)

Although at the outset the actors do not know how the dialogue will develop,
when they use the 'Yes and ...' rule to respond to and frame each other's
turns, a novel scenario will begin to emerge. It is not possible to predict in
advance what this will look like, as the scenarios that emerge from the

improvisational processes are greater than the sum of actors' individual contributions.

It could be argued that the dialogue in Extract 2 demonstrated an improvisational quality. Although initially, the children offer individual suggestions of events and problems for the History Mystery Investigators to investigate, some of which are explicitly rejected by other children, between lines 13 and 28 a collective narrative about a flooded office building gradually began to emerge. Starting with line 13, the conversational turns began to obey the 'Yes and ...' rule when girl 1 volunteered an idea for the second mystery, 'No one is getting any water out of the taps.' In the next line, Sally accepted this offer, and contributed some new information: 'So there's a problem with a water leak in the building, and it hasn't been fixed, and your building is now left without water.' Girl 1 built on this with 'And no water to drink.' In line 19, boy 4 started to develop Sally's 'water leak' idea and proffered the information that there was a burst pipe. The children did not respond to Sally's attempts (in lines 18 and 22) to remind them that in a meeting they needed to come up with some clear ideas. Instead they continued to add new ideas and to elaborate their chosen theme of a burst pipe that was flooding the building. Finally in line 27, boy 5 proposed an innovative course of action of buying some Hoovers (vacuum cleaners) to suck up the water.

Although the role-play was not a success from Sally's point of view, as the children did not stick to the 'agenda meeting' structure, Extract 2 offers an example of how a shared, creative narrative can emerge from improvisational play, and demonstrates how children manage the unpredictable process of collaborative emergence. Once again, this seems to challenge the view that young children need training in creative thinking techniques. Paradoxically, although Sally felt that she did not offer the children enough guidance in this session, she may actually have offered too much. When the children took active control of the role-play and moved away from the constraints of the agenda meeting, some creative improvisation began to emerge.

Discussion and conclusion

Although these two extracts can offer only a limited window on Sally's teaching and the many inventive ways she found to incorporate Synectics process tools and techniques into her teaching, the observations of her class over the course of the school year demonstrated that that she was a highly talented teacher. Her teaching methods were innovative and adventurous. She did not simply accept Synectics uncritically; she adapted the techniques to suit her own aims and objectives, and she combined them with other powerful teaching methods such as P4C and drama. Most of the time, she was able to achieve the kind of balance between structure and freedom that Craft et al. (2007) identify as the one of the hallmarks of teaching for creative learning. Although the discussions that took place in her lessons revealed a great deal of creative thinking, on the part of the children, however, it might be legitimate to ask whether they were also learning, and if so, what they were learning. If one accepts Prince and Logan's (2005: 155) argument outlined towards the beginning of this chapter that 'Learning and creativity are both basically, the ability to make connections to create meaning or significance' and that the process of thinking to learn is akin to creative thinking, then yes, these extracts suggest that the children were learning. This position, however, seems a little unsatisfactory. Critics might say that it is too easy to claim that creative thinking is the same as 'learning', particularly where learning is understood in the sense normally used in formal educational contexts. Perhaps a more precise definition of creative learning might be more helpful.

In *Creativity: Find it, promote it*, the QCA (2005) identified the following five elements as characteristic of creative learning:

* asking questions
* making connections
* imagining what might be
* exploring options
* reflecting critically.

With the possible exception of 'reflecting critically', examples of all five elements can be identified in Extracts 1 and 2. According to this view, therefore, one can accept that the children in Sally's class were learning as well as thinking creatively. As discussed above, however, it is not clear from these extracts whether the children needed the support of a formal creativity training programme in order to make creative connections, to invent story scenarios and to engage in dramatic improvisation. As Engel (2005) and Gellman and Gottfried (2006) argue, the features that demonstrate creative thinking emerge in early childhood in parallel with the emergence of language. It does not appear that children need special training to think in this way, it seems to come naturally. Similarly, as Sawyer (this volume) argues, young children are accomplished at improvisation and story telling from an early age and demonstrate this through their socio-dramatic play and pretence. This suggests that when children first start school, they are already competent creative thinkers and storytellers.

Both creative and narrative modes of thinking seem to involve abductive rather than deductive inferential reasoning. Paradigmatic thinking is difficult; it is based on formal logic and deductive inference, and is used for mathematical and scientific thinking as well as some forms of philosophical thinking. As Oatley (1996: 123) comments: 'The mind is more resistant to objects based on the paradigmatic mode …. Such objects need elaborate cultural assistance to allow them to enter the mind,' Piaget (1926) maintained that this kind of thinking does not develop until early adolescence. Somewhat more recently, it has become apparent that, even in adulthood, many people find this kind of thinking problematic or counter-intuitive, (see Johnson-Laird 1999 for a review). Many developmental psychologists and educational researchers would argue, however, that even in middle childhood, children can demonstrate causal reasoning and deductive thinking if they receive appropriate training (e.g. Burke and Williams 2008; Toth, Klahr and Chen 2000). If we accept the arguments offered by researchers such as Bruner, Gellman and Gottfried, and Engels and Oatley, then it seems reasonable to suggest that although children may need training in paradigmatic modes of thought, they do not necessarily need further training in narrative modes of thought. The examples of young children's thinking discussed in this chapter would seem to bear this out.

So what does Synectics bring to the educational experiences of children and their teachers? The Synectics programme claims to offer training to groups and organisations in process skills that facilitate innovation and that allow productive creative collaborations to develop in team-working contexts. It also offers strategies for maintaining a positive emotional climate, as well as a structured framework that permits people to harness and evaluate ideas in a disciplined manner. It does not claim to 'teach' creative thinking per se. Perhaps then, under Sally's guidance, the children in her class were learning how to collaborate rather than learning how to think? Sally's own view of what they were learning was that they were learning the kinds of communication skills that would allow them to work together more effectively in the future:

> The more work we do on dialogue, the better that the children get at crediting other people's ideas and taking an idea, and tweaking it to become their own. I think it's very important for creativity and innovation and things like that. And the speaking and listening; really, the better focus you have when you are listening and … able to speak very coherently about things, [these] are all those sorts of skills that you need to be able to make Synectics work.

Moran and John-Steiner (2004: 11) maintain that genuine creative collaboration 'involves an intricate blending of skills, temperaments, effort and sometimes personalities to realise a shared vision of something new and useful'. Based on their studies of well-known artistic and scientific collaborators they claim that transformational creative work and collaboration that pushes at boundaries takes time and is only realised through sustained effort. What one sees in schools, according to Moran and John-Steiner's definition, is more likely to be cooperative group work than creative collaboration. Nevertheless, the activities and language that support critical and creative thinking, together with the speaking and listening skills that Sally practised with her five-year-old children, are precisely the kind of 'culturally valued practices' (Gauvain 2001), that are seen as desirable by knowledge societies and innovation economies. The evidence presented in this chapter (and in the EXCITE! reports more generally) suggests that for her pupils, Sally's appropriation of Synectics processes and the way she used these to inform her practice and to create a positive, emotional climate in her classroom, began to equip them with some of the skills they will need as future workers and citizens in the knowledge society.

Acknowledgements

I would like to thank and acknowledge Sally Kynan and Matilda Joubert who contributed to the original EXCITE! report, and Vincent Nolan of Synetics Education Initiative. Acknowledgements are also due to the Department for Education and Skills and the Esmée Fairburn Foundation who funded the research reported in this chapter.

Notes

1   Details of Synectics and the Synectics Education Initiative can be found at http://www.synecticsworld.com/ and http://www.creativity-unlimited.org.uk/
2   Mathilda Joubert now runs the educational branch of the Synectics Education Initiative. Details of its training activities and methodology can be found at http://www.softnotes.com/
3   The EXCITE! reports are available through Open Research Online at http://oro.open.ac.uk
4   Guy Fawkes was a Catholic conspirator who received lasting notoriety for his part in what became known as the Gunpowder Plot, an attempt to blow up King James I and his members of Parliament during the formal opening of the 1605 session of Parliament. The anniversary of this event is still remembered every year on 5 November when UK families and communities celebrate by lighting bonfires, burning effigies of Guy Fawkes and letting off fireworks.
5   In this and subsequent extracts the name of the teacher has been changed. The names of the children she addresses or mentions have not been changed.
6   In these extracts and subsequent extracts (…) indicates sections of talk that were unclear and […] indicates where sections of the complete transcript have not been included in the extract where the talk is simply a repetition of the previous phrase or where it the teacher is using behaviour management language (e.g. 'Can you wait until she's had her turn', 'I'm hearing too many people talking at once').

References

Bruner, J. (1986) *Actual Minds, Possible Worlds*, Cambridge, Mass.: Harvard University Press.

Bruner, J. (1990) *Acts of Meaning*, Cambridge, Mass.: Harvard University Press.

Burke, L. A. and Williams, J. M. (2008) 'Developing young thinkers: an intervention aimed to enhance children's thinking skills', *Thinking Skills and Creativity*, **3**(2), pp. 104–24.

Cesarani, J. (2003) *Big Ideas: Putting the zest into creativity and innovation at work*, London: Kogan Page.

Comber, M., Galton, M., Hargreaves, L. and Wall, D. (1999) *Inside the Primary Classroom: Twenty Years On*, Abingdon: Routledge.

Craft, A. (2005) *Creativity in Schools: Tensions and dilemmas*, Oxford: Routledge Falmer.

Craft, A., Cremin, T., Burnard, P. and Chappell, K. (2007) 'Teacher stance in creative learning: a study of progression', *Thinking Skills and Creativity*, **2**(2), pp. 136–47.

Creativity Culture and Education (CCE) (2010) Online. Available at: http://www.creativitycultureeducation.org/ [accessed 19 August 2010].

Creative Partnerships (2010) Online. Available at: http://www.creative-partnerships.com/ [accessed 19 August 2010].

Department of Culture Arts and Leisure (DCAL), Department of Education (DE),

Department for Enterprise Trade and Industry (DETI), and Department of Higher and Further Education Training and Employment (DHFETE) (2000) *Unlocking Creativity: A strategy for development*, Belfast: DCAL.

Department for Education and Employment (DfEE) (2000) *The National Curriculum Handbook for Primary Teachers Key Stages 1–2*, London: The Stationery Office.

Dewey, J. (1991) *How We Think*, New York: Prometheus (original edn 1910).

Engel, S. L. (2005) *Real Kids*, Cambridge, Mass.: Harvard University Press.

Fryer, M. (2003) *Creativity Across the Curriculum: A review and analysis of programmes designed to develop creativity*, London: Qualifications and Curriculum Authority.

Gauvain, M. (2001) *The Social Context of Cognitive Development*, New York: Guildford.

Gelman, S. A. and Gottfried, G. M. (2006) 'Creativity in young children's thought', pp. 221–43 in J. C. Kaufman and J. Baer (eds), *Creativity and Reason in Cognitive Development*, New York: Cambridge University Press.

Jeffrey, B. (ed.) (2006) *Creative Learning Practices: European experiences*, London: Tufnell Press.

John-Steiner, V. (2000) *Creative Collaboration*, Oxford: Oxford University Press.

Johnson-Laird, P. N. (1999) 'Deductive reasoning', *Annual Review of Psychology*, **50**, pp. 109–35.

Kendall, L., Morrison, J., Sharp, C. and Yeshanew, T. (2008) *The Impact of Creative Partnerships on Pupil Behaviour*, Slough: National Foundation for Educational Research.

Learning and Teaching Scotland and IDES Network (2004) *Creativity Counts: Portraits of practice*, Glasgow: Learning and Teaching Scotland.

Learning and Teaching Scotland (LTS) and IDES Network (2004) *Creativity Counts: A report of findings from schools*, Glasgow: LTS.

LTS and the IDES Network (2001) *Creativity in Education*, Glasgow: LTS.

LTS and IDES Network (2001) *Creativity in Education: Case studies*, Glasgow: LTS.

Lipman, M. (2003) *Thinking in Education*, 2nd edn, Cambridge: Cambridge University Press.

Moran, S. and John-Steiner, V. (2003) 'Creativity in the making: Vygotsky's contemporary contribution to the dialect of development and creativity', pp. 61–90 in R. K Sawyer, V. John-Steiner, S. Moran, R. J. Sternberg, D. H Feldman, J. Nakamura and M. Csikszentmihalyi (eds), *Creativity and Development*, Oxford: Oxford University Press.

Moran, S. and John-Steiner, V. (2004) 'How collaboration in creative work impacts identity and motivation', pp. 11–25 in D. Miell and K. Littleton (eds), *Collaborative Creativity: Contemporary perspectives*, London: Free Association Books.

National Advisory Committee on Creative and Cultural Education (NACCCE) (1999) *All Our Futures: Creativity culture and education*, London: Department for Education and Employment.

Oatley, K. (1996) 'Inference in narrative and science', pp. 123–40 in D. Olson and N. Torrance (eds), *Modes of Thought: Explorations in Culture and Cognition*, New York: Cambridge University Press.

Office for Standards in Education (OfSTED) (2006) *Creative Partnerships: Initiative and impact*, HMI 2517, London: OfSTED Publications.

Perkins, D. N. (1985) 'Reasoning as imagination', *Interchange*, 16, pp. 14–26.

Piaget, J. (1926) *The Language and Thought of the Child*, New York: Harcourt Brace.

Prince, G. M. and Logan, V. (2005) 'Thinking, learning and creativity', pp. 155–65 in V. Nolan and G. Darby (eds), *Reinventing Education: A 'thought experiment' by 21 authors*, Stoke Mandeville: Synectics Education Initiative (SEI).

Qualifications and Curriculum Authority (QCA) (1999) *The National Curriculum Handbook for Primary Teachers in England*, London: DfEE and QCA.

QCA (2005) *Creativity: Find it, promote it! Promoting pupils' creative thinking and behaviour across the curriculum at key stages 1, 2 and 3 – practical materials for schools*, London: QCA.

Sawyer, R. K. (2003) 'Emergence in creativity and development', pp. 12–60 in R. K Sawyer, V. John-Steiner, S. Moran, R. J. Sternberg, D. H. Feldman, J. Nakamura and M. Csikszentmihalyi, (eds), *Creativity and Development*, Oxford: Oxford University Press.

Sawyer, R. K. (2006) 'Educating for innovation', *Thinking Skills and Creativity*, 1 (1), pp. 41–8.

Scottish Executive Education Department (SEED) (2006) *Promoting Creativity in Education: Overview of key national policy developments across the UK*, Edinburgh: Scottish Executive, Online. Available at: http://www.hmie.gov.uk/documents/publication/hmiepcie.html [accessed 19 August 2010].

Toth, E. E., Klahr, D. and Chen, Z. (2000) 'Bridging research and practice: a cognitively based classroom intervention for teaching experimentation skills to elementary school children', *Cognition and Instruction*, **18**(4), pp. 423–59.

Vygotsky, L. S. (1978) *Mind in Society: The development of higher psychological processes*, Cambridge, Mass.: Harvard University Press.

Chapter 4

Children's creative collaboration – a view of narrativity

Marjaana Kangas, Annakaisa Kultima and Heli Ruokamo

Introduction

It is assumed that one of the core drivers of knowledge and progress in society is creativity, and that one of the key missions of schools is to educate for the creation of knowledge and innovation (Craft 2005; Sawyer 2006, 2008). Innovations that spring from groups and teams that contain diverse perspectives, share goals and knowledge, and engender creative collaboration in classrooms are regarded by many scholars as being aligned with the important and pivotal nature of innovation in today's economy and society (e.g. Claxton, Craft, and Gardner 2008; Sawyer 2006, 2008). Children's worlds are increasingly populated by intelligent technologies, and formal and informal technology-enriched play and learning environments. If we think of the global society of the future as being based on collaborative creativity, what becomes relevant is not only the new technology, but also the modes and processes of acting and participating in collaborative activity and knowledge co-creation.

In this chapter, we argue that narration is a key aspect of meaning-making (Bruner 1996, 2002) and a specific kind of interaction (Becker and Quasthoff 2004) which provides an important viewpoint from which to discuss collaborative activity and creativity (cf. John-Steiner, Shank and Meehan 2004). We examine the roles of narrativity and narrative thinking within the creative and collaborative process, as well as the challenges for the future innovative learning environment from this perspective. We will present a study that started the research and development process whereby children were given a voice for gaining information for the real and meaningful purpose of developing and creating innovative learning environments that correspond with today's technology, and that provide the children with novel tools and skills for them to act confidently in a creative society.

The study presented here has two aims. One is to study children's creative collaboration and the role of narrativity in authentic co-design processes; the other is to use the findings as a basis for developing a 'playful learning environment' (PLE) and a theoretical framework for it. A PLE is defined as 'a technology-enriched play and learning environment' which provides novel opportunities for integrating creativity, playfulness and physical activities with a curriculum-based education (e.g. Kangas 2010; Kangas, Randolph and Ruokamo 2009). The pedagogical conception of the PLE as including a technology-enriched playground derives from multidisciplinary Finnish research and design projects[1] for developing an innovative outdoor playground in which learning can take the form of play and games, as well as own content creation. The PLE is also referred to as SmartUs – a commercial technology-enriched playground complex that integrates not only modern technology and playground equipment, but also outdoor playgrounds and computers inside the classroom. Hence, the affordances of the environment are subsequently extended to the classroom, providing tools, including the Internet, through which students can themselves create content and design games. Pilot outdoor environments consist of a novel playground facility located in the schoolyard and enhanced with RFID (radio frequency identification device) technology. The technological elements of SmartUs can be integrated into non-technological playground equipment, or located in a natural environment near the school, such as in woods.

One crucial point in designing and developing new learning environments is that they should support the play, learning, and physical activities of children in a variety of ways. The starting point from an educational point of view for this research study was to listen to children's voices, and to let them contribute to our research and design work. The data collection started with children of six and seven years of age (i.e. pre-primary children in Finland) because their viewpoint is usually missing in the design of play provision (Armitage 2001); for children of that age, play is a natural way of expressing oneself. The empirical data were collected from five preschools in 2003. The goal was to discover what children expect from a favorable and ideal play environment, and the activities that would be involved in play. This information was needed to better understand the features of the PLE, and related play and learning activities. Later, in the next phase of the PLE studies, children participated in testing the pilot environments in various play and learning settings. These empirical studies have been reported in other research articles (e.g, Kangas, Hyvönen, and Latva 2007; Hyvönen 2008; Kangas 2010).

In this chapter, we draw on an empirical study in which children (in small groups) designed the features of their ideal outdoor play environment by drawing and talking. We asked children in 'playful co-design sessions' to imagine, conceptualize, and describe the environment in which they would most like to play, what kinds of activities it would afford, and what kinds of elements there would be (see also Hyvönen and Kangas 2007). These situations provided us with a rich context from which to study children's creative collaboration and the role of narrativity in authentic and playful settings. The group of children worked around a large drawing sheet that was spread on the floor. A total of fifteen playful co-design sessions were arranged, each lasting 30 to 45 minutes and involving six groups of boys, five groups of girls, and four mixed groups of children. The sessions were video recorded, the discussions were transcribed, and the drawings were photographed.

Analysis of 'what' children expected from their ideal play environment revealed play environments, or rather 'play worlds,' that provided physical activities with friends, that were close to nature, and that were emotionally rich and vivid (Hyvönen and Juujärvi 2005; Hyvönen and Kangas 2007). The children prefer play environments that consist of several physical structures, such as those related to sport and nature, and playground artifacts (such as soccer fields, forests, various slides, and huts). In nature, children emphasize animals, trees, woods, flowers, rocks, and mountains. An interesting result of the data collection was the discovery that children's play environments in fact reflect rich emotional play worlds. Although the children designed accurate artifacts and play areas, their play worlds and the design process were generally rather more emotional than physical (Hyvönen and Kangas 2007, 2010).

In answering the question 'What did the playground designers suggest?,' six different emotional types of play world were found, which bring out happiness, scariness, care, aggression, excitement, and amusement (Hyvönen and Juujärvi 2005; Hyvönen and Kangas 2007). These emotional tensions were involved in and evident from the narratives that the children created during the sessions. The girls preferred to design play worlds that were characterized by both 'scariness' – with various bogey features and episodes – and 'happiness' – with summer and beauty. Boys had worlds of 'care,' with domestic play, 'aggression,' and 'competition.' Play worlds shared by boys and girls represented 'excitement' and 'amusement.' Nature, including animals, provided fascinating environmental features for both boys and girls (Hyvönen and Kangas 2007; Hyvönen 2008). The findings also show that in many cases children were collaboratively engaged in mutual design and story creation during the co-design sessions: they created a large number of stories around the play worlds. In other words, the co-design sessions inspired or gave an opportunity for the children to co-create and insert plot-shaped narratives into their designed and drawn play environments. Thus, in addition to discerning 'what' the children designed and created (see Hyvönen and Juujärvi 2005; Hyvönen and Kangas 2007), it was also meaningful to explore 'how' the play worlds were generated in small groups.

On the above basis, we will discuss, in this chapter, the role of narrativity and narrative thinking within the co-design processes of children. We will also consider the challenges for future innovative learning environments from this angle. Following Jerome Bruner (2003: 45), the founder of narrative psychology, we are interested in how narrative as an instrument of mind operates in the construction of reality, and how this emerges in children's creative and collaborative activity. We endeavor to intertwine the educational and philosophical aspects of narrativity, and to get closer to a versatile theoretical examination of both the phenomenon of narrativity, and collaborative creativity. However, as put forward by Sawyer (2008), to explain and understand the creativity of complex collaborating groups, we need a theoretical framework that allows us to better understand how groups of people work or design together, and how the collaborative activity results in a final created product.

Narrative thinking within creative and collaborative processes

One of the central aspects of narrativity is its inherent interdisciplinary nature; many different disciplines, such as art psychology, cultural studies, and literary studies, have an interest in narrative (Mateas and Sengers 2003). The words 'narrative, narration' and 'narrate' have Latin roots which suggest a close connection with knowledge and skilful practice (Whyte 1981). Recently, narrative is defined as 'a mode of thinking': a continuous account of a series of events or facts that shapes them into an emotionally satisfactory whole (Bruner 1996; Egan 2005). Narrative thinking refers to the thought process involved in creating a story; events and experiences are organized into plotted structures (Bruner 1990). Hence, the concept of narrative thinking relies on an argument that it is a key way of making sense of experience and the world (Bruner 2003, 2002, 1996; Egan 2005). With the help of a plot and characters, surroundings and activities are connected to each other (Bruner 1986). This kind of thinking is also evident in children's pretend play. In this way, story functions as a tool for constructing meaning about the surrounding world, and thinking gains a narrative form, and becomes explicit and easier to manage (Bruner 1996; Egan 1986). Stories also help one in dealing with more complex meanings (Schwartz 1996).

According to Bruner (1990, 1996), narrative thinking is natural and is one of the earliest forms of thinking for the human mind. It is not only connected to linguistic structures because it is present in the pre-linguistic stage of child development. This can be observed in children's play, when they mould the story verbally and with different creative actions such as drawing or making gestures. Thus, in narrative thinking, emotions, imagination, memory, and thinking are combined (Bruner 1996, 2002). Narrative thinking is not only something that is present in the early development of thinking processes in children. It is also pertinent to story-like experiments within science and philosophy; these are termed 'thought experiments.' It is believed that thought experiments play an essential role in testing a theory's consistency and explanatory power (Bokulich 2001; Gendler 2000). Hence, it can be assumed that narrativity has a close relationship with several possible worlds.

When constructing a story, one can build parts of a possible world. Understanding that things can be different requires the existence of elaborative thinking, constructing, and active thinking constructs that can be thought of as 'worlds.' As we will show later, the play worlds designed by the children provide examples of these 'worlds.' Thinking of other worlds involves considering more complicated notions, such as the relations between individuals, causality, and time. One may perceive that possible worlds are only stipulated entities (Kripke 1972), or that they are physical entities (Lewis 1986). In the latter case, the limits of language do not limit the possibilities – imagining a possible world does not have to be only a verbal act. In this respect, play can be thought of as making a thought experiment whereby an imaginary setting puts certain views regarding the actual world to the test. In this research study, playful co-design sessions were organized in a playful way, because such an environment affords greater possibilities for creating hypotheses and generating inventions in collaboration. The sessions were constructed with an atmosphere that allowed and nurtured children's creativity and imagination.

Although creativity is interpreted in many different ways, recent scholars see it as involving the generation of novel and imaginative ideas (e.g. Craft 2005; Cropley 2001). Imagination has an essential role in this process, with a close relationship between imagining possible worlds and generating novel ideas. Vygotsky (1998) considered imagination as a process directly connected with meaning-making. It is 'the ability to think of things as possible – the source of flexibility and originality in human thinking' (Egan 2005: 220). Hence, we assume imagination as well as narrative thinking are both the source of, and the vehicle for creativity rather than synonymous processes.

Creativity and play are linked in numerous ways, as are creativity and playfulness (e.g. Russ 2003; Liebermann 1977). Considerable evidence demonstrates that a playful approach to the task at hand increases the likelihood of producing creative results (Amabile 1983; Bruner, Jolly and Sylva 1976). Liebermann (1977) was among the first who proposed a relationship between playfulness and creativity, and identified five aspects of the quality of playfulness: cognitive, social, physical spontaneity, the manifestation of joy, and a sense of humor. Physical spontaneity refers to coordination and motor activity levels. Social spontaneity refers to qualities of interaction, and cognitive spontaneity refers to the use of imagination. Manifestation of joy involves enthusiasm, exuberance, enjoyment, and lack of restraint. Sense of humor captures behaviors such as joking and clowning. Playfulness can be associated with the creation of imaginary play worlds through role-play, and being open to playing with ideas and new possibilities (Egan 2005; Craft 2001). Hence, playfulness may help children think about and reflect on the world in a way that is free from constraints. One form that this can take is word play or humor between participants to create common ground. Playing with words and ideas assumes a context of mutual trust and support, where each participant knows that what they say (or draw, perform, and so on) will be accepted (Wegerif 2005).

Recently, as with learning, scholars consider creativity not only as an individual phenomenon, but also as a socially shared phenomenon (e.g. Littleton and Miell 2004; Sawyer 2006; Vass 2004). Creativity cannot simply be reduced to processes of individual thinking. Rather, a proper study of creativity necessitates an understanding of both personal factors and how the individual engages in collaborative activity. When children's creative acts manifest collaboration, this requires the participants' commitment to the same task during the collaborative process. For instance, Schrage (1990) defines collaboration in terms of two or more individuals with complementary skills interacting to create a shared understanding that no one had previously possessed, or that they could not have acquired on their own. The term 'knowledge co-creation' illuminates this phenomenon, referring to jointly constructed knowledge, interaction with others and with cultural tools (Vygotsky 1986), and the collective construction of artefacts (Paavola, Lipponen, and Hakkarainen 2004). In this study, knowledge is represented by ideas and narratives that children co-create; knowledge and understanding are not only shared, but also socially generated and validated in groups of children. Following Rojas-Drummond and colleagues (2006), knowledge can be defined as the product of the joint negotiation of the participants, using a variety of communicative strategies to construct a shared understanding. The research discussed in this chapter illustrates how, using a play framework, co-design sessions provided children with an opportunity to create knowledge collaboratively through the discussions and stories, and to create artefacts, such as drawings, of their ideal play environments. In this case, a large sheet of paper on the floor and colored pencils represented the cultural tools.

Collaborative creativity and creative collaboration have been the focus of considerable educational research, and are of great interest to research of both play and learning (e.g. Littleton and Miell 2004). In joint activity, learners can become more reflective by serving as 'revealing mirrors' to each other (John-Steiner 2000). An advantage of collaborative activity is also illustrated by Vygotsky's (1978) concept of the zone of proximal development (ZPD), in which children are challenged with graduated zones that are slightly above their current individual level of functional competence. However, in collaborative endeavor, the role of each participant as learner and tutor is emphasized (e.g. Wells 1999); in such a case, the ZPD, which consists of action, thinking, and emotions, is at the same time a potential challenge for everyone. It is argued that shared activity in collaboration with others gives rise to 'inter-mental understanding' which then leads to the development of individual (intra-mental) knowledge and skills (Vygotsky 1978; Mercer 2002). It is also argued that joint activities in learning and creativity are enhanced when the interactions between participants are supported by 'the gift of confidence,' the sharing of risks in the presentation of new ideas, constructive criticism, and the creation of a safety zone (Mahn and John-Steiner 2002).

Methodological considerations

At the beginning of the co-design sessions, a frame story was told to the children in order to stimulate their imaginations and provide an atmosphere of creativity. The frame story made the situation more playful, while at the same time it oriented the children to think about the world in a way essentially free from constraints. The approach of each frame story was decided on according to the situation, since the children's readiness to engage with the sessions varied among the groups. In an imaginary world, any kind of play is possible and any kind of environment can be ideated. After the frame stories were established, the children drew pictures and discussed vividly, adopting the roles of designers and players.

The playful nature of the design sessions was similar to Stig Broström's (1996, 1999) description of frame play, in which an adult may also participate in the construction of the plot and imaginary situation. The 'frame' refers to the participants' conscious and joint plan of the imaginary play situation. During the design sessions, the researchers participated by listening, discussing, and drawing with the children. The researchers' role was to orient the children into the task, listen to them carefully, and encourage and inspire them to imagine and draw. Researchers also asked questions about different aspects of the playing environment, and what the children would like to do there. Adults contributed to the storyline, but the children's ideas and initiatives held the main role around the drawing paper (see Figure 4.1).

The method used for the design sessions is called 'playfulness-based research' (PBR) (Hyvönen and Kangas in press). The method provides a meaningful way of gathering data from children by engaging them to work and design in creative collaboration. It is a tool to facilitate young children's meaning-making, to encourage and solidify their ideas and creative thoughts, and to understand their construction of reality. It can also serve as a valuable basis for research where sharing understandings among children and researchers is valued. Participating in playful co-design sessions suits children, because imagining, drawing, coloring, and playing are natural ways for them to express their intentions and desires. Thus, the idea of the research method follows Kieran Egan's (2005) underlying idea that the learner works as an integrated whole, with the inclusion of not only the mind but also the body, emotions, and imagination.

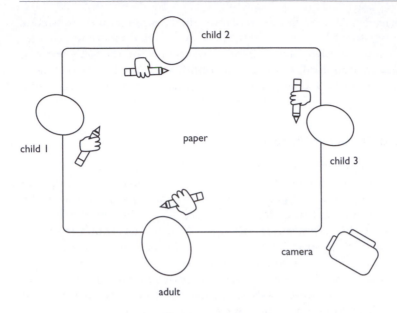

child 2

child 1

paper

child 3

camera

adult

Figure 4.1 Arrangement of children in relation to drawing paper and camera

For the purposes of the narrative analysis, the data from the discussions about play environments were restructured in the form of narratives so that the talk around a certain play idea formed one narrative episode. The built narratives were set apart so that one narrative unit consisted of one story with a clear plot or a connected whole. Thus, one narrative could be a short description of the environment and an activity, or the whole environment ideated on the paper. In addition, the narratives were analyzed according to whether they were generated in collaboration, or were individually constructed. The criteria for collaboration included jointly generated ideas and plots of the play environment, shared emotions, and reciprocal activity in the design situation. From all the sessions, nineteen narratives out of thirty in total were generated in collaboration, showing that two or more children constructed the storyline and shared an imaginary situation in a collective way. This was based on the assumption that collective thinking, where ideas are not just shared but also jointly generated, is closely based on children's narrative thinking and its appearance in playful co-design sessions.

Empirical findings: narrative thinking in creative collaboration

The pre-school-aged children were eager to ideate the environments of their dreams. In these processes, the children often amalgamated their play ideas, shared their narrative thinking, and constructed narratives with a high level of collaboration. Narratives emerged at the levels of playfulness, verbal action, and emotions, and these became more and more complex and emotional as the collaborative process proceeded. We will now present the results, starting with the issue of playfulness in the sessions and finishing with descriptions of the characteristics of narrative thinking, and the concept of shared narrative thinking. We then introduce our conclusions regarding the role of narrative thinking in creative activity at a theoretical level.

Narrative thinking as playing

Playful design sessions inspired the children to insert narratives into the play environments under generation. Narratives were represented as drawings, descriptions, and discussions about the play environment of their dreams and connected activities. Many stories were born of the creative and playful processes. Such stories can be thought of as an indication of children's narrative thinking, and a way of organizing new experiences into a plot-like shape. Sometimes, narratives were born with children imagining activities in the environments, and acting as the narrators of those situations. Sometimes, the design process became increasingly integrated into play activities during the episode, and children shared their common narratives. Extract 1 illustrates the design process in which the researcher has an important role in creating appropriate conditions for children's collaborative creativity by being encouraging, inventive, and creative.

Extract 1

Caroline, Sabrina, and Madeleine are designing the play environment of the 'Volcano slide.'

Caroline (to researcher) 'Would you draw here, sand for instance? Make it a volcano, for instance. Use red color here.'
Researcher 'Would you help me a little bit?'
Caroline 'Yeh, I will.'
Researcher (suggesting) 'Would it probably be a play park with a volcano? Isn't that at all frightening?'
Caroline 'Sure! It would be frightening.'
Researcher 'But if it were a false volcano?'
Madeleine 'It would be made of sand.'
Researcher 'Would it then provide lava?'
Caroline 'Yes, it will.'
Sabrina 'It is false lava indeed, which is not burning at all.'
Caroline 'Yeah!'

Sabrina   'Would we pretend that ...'
Caroline   'Here as well, lava erupts'
Sabrina   'Would we figure out that this lava is a certain slide?'
Researcher   'It would be quite nice ... slide made of lava, it's a really good idea!'
Caroline   'That kind of spiral lava ladders (twisted ladders composed of lava).'
Researcher   'Spiral lava ladders?'
Caroline   'Yes.'
Sabrina   'Yeh, we could climb upwards by using those spiral lava ladders.'

The extract shows that the children are increasingly involved in a collaborative design process that starts to resemble play (Juujärvi, Kultima, and Ruomako 2005). Generating a common narrative leads them to the possibility of engaging more intensely in the play world and acting as players. Sometimes, children played the roles of the narrative, and it was more difficult to distinguish drawing and ideating from role-play activities (Kieff and Casbergue 2000). This is illustrated in Extract 2.

Extract 2

Alex, Tom, and John are structuring the narrative 'Fighting pirates' (where a ship fires at another ship, and a rocket fires at a park) by playing (see Figure 4.2).

Alex   'What am I gonna do? ... Well there is no cannon!'
Tom   'Yes, there is none.'
             (Notices that he also has none, and draws a cannon on his ship.)
Alex   'There's going to be a bang!'
Tom   'Mine is shooting there, look at it, it shoots directly at the pirate ship.' (Indicates Alex's pirate ship.) '... Big ammo ... shoots kind of really far, doesn't it?'
Alex   'Mine too ...'
Tom   'Little rocket!'
John   'Oh geez! If that rocket ... oh no!'
Alex   'Rocket goes, it breaks that in a minute, and then all of those!'
Tom   'Yes it does! The ship shoots ship, and rocket shoots park.'
Alex   'Look.'
John   'My pirate ship gets revenge.'
Tom   'Yeah! But not this, this shoots you into outer space. And that flies to space certainly.'

Figure 4.2 Fighting pirates

In Extract 2, destructive, noisy, and competitive patterns of behavior emerge when the children are playing fighting pirates on the sea. Although the activity was based on competition and the confrontational topic of fighting, it transformed into collaborative role-playing in the same narrative context. Play and playful situations facilitated creativity and the use of the imagination. Children's imaginations and their whole bodies were involved in the activity; they talked, played, drew, suggested, and acted out their images in an integrated manner.

Narrative thinking as collective thinking

Through narratives, children structured and organized their experiences and the products of their imaginations into entities through which their created environments acquired meaning. From these narrative episodes, we distinguished four features in children's narrative thinking, namely 'entity, fascination with surprise, integration of fact and fiction,' and 'emotions.' In addition, we perceived five properties of children's 'shared narrative thinking,' and built this concept into the study (see Table 4.1).

Once the children simultaneously drew, discussed, and played in the situation, their 'narratives formed meaningful entities.' Children also made perceptions about the affordances of play worlds (Hyvönen 2008; Hyvönen and Kangas 2010), and the possibilities for action that their ideas provided. They constructed affordance compilation; in other words, they connected

Table 4.1 The main features of narrative thinking and shared narrative thinking

Narrative thinking		Shared narrative thinking	
Category	*Implication*	*Category*	*Implication*
Entity	Tendency to form meaningful entities	**Imitative**	Creating narratives through imitations for construction of common ground
Surprise	Meaning in the stimulation of thinking		
Integration of fact and fiction	Tendency to generate imaginative situations around formal knowledge	**Associative**	Creating narratives through associations
		Productive	Creating narratives productively through collaboration
Emotionality	Essential role of emotions in the play worlds	**Transformative**	Refining and elaborating ideas through collaboration
		Emotional	Emotional commitment to shared idea

various play affordances in order to create a larger entity for play – a 'play world.' This happened collaboratively in many sessions.

In narrative thinking, an element of surprise – that is, presenting surprising alternatives – inspired the children's imagination and narrative thinking. For example, in one session, each of the children first drew a tiger, and when the researcher asked if the animals could speak, the children did not react much to the question. Shortly afterwards, however, the animals became climbing frames from which you could slide down from the animal's tongue. In this narrative episode, the children integrated fact and fiction, and created a slide that was part of the 'bogey mountain'; it was a lion-like animal with a very long tongue. Children climb to the mountain on the back of the animal, they become very excited, and they finally slide down on the long tongue. Slides, as a whole, were a very fascinating element for children to modify with their knowledge of nature, for instance with volcanoes (Extract 3). Therefore, we argue that surprise – such as asking if tigers could speak – stimulated the children's imagination, but this only happened when the children found the ideas proposed appealing.

We also noticed that surprise is closely connected to the 'integration of fact and fiction' in narrative thinking. Extract 3 illustrates how formal knowledge is intensely integrated with fiction. Indeed, combining fact and fiction seemed to inspire the children, and tended to exclude the conventional in the narratives. Figure 4.3 shows the children's ideal playground corresponding to this narrative.

Extract 3

The children are structuring the narrative of 'Volcano land.'

Paul	'I'll make a volcano!'
Nico	'Yeah, I'll make volcanoes, too!' (Giggles.)
Paul	'But these are not real ones. They're fake volcanoes!'
Nico	'I'll make a big one, at least! Lava is splattered there!'
Paul	'Hmm, this is fun!'
Researcher	'Why is there lava?'
Nico	'Hmm … you can swim there.'
Researcher	'In lava?'
Nico	'Yeah.'
Paul	'Then swimming trunks are needed!'
Nico	'Yes!'
Paul	'And lava proof ones!'
Researcher	'Ooh. Super trunks.'
(The boys laugh.)	
Paul	'There could be colored water, red water.'
Researcher	'Yeah, it could be fake water.'
Paul	'Yeah, is it OK, Nico?'
Nico	'Yes.'
Paul	'Like red cloth you could jump into.'
Researcher	'Exactly. So your clothes don't get wet and the lava doesn't burn.'
Paul	'Then we could play volcano climbing! … What an unusual climbing place!'

Figure 4.3 Ideal playground

In Extract 3, the children differentiated between reality and fiction, but seemed to be fascinated with the more fictitious surroundings. The more fantastic assumptions, like swimming in lava, stimulated a greater refining and elaboration of the narrative, turning it into descriptions of other possible worlds. Integrating fact and fiction turns views of reality into a test of possible worlds by making thought experiments. An adult joined the imaginative situation, but allowed the children to construct a common narrative for themselves. Thus, in one socially shared story, narrative thinking, or some aspects of it created by many children, was represented. Extract 4 illustrates another situation where children's prior knowledge and fiction are intertwined. However, certain cognitive and emotional conflicts are in evidence (Hyvönen and Kangas 2010); the children have a knowledge base about foxes, but they lack confidence in how to use the information in this playful situation (Extract 4). The children are generating the play world of 'Lovely animals' (see Figure 4.4), where possibility thinking starts from the conflict of fact and fiction.

Extract 4

The children are structuring the narrative of 'Lovely animals.'

Researcher	'Do you think if there would be any animals in the forest?'
Sandra	'Yeah, there are foxes, I guess.'
Researcher	'Foxes?'
Sandra	'They are kind of nice foxes.'
Researcher	'Kind foxes.' (Repeats.)
Caroline	'… which are afraid of people.'
Researcher	'They are afraid of people?'
Sandra	'No, no. They are nice, they won't be afraid.'
Madeleine	'Animals, indeed, they are afraid of people.'
Sandra	'Yeah, they easily do so. However, these animals are such as they are not afraid of people.'
Researcher	'It can be possible.'
Caroline	'Except for leopards.'
Madeleine	'Bears are afraid as well.'
Sandra	'Yes, but once they have a baby bear and it is newly born, which they have to protect against humans, then they won't be afraid.'
Researcher	'What would the foxes do there?'
Caroline	'One can only stroke them, otherwise their mother gets angry.'
Sandra	'No, I wouldn't suggest to stroke either.'
Caroline	'But can.'
Sandra	'Yes but … pretending could, but not for real.'

Figure 4.4 Lovely animals

In this conversation, the children propose formal knowledge about animals and their behavior. They also propose fictional knowledge about animals. The episode illustrates the negotiation, whereby the children's narrative thinking, by means of possibility thinking and creating possible worlds, is formed step by step. At the end of the episode, Sandra's utterance 'Pretending could, but not for real' involves the suggestion of an imaginary play world where everything is possible. The same children later continue the discussion of the same play world, and finally successfully generate a common play environment with which each child is very satisfied. In this case, the conflict of fact and fiction facilitated the creation of imaginative situations around formal knowledge, and inspired the children to think about possibilities. This kind of interaction is valuable from the viewpoint of knowledge co-creation. The talk identifies a meaningful learning space whereby one child's imagination feeds that of another, and nurtures the possibility of thinking (Kangas 2010).

We assume that high-quality collaboration arose where a story was constructed based on collaborative creativity and on shared narrative thinking. In other words, it was assumed that stories that were versatile and rich in content were mostly constructed collaboratively. Especially in situations where the children's narrative thinking was socially shared, their imagination, memory, thinking, and emotions came together. Representations of shared narrative thinking are not only verbal, but also included the movements, actions, and drawings during the process. Based on an analysis of the narratives that were built with a high level of collaboration, shared narrative thinking is characterized as being 'imitative, associative, productive, transformative,' and 'emotional.'

When children shared ideas for the narrative, refined them, and developed them further, they were acting as guides and innovators, but also as targets for copying and learning from each other. In all sessions, shared ideating was based on 'imitation,' which appeared to be meaningful (especially in the shared reciprocal state), on collective imagination, and on constructing a common view and ground. It is possible that, for children at this age, imitation is one of the ways in which they signal to their partner that they have accepted the stated idea (Faulkner and Miell 2004). It was also typical that the stories were created associatively. For example, in one session, a child drew a house upside down and the other elaborated on it by turning it into an amusement park, building associatively from her own experiences. 'Associative' refers to narration construction through reciprocal associations.

In addition, shared narrative thinking can be said to have been productive when it pertains to numerous ideas formed in collaboration. This is manifested in the sessions as rich and imaginative play worlds. Due to the collaborative nature of elaborating and refining ideas, shared narrative thinking seems to be transformative. During the collaborative process of constructing a narrative, the ideas of others were not taken as themselves, but rather were constructed and refined further. In this case, transformative narrative thinking is connected to the idea of reciprocal creativity; ideas are refined in such a way that none of the children could ever create them alone.

The data support the assumption that emotions are closely linked to imagination (Egan 2005) and narrative thinking (Bruner 1996). During the sessions, children welcomed the ideas that attracted them emotionally: the findings support Egan's (1992) notions that children's imagination is best stimulated by stories with content that influences them at the emotional level. Shared narrative thinking represents 'emotional commitment to the same idea.' This supports the arguments of John-Steiner and colleagues (2004), and originally from Vygotsky (1986), that verbal patterns, and in this case also play patterns, vary according to the degree of emotional and intellectual closeness. For example, if one of the children or adults came up with an exciting idea, the others took part in the imaginary situation by eagerly making gestures and empathizing intensely with the idea. Common humor and excitement functioned as emotional stimulants to the collective imagination and play.

The study also showed that shared narrative thinking was reached especially in situations where the children knew each other well, and where they were used to collaborating and playing with each other. This notion supports Vygotsky's (1986) argument that depth of understanding emerges between people who have close psychological contact, and who are able to communicate with each other using condensed verbal means. These results provide an interesting standpoint for a consideration of the situations and conditions required for successful knowledge co-creation.

Towards a model of narrativity

In the co-design sessions, the children generated play environments spontaneously, sharing only relevant thoughts. This is enough for understanding, because in social interaction a story can carry both meaning and context (that is, the surroundings for the meaning). The story itself is actually broader than is explicitly expressed. For example, in the session (Extract 3) where Nico and Paul created the volcano environment, Nico's 'You can swim there,' was based on the assumption that you will need swimming trunks, and that swimming in lava is possible in play. Such implicit assumptions start to broaden the story into a whole other possible world.

Based on the perspectives that arise from the data and the theories of narrativity, we developed a three-dimensional model of narrativity (see Plate 1). This model incorporates the dimensions of meaning, activity, and collaboration. The model introduces a flexible idea of narrativity; it starts from separate entities and moves towards whole worlds, with narrativity lying in between these two poles. The thirty narratives found during the sessions were situated in this model.

At the bottom of the model are the simplest meanings, such as characters and things. Moving up, we see the act of combining simple elements with different kinds of relations, such as time, causality, and so on, introducing a narrative. At the top, the narrative expands into a whole possible world. As we approach the narrative level, which should not be thought of as a definite level with real borders but rather as a continuum, the meaning of the axes of collaboration and creativity grows. The narratives that emerge in collaboration were hard to fit into the figure because of the very complex nature of all three dimensions. Most of the narratives (nineteen) are located in the 'creative-collaboration' corner (that is, the corner of 'shared narrative thinking'). In the small-group design sessions, the children were not told to collaborate. The collaboration happened naturally through stimulation by the entities contributed by the peers and researchers, and through association, surprise, or the integration of fact and fiction. The activities observed can be categorized as imitative, productive, and transformative. Presumably, expansion into broader worlds occurred, but the more explanatory level (in other words, the level of narrative) was our main focus in this study. We also assume that shared narrative thinking is an ideal state for knowledge co-creation. We separated the concepts of shared narrative thinking and creative collaboration. Narrative thinking emphasizes a state of joint thinking embedded by emotional factors, and is a vehicle for creative collaboration, whereas creative collaboration is a more target-oriented activity.

Discussion and conclusion

In this article, we have presented the findings of a study in which we paid attention to the narrativity of the co-design sessions where children designed their ideal play environments. We took for a starting point that narrativity and a tendency to create plot-shaped stories are essential elements of creative and collaborative action. We concentrated on how these narratives were constructed through creative and playful processes, and on the effect that narrative thinking has on the processes. We were not trying to define the borders of a story – namely what is considered as a story and what is not – but rather accepted it as a relative term. Following Bruner (2003, 2002, 1996), we were interested in how narrative as an instrument of mind operates in children's playful co-design processes, where in small groups they create their own ideal play environments.

The study showed that most of the children created the play environments of their dreams through creative collaboration, and they included in them meaningful narratives in the shape of actions. The study also showed that children's narrative thinking can be shared, and that joint activity arose especially by playing and refining imaginative situations. Through shared narrative thinking, the children crossed the borders and limitations of individual imagination. As our data showed, surprise and integration of fact and fiction were among the most important factors in narrative thinking. We noticed that combining fact and fiction seemed to inspire children, and tended to exclude the conventional in the narratives. Interesting and exciting conflicts between fact and fiction produced more shared narrative thinking. Possibility thinking emerged as an imaginative way of testing and integrating fact and fiction while the children drew and talked in small groups.

In their investigations of the dynamics of creative collaboration, John-Steiner and colleagues (2004) found that collaborators who established the most integrative relationships relied on the largest number of jointly constructed utterances. The authors note that it was as if the collaborators were inside each other's heads, and were completing their partner's unfinished thoughts. In our case, this refers to the children's commitment to the creation and design of the same play environment by connecting their own ideas or thoughts with the ideas of others. Narratives from the viewpoint of collaborative activity are thus not only the sum of the narratives of individuals, but the active collaborative building of narratives. Further, in this case the focus was not on individuals transforming their own structures of mind, but on contributing to and refining shared narrative information (Bereiter 2002).

The study has theoretical and methodological advantages. It has contributed substantially to the development of the theoretical and pedagogical approaches underpinning creative and playful learning (CPL) by generating further interest and understanding in how narrativity, creativity, and imagination should be included in learning in the PLE setting (Kangas 2010). On the basis of the findings, we concluded that the PLE should be adaptive, flexible, and customizable if it is to support children's own narrative activity and creative collaboration. It is important to give children the opportunity to refine possible worlds that are relevant to their current views of reality and their interests. When constructing possible worlds by means of narrative, children gain an understanding of more complex meanings and learn to create new meaningful worlds. This was tested in the pilot teaching experiment in the PLE setting in a week-long intervention where curriculum-based learning was extended from the classroom to an outdoor playground, and where children's narrativity and imagination were supported by various fact-and-fiction-based learning methods (e.g. Kangas, Kultima, and Ruokamo 2006; Kangas 2010). The results of the teaching experiment were encouraging, although further empirical research is required.

In addition, the theoretical model of narrativity introduced here requires further interdisciplinary research. Considering thought processes from a narrative viewpoint has aroused special interest in recent years. As a theoretical support for narrative thinking, one can also use the philosophical analysis of the semantics of possible worlds. This is related to Jerome Bruner's argument, which states that the essence of narrative thought processes is to clarify anything that deviates from the ordinary practice.

The 'playful co-design sessions' provided us[2] with a fascinating opportunity to explore creative collaboration and knowledge co-creation in authentic settings. Hence, another advantage of the study lies in the richer understanding that it yielded of the role of peers and adults in creative collaboration. The study showed that collecting data from groups of young children is a meaningful way of encouraging children to present their views and images, as well as of generating new suggestions and ideas collaboratively. However, interacting with children in this way often requires a good tutor (an adult or a peer) who is sensitive to the creative situation, and who can stay in the background and actively participate in discussions and activities when needed. Indeed, the researchers' participation and engagement in the design sessions was very important. They acted as interviewers, designers, and researchers, but first and foremost as facilitators, inspirers, and motivators.

Play and playful situations are rich grounds on which to develop children into flexible thinkers and actors for the future. Innovations spring from groups and teams that contain diverse perspectives, and that share goals and knowledge (Claxton et al. 2008; Sawyer 2006, 2008). We also concluded, consistent with the assumption of Egan (2005), that playfulness during activity may help children to think about and reflect on the world in a way that is free of constraints.

Notes

1 The SmartUs project included Let's Play (education), WePlay (industrial design), UbiPlay (software), Moto+ (physical exercise) and PlayTech (technologies). The products and software were produced by Lappset R & D of Lappset Group Ltd, a playground manufacturer (http://www.smartus.com/play/).
2 Marjaana Kangas, Annakaisa Kultima, and Heli Ruokamo.

References

Amabile, T. (1983) *The Social Psychology of Creativity*, New York: Springer-Verlag.

Armitage, M. (2001) 'The ins and outs of school playground play: children's use of "play spaces",' pp. 37–57 in J. Bishop and M. Curtis (eds), *Play Today in the Primary School Playground*, Buckingham: Open University Press.

Becker, T. and Quasthoff, U. M. (2004) 'Different dimensions in the field of narrative interaction,' pp. 1–11 in U. M. Quasthoff and T. Becker (eds), *Narrative Interaction*, Amsterdam: John Benjamins.

Bereiter, C. (2002) *Education and Mind in the Knowledge Age*, Hillsdale, N.J.: Erlbaum.

Bokulich, A. (2001) 'Rethinking thought experiments,' *Perspectives on Science*, **9**(3) pp. 285–307.

Broström, S. (1996) 'Frame play with 6 year-old children,' *European Early Childhood Education Research Journal*, **4**(1), pp. 89–101.

Broström, S. (1999) 'Drama games with 6-year-old children: possibilities and limitations,' pp. 250–63 in Y. Engeström, R. Miettinen, and R-L. Punamäki (eds), *Perspectives on Activity Theory*, New York: Cambridge University Press.

Bruner, J. (1986) *Actual Minds, Possible Worlds*, Cambridge, Mass.: Harvard University Press.

Bruner, J. (1990) *Acts of Meaning*, Cambridge, Mass.: Harvard University Press.

Bruner, J. (1996) *The Culture of Education*, Cambridge, Mass.: Harvard University Press.

Bruner, J. (2002) *Making Stories: Law, literature, life*, New York: Farrar, Strauss & Giroux.

Bruner, J. (2003) 'The narrative construction of reality,' pp. 41–62 in M. Mateas and P. Sengers (eds), *Narrative Intelligence*, Amsterdam: John Benjamins.

Bruner, J., Jolly, A., and Sylva, K. (1976) *Play*, London: Penguin.

Claxton, G., Craft, A., and Gardner, H. (2008) 'Concluding thoughts. Good thinking – education for wise creativity,' pp. 16–34 in A. Craft, H. Gardner, and G. Claxton (eds), *Creativity, Wisdom and Trusteeship: Exploring the roles of education*, Thousands Oaks Calif.: Corwin.

Craft, A. (2001) 'Little c creativity,' pp. 45–61 in A. Craft, B. Jeffrey, and M. Liebling (eds), *Creativity in Education*, London: Continuum.

Craft, A. (2005) *Creativity in Schools: Tensions and dilemmas*, Abingdon/New York: Routledge.

Cropley, A. J. (2001) *Creativity in Education and Learning*, London: Routledge.

Egan, K. (1986) *Teaching as Story Telling. An alternative approach to teaching and curriculum in the elementary school*, Chicago, Ill.: University of Chicago Press.

Egan, K. (1992) *Imagination in Teaching and Learning Ages 8–15*, London: Routledge.

Egan, K. (2005) *An Imaginative Approach to Teaching*, San Francisco, Calif.: Jossey-Bass.

Faulkner, D. and Miell, D. (2004) 'Collaborative story telling in friendship and acquaintanceship dyads,' pp. 7–29 in K. Littleton, D. Miell, and D. Faulkner (eds), *Learning to Collaborate, Collaborating to Learn*, New York: Nova Science.

Gendler, T. S. (2000) *Thought Experiment. On the powers and limits of imaginary cases*, New York: Garland.

Hyvönen, P. (2008) *Affordances of Playful Learning Environment for Tutoring Playing and Learning*, Ph.D. thesis, Acta Universitatis Lappoensis 152, Rovaniemi, Finland: University of Lapland.

Hyvönen, P. and Juujärvi, M. (2005) 'Affordances of playful environment: a view of Finnish girls and boys,' pp. 1563–72 in *Proceedings of ED-MEDIA 2005: World Conference on Educational Multimedia, Hypermedia and Telecommunications, Montréal, Canada, 26 June–2 July 2005* (CD-ROM).

Hyvönen, P. and Kangas, M. (2007) 'From bogey mountains to funny houses: children's desires for play environment,' *Australian Journal of Early Childhood*, **32**(3), pp. 39–47.

Hyvönen, P. and Kangas, M. (2010) 'Children as experts in designing play environment,' pp. 143–70 in E-L. Kronqvist and P. Hyvönen (eds), *Insights and Outlouds: Childhood research in the North*, Acta Universitatis Ouluensis E 107, Oulu, Finland: Oulu University Press.

Hyvönen, P. and Kangas, M. (in press) 'Playfulness-based research: involving children in research process of designing a playful learning environment,' proposal accepted for an edited collection of Barn och ungas användning av digital teknologi i vardagen.

John-Steiner, V. (2000) *Creative Collaboration*, Oxford: Oxford University Press.

John-Steiner, V., Shank, C., and Meehan, T. (2004) 'The role of metaphor in the narrative co-construction of collaborative experience,' pp. 169–95 in U. M. Quasthoff and T. Becker (eds), *Narrative Interaction*, Amsterdam: John Benjamins.

Juujärvi, M., Kultima, A., and Ruokamo, H. (2005) 'A narrative view on children's creative and collaborative activity,' pp. 203–13 in H. Ruokamo, P. Hyvönen, M. Lehtonen, and S. Tella (eds), *Proceedings of the 12th International Network-Based Education (NBE) Conference: Teaching-studying-learning (tsl) processes and mobile technologies – multi-, inter- and transdisciplinary (MIT) Research approaches*, Rovaniemi, Finland: University of Lapland Press.

Kangas, M. (2010) 'Creative and playful learning: learning through game co-creation and games in a playful learning environment,' *Journal of Thinking Skills and Creativity*, **5**(1), pp. 1–15.

Kangas, M., Hyvönen, P., and Latva, S. (2007) 'Space treasure outdoor game in the playful learning environment: experiences and assessment,' pp. 181–94 in H. Ruokamo, M. Kangas, M. Lehtonen, and K. Kumpulainen (eds), *The Power of Media in Education: Proceedings of the 2nd International Network-Based Education Conference, Rovaniemi, Finland, 13–15 June 2007*, Publications in Education 17, Rovaniemi, Finland: University of Lapland.

Kangas, M., Kultima, A., and Ruokamo, H. (2006) 'Co-creative learning processes (CCLP) – children as game world creators to the outdoor playground contexts,' pp. 14–21 in J. Multisilta and H. Haaparanta (eds), *Proceedings of the Workshop on Human Centered Technology HCT06*, Publication 6, Pori, Finland: Tampere University of Technology.

Kangas, M., Randolph, J., and Ruokamo, H. (2009) 'An international mixed-method investigation into student satisfaction with playful learning environments,' Paper presented at 2009 AERA (American Educational Research Association) annual meeting, San Diego, California, 13–17 April 2009.

Kieff, J. E. and Casbergue, R. M. (2000) *Playful Learning: Integrating play into preschool and primary programs*, Boston, Mass.: Allyn & Bacon.

Kripke, S. A. (1972) *Naming and Necessity*, Cambridge, Mass.: Harvard University Press.

Lewis, D. (1986) *On the Plurality of Worlds*, Oxford: Blackwell Publishing.

Lieberman, J. N. (1977) *Playfulness: Its relationship to imagination and creativity*, New York: Academic Press.

Littleton, K. and Miell, D. (2004) 'Collaborative creativity: contemporary perspectives,' pp. 1–10 in D. Miell and K. Littleton (eds), *Collaborative Creativity: Contemporary perspectives*, Sidmouth: Chase.

Mahn, H. and John-Steiner, V. (2002) 'The gift of confidence: a Vygotskian view of emotions,' pp. 46–58 in G. Wells and G. Claxton (eds), *Learning for Life in the 21st Century: Sociocultural perspectives on the future of education*, Cambridge, Mass.: Blackwell.

Mateas, M. and Sengers, P. (2003) 'Narrative intelligence,' pp. 1–25 in M. Mateas and P. Sengers (eds), *Narrative Intelligence*, Amsterdam: John Benjamin.

Mercer, N. (2002) 'Developing dialogues,' pp. 141–53 in G. Wells and G. Claxton (eds), *Learning for Life in the 21st Century: Sociocultural perspectives on the future of education*, Cambridge, Mass.: Blackwell.

Paavola, S., Lipponen, L., and Hakkarainen, K. (2004) 'Models of innovative knowledge communities and three metaphors of learning,' *Review of Educational Research*, **74**(4), pp. 557–76.

Rojas-Drummond, S., Mazon, N., Fernandez, M., and Wegerif, R. (2006) 'Explicit reasoning, creativity and co-construction in primary school children's collaborative activities,' *Thinking Skills and Creativity*, **1**(2), pp. 84–94.

Russ, S. W. (2003) 'Play and creativity: developmental issues,' *Scandinavian Journal of Educational Research*, **47**(3), pp. 291–303.

Sawyer, R. K. (2006) 'Educating for innovation,' *Thinking Skills and Creativity*, **1**, pp. 41–8.

Sawyer, R. K. (2008) 'Learning music from collaboration,' *International Journal of Educational Research*, **47**(1), pp. 50–9.

Schwartz, P. (1996) T*he Art of the Long View: Planning for the future in an uncertain world*, New York: Bantam Doubleday Dell.

Schrage, M. (1990) *Shared Minds: The new technologies of collaboration*, New York: Random House.

Vass, E. (2004) 'Understanding collaborative creativity: young children's classroom-based shared creative writing,' pp. 79–95 in D. Miell and K. Littleton (eds), *Collaborative Creativity: Contemporary perspectives*, Sidmouth: Chase.

Vygotsky, L. S. (1978) *Mind in Society*, Cambridge, Mass.: Harvard University Press.

Vygotsky, L. S. (1986) *Thought and Language*, Cambridge, Mass.: MIT Press.

Vygotsky, L. S. (1998) *The Collected Works of L. S. Vygotsky, Vol. 5: Child Psychology*, ed. R. W. Rieber, New York: Plenum.

Wegerif, R. (2005) 'Reason and creativity in classroom dialogues,' *Language and Education*, **19**(3), pp. 223–38.

Wells, G. (1999) *Dialogic Inquiry: Towards a sociocultural practice and theory of education*, Cambridge: Cambridge University Press.

Whyte, H. (1981) 'The value of narrativity in the representation of reality,' pp. 1–24 in W. Mitchell (ed.), *On Narrative*, Chicago, Ill.: University of Chicago Press.

Chapter 5

The subjects and meanings of young children's drawings

Elizabeth Coates and Andrew Coates

In 1955 Rhoda Kellogg in America suggested that:

> The reality objects drawn by children under five years of age are ones which most easily evolve out of their earlier abstractions and are recognisable by adults as well as by the child. Autos, boats, flowers, airplanes soon join the sun, human, animal and house. These objects then get compiled into one drawing.
>
> (Kellogg 1959: 119)

Our examination of upwards of 800 drawings and related audiotape recordings, collected as a result of an ongoing research project observing three to seven year old children, in pairs, making self-directed drawings (in other words, making images of subjects of their own choice) (Coates and Coates 2006) although supporting in principle the production of Kellogg's 'reality objects', has provided valuable insights into children's thinking about their works which goes beyond her simple definition of theme and content. In this chapter we argue that the narratives that accompany these drawings provide evidence of individual trains of thought which not only derive from significant first-hand experiences but also indicate a highly complicated and informed knowledge and understanding of contemporary popular visual culture. Aspects of this may well include picture books produced specifically for children as role models for the successful marriage of Plate and story, television cartoons in which inanimate objects and animals achieve human status by acquiring language, characters on television and DVD/video productions such as Darth Vader and Sleeping Beauty which provide experiences and stories outside children's normal potential to imagine, and television documentaries containing facts and insights into a range of subjects and diverse cultures. It would seem, therefore, that this enriched cultural awareness has had a profound influence on children's drawings as it has enabled them to extend their subject matter beyond the boundaries of first-hand experience.

In 1921 Franz Cizek, an artist/teacher in Vienna, and one of the most important pioneers in the discovery of child art as someone primarily concerned with preserving the innocence of childhood, was reported as saying that:

> Children live nowadays altogether too sophisticated a life – they see and hear too much – they are taken to cinemas and theatres, and all sorts of alien influences play upon them.

(Wilson 1921: 4)

Despite the rise of the 'shocking' practice of providing children with rich wide-ranging experiences, and a more recent explosion of the products of the media industries which could not have been envisaged even by Kellogg in the 1950s, young children's spontaneity and their ability to invent symbolic representations of their visual world have not been inhibited. Their new subjects from the media are naturally incorporated into an enriched iconography along with such as 'A portrait of me flying a kite' (Alex, age 5:5) and 'A picture of me with a pony tail and pink shoes' (Phoebe, age 4:9).

It was exactly this innocence, instinctive expressiveness and freedom to invent unconstrained by academic rules, however, which led avant-garde European visual artists in the first two decades of the twentieth century to investigate the drawings of children. In 1902 André Derain wrote to Maurice de Vlaminck that he would like to study the art of children 'as truth is doubtless there' (Flam 1984: 216) and Pablo Picasso remarked about Henri Matisse's work of 1906 that what Matisse aimed to achieve 'was the straightforward simplicity of children's art' (Flam 1984: 224). Their interest was one aspect of a movement in nineteenth and early twentieth-century art broadly called 'primitivism' – the study of exotic and primitive artefacts based largely, though not exclusively, on the tribal arts of Africa and Oceania – as a means by which the western classical tradition might be challenged and the nature and purposes of art reassessed. In particular, this challenge applied to the post-Renaissance obligation to pursue an art of imitation, the skilful and faithful representation of the visible and tangible world, (Stolnitz 1960), as instead artists set out to find ways to make visible their emotional responses to it. This term, the invention of western anthropology, arose in relation to eighteenth and nineteenth-century European colonial expansion and the discovery of a wealth of cultures new to the West 'set within a system of unequal power relations which determined that the primitive, or more often in contemporary writings, the "savage", was invariably the dominated partner' (Rhodes 1994: 7). It is even now, at least in popular thought, regarded as meaning something inferior to the culture of western civilisation, but its influence on the development of twentieth-century visual art has been profound.

The movement's ultimate victory was a negation of the great tradition of

Renaissance thinking, and modernism, the name given to the succession of avant-garde styles in art and architecture that dominated western culture throughout most of the twentieth century, became the establishment (Lucie-Smith 1990). A direct consequence was that the art of the child became more widely recognised as possessing qualities as valid as those of adult artists, a relationship recognised by Kellogg with O'Dell when they wrote:

> Now that Kandinsky and Klee, Chagall, Picasso and Miro have returned to the sources of child art and manipulated these shapes and patterns in sophisticated ways, the creations of the young receive some of the attention they deserve. Scribblings that once were thrown in the waste basket are looked at with respect and even pleasure by those who have become sympathetic to the aims and needs of the child.
>
> (Kellogg and O'Dell 1967: 93)

Ultimately, however, the modernist revolution has profoundly and conclusively influenced the visual environment experienced by children through the education and thinking of those responsible for designing, making and providing the products of the media industries. It would seem therefore that child art has come full circle, in that what children are now experiencing in the media and expressing in their drawings is at least in part a result of previous children's expression. What follows provides grounds for this premise, with evidence taken from a range of sources. These include the disciplines of art history, psychology and the history of art education, as well as our current research with young children which has provided drawings with subjects related to such as children's books, television programmes and cartoons. The discussion is structured according to the following broad headings:

- the recognition of the child as artist
- primitivism as a challenge to the western classical tradition, including further reference to the role played by the art of children
- the influence of the drawings of young children on the art of Paul Klee
- the main means by which young children structure their drawings and represent space
- the subjects of young children's drawings
- the role of narrative as an accompaniment to the drawing process
- significant first-hand experiences as revealed through quality talk
- sources for imaginative stories
- heroes and subjects from the media.

The recognition of the child as artist

During the second half of the nineteenth century, a revolution took place in the field of psychology which was going to affect both the nature of early years education and how we came to regard the art of children. Perhaps as a response to Rousseau's maxim that 'the child is not a small grown-up, he has needs of his own, and a mentality adapted to those needs' (cited in Viola 1944: 7), and sparked by a number of recently published 'reminiscences of early years' (Sully 1895: 4) , the child became worthy of study.

Herbert Spencer was the first to recognise the child as artist, certainly in England, when his views on art education were published in the *North British Review* in May 1854 and subsequently republished in his book *Education* in 1878 (Macdonald 1970). Spencer wrote:

> What is that the child first tries to represent? Things that are large, things that are attractive in colour, things round which its most pleasurable associations most cluster – human beings from whom it has received so many emotions; cows and dogs which interest by the many phenomena they present; houses that are hourly visible and strike by their size and contrast of parts.
>
> (Spencer 1854/1929: 82–3)

John Ruskin in his seminal book *The Elements of Drawing*, first published in 1857, also recognised the value of young children engaging in the activity of drawing. He wrote:

> It should be allowed to scrawl at its own free will [and] should be gently led by the parents to try to draw, in such childish fashion as may be, the things it can see and likes, – birds, or butterflies, or flowers, or fruit.
>
> (Ruskin 1892)

These ideas, as well as publications by Corrado Ricci (1887) in Italy, Bernard Perez (1888) in France and Ebenezer Cook (1885–6) in England (MacDonald 1970), which considered the nature of young children's art, both impressed and influenced James Sully, who in 1895 published his *Studies of Childhood*. He regarded the beginnings of art activity as 'one of the most interesting, perhaps also one of the most instructive phases of child life' (Sully 1895: 298) stating that 'the most obvious source of interest in doings of infancy lies in its primitiveness' (Sully 1895: 4). He made analogies between the characteristics of children's drawings and the drawings of 'untutored savages' (Sully 1895: 385) collected from primitive races, and drawings by unskilled adults and those from archaic civilisations, many of which he viewed in the collection of General Pitt-Rivers. Sully spearheaded a movement which was to have a profound affect on our understanding of how children learn as well as informing the development of 'child-centred' education, and recognised that children use drawing to order their experience and explore ideas as a fundamental element in their developing sentience. His work was closely followed by such as Levinstein (1905) and Krotzsch (1917) in Leipzig; Kerschensteiner (1905) in Munich; Rouma (1913) in Brussels; Luquet (1913) in Paris and Burt (1921) in London (Steveni 1968). More recently a range of theories have been put forward regarding the development of children's art, perhaps the most notable being those of Lowenfield and Brittain (1964, 1987) (first published in 1947), Kellogg (1959, 1969) and Gardner (1980) .

In order to begin to understand the relationship between the discovery of the art of children and the study of the visual arts of cultures outside the western classical tradition – both regarded as 'primitive' – it is necessary to know something about the ideas that informed the rise of modernism in the twentieth century.

Primitivism as a challenge to the western classical tradition – including further reference to the role played by the art of children

By the beginning of the nineteenth century the language of classicism was losing its centrality, and other western cultures such as those of the Middle Ages and Nordic Europe, the Middle and Far East and later the art of 'savages' began to be studied as serious viable alternatives (Lynton 1989). For instance, Vaughan (2005) defined primitivism as a series of movements in art responding to Rousseau's notion of the 'noble savage', which sought to recapture the conditions of a simpler and more truthful age. He cited Samuel Palmer as an example of one of the earliest of those artists who reflected his generation's response to the richness and moral superiority of the mediaeval world.

Paul Gauguin, however, is normally considered the starting point for a serious study of primitivism as a potential challenge to the western classical tradition, and even though his assertion that he considered himself 'a savage beyond the taint of civilisation' (cited in Chipp 1968: 51) was largely affectation, it did not mask a genuine desire to reinvent both himself and his art. To this end, therefore, he moved first to Brittany to immerse himself in the simple life and superstitions of the peasants, and subsequently to Tahiti in 1891 to make:

> simple, very simple art … to immerse myself in virgin nature, see no-one but savages, live their life, with no other thought in mind but to render, the way a child would, the concepts formed in my brain, and to do this with nothing but the primitive means of art, the only means that are good and true.
>
> (cited in Varnedoe 1984: 187)

As a result of the European colonisation of the third world, tribal art became available for appraisal, not only by the anthropologists responsible for its acquisition, but also by vanguard artists, particularly in Paris, who discovered it in the Musée d'Ethnographie du Trocadéro. Pablo Picasso who came to own a significant collection, promoted it to the status of art. He described what he had discovered as giving him 'the right to the arbitrary and the right to freedom' (Malraux 1974: 15). Subsequently, twentieth-century artists gained the freedom to invent without the constraints of a stifling academic tradition, and moved towards a conceptual rather than a perceptual way of working.

In Germany, primitive art was discovered by the artists of both the Die Brücke group in Dresden, and the Blaue Reiter group in Munich. No doubt this was made possible by the ethnographic collections of the great museums in Hamburg, Berlin, Leipzig and Dresden (Newton 1980). It is in the publications of the Blaue Reiter group, however, that references to the art of children were made consistently, for they believed that 'the primitive could just as readily signify Archaic court art, folk art, or children's art as it could tribal art [as one of its purposes] according to Wassily Kandinsky, was to foster the assimilation of all expressive art forms' (Gordon 1984: 374). Originally centred on Wassily Kandinsky, Franz Marc and Auguste Macke, the Blaue Reiter stated in their manifesto in 1906, that they wanted to 'gain freedom of movement and life against the well-entrenched older forces [to create] directly and without adulteration' (Guenther 1989: 2). In 1912 they published an almanac and organised two art exhibitions under the banner of Der Blaue Reiter supporting a generally agreed philosophy. The almanac contained a series of essays, mostly about art, but also included articles about new ideas in music, and was profusely illustrated with Bavarian paintings on glass, European folk art, Russian secular and religious prints, primitive masks and figures and children's drawings. Marc wrote in this publication that the almanac 'reveals subtle connections with gothic and primitive art, with Africa and the vast Orient, with the highly expressive, spontaneous folk and children's art' (Lankheit 1974: 252).

Paul Klee joined the group in that year, and exhibited with them along with a large number of artists such as the French cubists and representatives from the Russian avant-garde. Although Rubin (1984) identified a number of examples that reflect how Klee also borrowed from primitive works, it is the profound influence that the drawings of young children had on his art and visual thinking that is of particular interest in the context of this chapter. Klee considered the art of children as the most primitive form of art, and examined it to discover 'how a primitive instinct finds a formal structure appropriate to content' (cited in Haftmann 1967: 50). It is the recognition of the parallel between the devices and structures used by both young children and Klee that has led to the following examination of his work.

The influence of the drawings of young children on the art of Paul Klee

Many of Klee's images and structures bear a remarkable resemblance to those of young children, and as Schmalenbach wrote, 'Klee belonged to those artists who delighted in the charm of children's drawings, but he was the only one of his generation who allowed his art to be influenced so directly by them' (1986: 26). The first evidence of Klee's interest in children's art is contained in a letter to his fiancée, Lily Stumpf, dated 31 March 1905, in which he described a recent drawing, 'Girl with a doll', made 'as children would draw it' (Franciscono 1998: 98). Six years later he expressed his support of primitive art, particularly extolling the virtues of the art of young children, when he wrote a review of the first exhibition of the Blaue Reiter group held in Munich in 1911 (Partsch 2003). This review was reiterated in a diary entry of 1912 as follows:

> For these are primitive beginnings in art, such as one usually finds in ethnographic collections or at home in one's nursery. Do not laugh, reader! Children also have artistic ability, and there is wisdom in their having it! The more helpless they are, the more instructive are the examples they furnish us; and they must be preserved free of corruption from an early age. Parallel phenomena are provided by the works of the mentally diseased; neither childish behaviour nor madness are insulting words here, as they commonly are. All this is to be taken very seriously, more seriously than all the public galleries, when it comes to reforming today's art.
>
> (Paul Klee, cited in F. Klee 1965: 266)

By this time it would seem that Klee's respect for the vitality and immediacy of the drawings of young children was well established, based as it was on perhaps the most potent imaginable source – the work of his own child which he diligently collected, as well as that of other children (Spiller 1961). He married in 1906. Felix, the couple's only child, was born in 1907, and for a number of years Klee acted as a 'house husband', looking after the child while his wife Lily earned money by working as a piano teacher. This arrangement is even now unusual, but a hundred years ago in western society a professional man acting in this capacity must have been almost unique. What better opportunity, however, given that the child was likely to have been playing in the studio in which his father was working, to observe – in a similar way that we, as artist and teacher observed and collected the works of our children during their formative years – how Felix responded to the painting and drawing materials given to him for his amusement, so that his father's work was not unduly interrupted. Little wonder, therefore, that the child's seriousness and focused concentration, coupled with a profound command of the means by which his images were produced, impressed his equally serious father to the extent that he began to examine them as a starting point for his own explorations.

Partsch is of the opinion that 'Art historians, most of whom are men, are only now beginning to allow that this aspect of Klee's art may also have something to do with the years he spent as a househusband' (2003: 15–16). After all, four-year-old children tend not to question the validity of their own inventions as representations of a person, animal or object, but accept them unequivocally as images of reality. What better role model in the circumstances if your aim is to reinvent both yourself and the nature of art?

Klee's contemporaries, however, often accused him of childishness, and likened his images to those of young children. (Schmalenbach 1986). Given his 'serious' artistic and pedagogical ambitions as a teacher at the famous school of design, the Bauhaus at Weimar, and the weight of academic prejudice which gave rise to such accusations, it was perhaps inevitable that he would want to deny them and at least claim to distance himself from such 'untutored' and 'subjective' works as sources of reference and inspiration.

Nevertheless, this debt is evident to a greater or lesser extent throughout most of his artistic career, and the following discussion provides evidence for this. It contains terms perhaps rarely used outside the study of the structure of young children's drawings. The meanings of these are discussed in some detail in the next section.

Klee's 'Composition on parallel horizontals' of 1920 (see Figure 5.1) is a promenade of trees, people, animals and machines placed on a complicated horizontal structure – much like railway tracks – and set between a rapidly scribbled baseline and a scribbled skyline. It is a clear example of the use of plan and elevation as a means of defining space (as discussed earlier). Each object occupies its own space and there is no overlapping. Even though the trees and lines may refer to 'a kind of musical notation' (Grohmann 1960: 24), do not children also draw 'lollipop' trees? Our research drawings provide many comparable examples, and Klee, like Lauren (age 5:2), whose drawing was based on a family holiday by the seaside (see Plate 2), works out a complicated imaginative story. Both compose their ideas in a remarkably similar way. Lauren's rows of people with flowers in their hands, beach bags and multicoloured birds, each occupying their own horizontal band of space, are firmly contained within a blue baseline as sea and a skyline with a shining sun.

Likewise, Klee transferred his ridicule of the people of Switzerland who thought he was not quite normal (Schmalenbach 1986) onto a work made towards the end of his life, 'The boulevard of the abnormal ones' of 1938 (see Plate 3), which depicts a group of diagrammatic people in top hats, and a dog, processing from right to left while looking directly at the beholder as they pass – like lemmings on their way to oblivion.

Figure 5.1 Paul Klee, 'Composition on parallel horizontals'

These works reflect the characteristic graphic inventions of four to seven-year-old children, placed by Lowenfield and Brittain in what they call the 'preschematic stage' of drawing development. This stage follows scribbling, and is described as the gradual realisation of how things are represented as the child is 'involved with the establishment of a relationship to what he intends to represent'. (1947/1964: 115)

This definition is far too simple to adequately describe what is a complicated period of children's development, as during that time they will have evolved and learned to use a variety of images, structures and processes as the building blocks of a graphic vocabulary with which to represent familiar objects. The literature that deals with this area is complicated, but despite its diversity there is sufficient consensus to enable us to draw on it to describe in broad terms the means by which young children structure their drawings, represent space and express their ideas and experiences. These are illustrated, where appropriate, by reference to examples taken from our research data.

The main means by which young children structure their drawings and represent their ideas

Line as the technical basis for drawing

The technical basis for young children's drawing is circumferential outline, which describes the main part of the figure or object as well as suggesting aspects such as arms, legs, fingers and flower stalks and petals. Children often 'fill in' these objects with colour.

The development of geometric symbols or schemas

As a progression from scribbling, children create their own highly personal geometric symbols or schemas as diagrammatic representations of their visual environment. Lowenfield and Brittain regard the schema as 'the concept at which the child has finally arrived' (1947/1964: 140) at around the age of seven years, but up to that age a range of ever-changing symbols are developed and used for a variety of purposes. Circles are the first shape as they are the easiest to draw, followed by squares, rectangles and when mastered, triangles.

Intellectual realism

In our experience young children base their drawings on what they have seen and remembered, and include aspects of what they know which are not necessarily visible. In 1927 Georges-Henri Luquet devised the term 'intellectual realism' to describe this phenomenon as including the details of objects drawn 'even if they are not visible either from the location from which they are observed or from any other viewpoint [as well as] abstract elements which exist only in the mind of the artist' (1927/2001: 102).

The mixing of plans and front elevations

Rather than using eye-level perspective to represent 'a three-dimensional object or a particular volume of space, on a flat or nearly flat surface' (Lucie-Smith 1990: 145), children create their own symbolic space by mixing together plans and front elevations in order to clearly express the significance of the information they wish to communicate. For instance, in relation to the effective delineation of space, a mixture of viewpoints is far more effective than the use of eye-level perspective and would be ineffectual say, in describing the positions of fielders on a cricket pitch. Bethanie (age 5:1) in 'Me and my friends at the swimming pool' provides a good example of this mixture, as the swimming pool is drawn in plan and Bethanie and her friends are drawn in elevation. (see Plate 4).

The base line and sky line

The base line is most often drawn at the bottom of the picture as grass or earth, and acts as a support for the objects it contains. This definition, however, is not used merely because of its low position on the paper, as one or more baselines can be added to reflect the complexity of the ideas being expressed. In some drawings space is represented as a stacking up of base lines one above the other 'so that the picture is divided into plane strips' (Lowenfeld 1939: 42). In this respect the relationship between a work by Paul Klee and a work by Lauren has already been discussed in some detail. Many drawings contain a strip of sky at the top of the paper, often with a space for the sun which actively shines by means of rays which extend out of it. 'Me and you in the Princess Land' by Caitlyn (age 4:10) contains grass as a baseline and a strip of sky at the top with a shining sun (see Plate 5).

A development of the base line is a circle or rectangle as a plan representation of a space such as a pond or a football field. This then acts as a support for buildings, trees, figures or goal posts, drawn at right angles and 'folded out' or 'folded in' from it. Perhaps the first and simplest example of this phenomenon is the chimney that folds out at right angles to the triangular roof.

The tendency to avoid overlapping

There is a tendency for young children to avoid partially obscuring a unit by overlapping with another. According to Arnheim this is because 'The need for a simple and clear picture requires the child neatly to separate visual objects from each other. They must not be allowed to mingle, because this would greatly complicate the visual structure,' (1956: 157). Bethanie in 'Me and my friends at the swimming pool' solves the problem of overlapping when drawing her friends at the pool side, one behind the other, by first drawing the heads in grey and then stacking up short orange bodies in the available space between the heads. She said: 'They are going to have little bodies because they go over the head … they might be in a line. These got big ones and these got little ones [bodies] … they're at the top' (see Plate 4).

Disjunctures of scale

Just as the head is invariably drawn proportionally large in the representation of a person, children also tend to exaggerate the conceptually important parts of a picture with little regard for visual appearance and proportional accuracy, as the scale of the elements largely depends on their emotional significance. For instance, in 'Me and you in the Princess Land', Caitlyn drew the princess much bigger than both herself and her friend Jay who flank her on either side, as well as exaggerating her head and hands. The blue castle is an almost insignificant part of the composition (see Plate 5).

X-ray pictures

Sometimes young children make transparent or X-ray pictures in which both the inside and outside of an enclosure are shown simultaneously, 'This can be seen whenever the inside is of greater importance for the child than is the outside of the structure' (Arnheim 1956: 159). Aidan (age 6:2) in 'My holiday in Wales' (see Plate 6) drew a rectangle with four wheels as an image of a caravan in which he and his family had stayed. He then proceeded to draw objects inside the caravan, not only its contents such as the kitchen, a television with a cat sitting on top of it and a Christmas tree, but also a swimming pool and five people 'dancing to the music'.

Writing that accompanies the drawing

Drawings made by three to four-year-old children often contain marks and patterns as a response to writing made by adults and older children, and reflect an awakening knowledge of the significance of letters and words. 'These independent marks, are often referred to as "emergent writing"' (Wilkinson 1996: 135). Archie (age 4:10) in 'I'm doing different colours for the writing' (see Plate 7) reflected this when he drew four 'tadpole' figures surrounded by red and grey letter shapes in a credible attempt to construct words and sentences.

As writing assumes greater importance in the curriculum and children become more aware of the nature of print, they often insist on including their name as part of the composition. Later, more complicated messages or the names of characters being represented become integral to the graphic imagery. For instance, Aidan (see Plate 6) included the names of those on holiday with him.

Running parallel to, and perhaps preceding theories that seek to describe and offer explanations for the technicalities relating to children's picture construction, are texts relating to the content of such pictures. The following section, therefore, deals with the subject matter reported in the literature, providing a platform upon which the content of our research drawings may be discussed.

The subjects of young children's drawings

It is surprising how little the reported subject matter of children's drawings has changed since the writings of Spencer, Ruskin and Sully in the nineteenth century. Spencer (1854/1929) suggested that young children's immediate environment, the significant people in their lives and the objects they see every day are fundamental to the content of their earliest work. This was echoed by Sully, who found similar evidence of humans, houses and animals, particularly 'the man on horseback' (1895: 377), and Margaret McMillan, who listed the objects that nursery-age children model in clay, her chosen medium for expression and 'the one most suitable for little children' (1919: 254), as marketing baskets, potatoes, cucumbers, children, men, women, nursery schools, aeroplanes, drays, horses and red-riding hoods or 'any or everything that passes through our busy little heads.' (1919: 105). Such images featured in a number of later studies (Kellogg 1959, 1969; Gentle 1985) with little variation apart from the change in emphasis from horses to motorised vehicles. The reasoning behind children's drawings concerned Gaitskell and Hurwitz (1975) and Gardner (1980), who both felt that content is dictated by experiences that weigh heavily on children's minds or form important relationships in their thoughts.

Certainly references to the subject matter of children's earliest drawings point to the importance of people, and figures labelled 'mummy' and 'daddy' are common. As Kellogg and O'Dell wrote, 'The favourite subject of people is people. And so it is with children and their art' (1967: 65). There would also seem to be a consensus that three to four year olds often depict a single figure, but by five or six years stories begin to appear which are influenced by events in their own lives, story books and fantasy worlds. It is at this stage that complete pictures occur with inter-related objects and figures.

The socialisation that occurs once children enter the school or nursery can in fact have a positive effect on the subject matter of their drawings. Gentle (1985) talked of the influences that come from society, while Thompson (1999) suggested that children discuss possible subject matter together, and this has an effect on the content as they clarify and extend concepts, or vie to outdo one another. This is a time when children's horizons are being extended in both formal and informal ways, and out of school popular culture becomes a vital part of this in the form of cartoons, pop stars and superheroes (Anning 2002). Marsh (1999) suggested that while what constitutes popular culture may vary from community to community, in this era of mass production particular media-based influences may be common to children across a wide range of social groups. The media technology available inside and outside the home with its urgent movements, fantastic creatures and explosive sounds provides a rich source of subject matter, and the more recent literature identifies DVDs, Play Stations and merchandise as references for both play and drawing activities (Ring 2006).

Many of the drawings we collected mirror the subject matter discussed in the literature, with its emphasis on figures, but each one is unique, reflecting the particular interest of the individual child. Furthermore, our investigation suggested that the iconography of children's books, and the images found in both children's cartoons and television programmes, have influenced and extended the subjects available as sources for children's drawings. Their visual environment now contains a range of images from rainbows, hearts, and animals and monsters based on both the real world and the world of the imagination, to characters from cartoons and films, all of these perhaps made possible by the modernist rejection of naturalistic representation. The advent of computer games and Play Stations adds yet another dimension to this environment, as the possibility of participating and manipulating characters' actions provides a bridge between real and imagined worlds. Marsh (1999, 2005), when examining nursery children's responses to the media, found that one of the biggest influences on their shared culture was the artefacts produced by large companies to go alongside their latest film, television series or game. This influence was confirmed by the narratives in our research, where children discussed with passion the actions of pirates and princesses, and superheroes from such as *Power Rangers* and *Star Wars*, translating their adventures onto paper as part of the shared experience.

The role of narrative as an accompaniment to the drawing process

Examination of our research sample's drawings suggested that they were often based on narratives related to the subjects of their imagery. The children had evolved graphic symbols by which to express the most important parts of their visual world. These symbols developed and changed constantly but were based on the knowledge they had at the time, extended and enriched by the social interaction which occurred as each pair engaged in the act of drawing. Many of the structures employed by these children have already been discussed, for they echo those used by Klee, as the highly personal invention of graphic symbols and the same surety of line which make our children's drawings so vivid can be seen in both his work and that of his contemporaries. Although some children stated at the outset what they intended to draw, the process was dynamic and its direction could be modified or even diverted by a chance remark, a conversation or the addition of different elements. Their narratives in fact operated at different levels, as they might be either simple descriptions of what the drawing contained, or highly complicated dialogues which encapsulated a complete remembered experience. On occasions an imagined situation was actualised visually, revealing whimsical or fantastical ideas as well as humour. These narratives if studied alongside the developing drawing, may be said to portray a desire on the part of the child to tell the story behind the completed image in a way that Arthur Rackham, possibly 'England's leading [children's] book illustrator' (Darrell 1972: 8) would have recognised, for he had a strong belief in the need for a balance between text and plate.

While there is no evidence of narrative to support their contention, Spencer's (1854/1929) and Sully's (1895) previously stated suggestion that children's immediate environment and the people who were important to them acted as favourite subjects for their drawings is still true over 100 years later, but of the drawings we collected, 'friends' often replaced 'mummy' and 'daddy' as children now enter the social world of the nursery at a much younger age and friendships become increasingly important. However, the subjects of many drawings focused upon wider media-based issues, ranging from story books to fantasy worlds based on technical and factual documentaries.

The next section discusses some of the subjects and themes derived from our observations and data collection, providing instances of the narrative accompanying them and suggesting possible sources of influence. The areas selected for consideration represent what would seem to be, in our experience, the most common themes:

- significant first-hand experiences as revealed through quality talk
- sources for imaginative story
- heroes and subjects from the media.

Significant first-hand experiences as revealed through quality talk

Some of the most significant drawings and narratives in our research originated from memories of events experienced at first hand. Although the quality of the drawings enabled them to be appreciated as works in their own right, it was the talk that revealed the depth of children's understanding in relation to their retention of facts and recollections, and illustrated how drawings can sometimes change as fresh memories surface. Aidan's drawing of 'My holiday in Wales' (as discussed earlier; see Plate 6) is a good example of the way that several events, occurring over a period of time, can be encapsulated simultaneously in one work, as he recalled a memorable holiday. He first drew a decorative frame round the edge of the paper based on looking at the display of work in the school corridor. His utterances can be grouped under three headings – factual information, aesthetic responses to the qualities of the environment, and his relationship to family:

> That's a chair, this is the kitchen .... I have blue water in that little square .... It's when it was Christmas, I've got the Christmas tree and a star at the top .... I like Christmas and got fifteen presents .... Oh yeah, my cat went too, Penny, that's my cat.
>
> This is the sunshine sky, blue, blue, sky .... I like Wales, I wish I went back there .... Wales is my bestest holiday so far, like a home, I wish I lived there .... It's so beautiful, so beautiful and good, so beautiful and precious.... Beautiful means you love something .... Wow! This is the life.
>
> And I was sitting watching all the television ... my bestest family ever, we was watching TV together ... we played chess, I was laughing .... This is daddy, dad's name is Arthur .... That's my mummy, she's got black hair and her name's Binny.

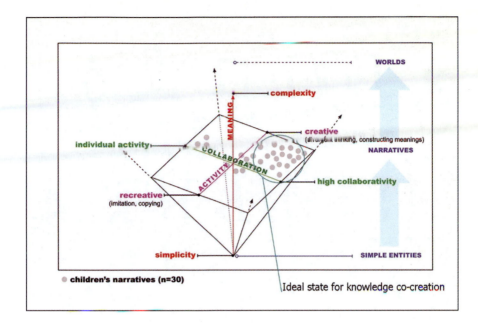

Plate 1 The ideal state for knowledge co-creation

Plate 2 Lauren (age 5:2), 'My family on holiday by the seaside'

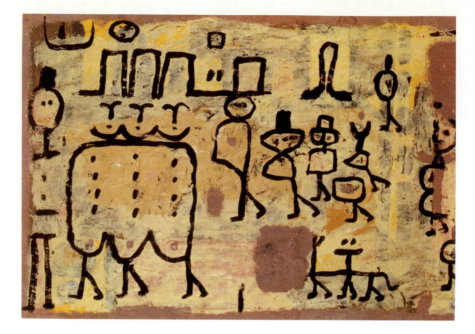

Plate 3 Paul Klee, 'The boulevard of the abnormal ones', 1938

Plate 4 Bethanie (age 5:1), 'Me and my friends at the swimming pool'

Plate 5 Caitlyn (age 4:10), 'Me and you in the Princess Land'

Aidan Binny arttelu Adrian
and
Cavan whales fluckey

Plate 6 Aidan (age 6:2), 'My holiday in Wales'

Plate 7 Archie (age 4:10), 'I'm doing different colours for the writing'

Plate 8 Alisha (age 5:1), 'Me and mummy paddling in the sea'

Plate 9 Lucy (age 4:11), 'My Georgina and her friends'

Plate 10 Amy (age 4:11), 'Treasure on the top of the rainbow'

Plate 11 Neil (age 5:3), 'They're my dogs – that's a dogs' home'

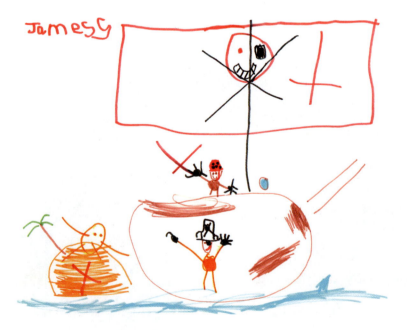

Plate 12 James (age 5:4), 'Pirates, pirate ships and buried treasure'

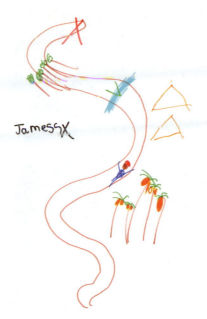

Plate 13 James (age 5:4), 'Treasure map'

Plate 14 Reception class children and an 'expert' teacher

Plate 15 A reception child's painting of a flying dinosaur

Plate 16 'Little wet license', example of a colouring page from a Czech pre-school for participation in a 'tadpole' swimming school

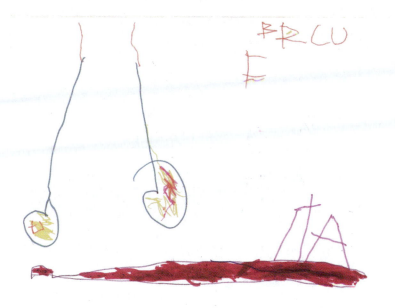

Plate 17 A child's comments on his artwork on the theme 'Stranger': 'That's why he steps on the snake. The snake wakes up and bites him on the foot.'

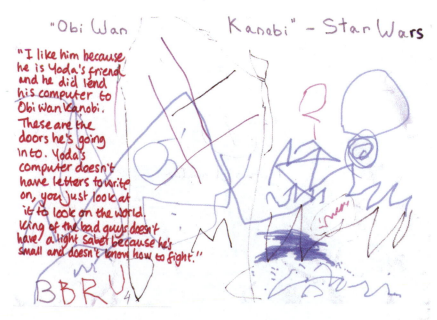

"Obi Wan   Kanobi" - Star Wars

"I like him because he is Yoda's friend and he did lend his computer to Obi Wan Kanobi. These are the doors he's going into. Yoda's computer doesn't have letters to write on, you just look at it to look on the world. King of the bad guys doesn't have a light sabet because he's small and doesn't know how to fight."

BBRU

Plate 18 Child B's favourite character, Obi-Wan Kenobi from Star Wars

Plate 19 Child B's illustration for the theme 'My territory, my place'

Plate 20 Child B's illustration for the theme 'My things'

Plate 21 Dual parks and pollution

Plate 22 Changing night into day

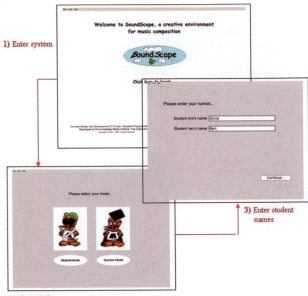

1) Enter system

2) Select Mode

3) Enter student names

Plate 23 Getting started with SoundScape

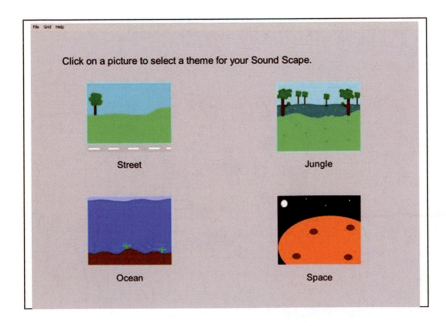

Plate 24 Setting the context for the composition – theme selections

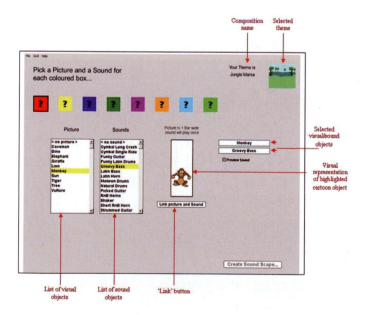

Plate 25 Encouraging reflexivity in learning

Plate 26 Setting up musical objects in the SoundScape environment

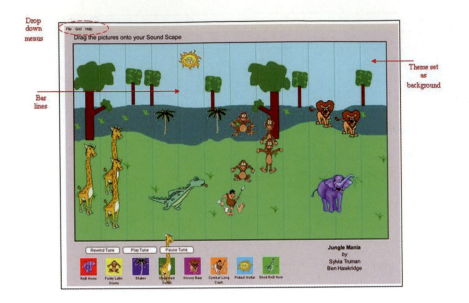

Plate 27 The composition interface

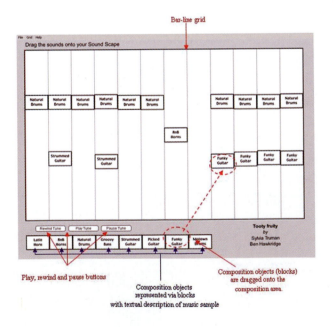

Plate 28 Abstract representation of music prototype

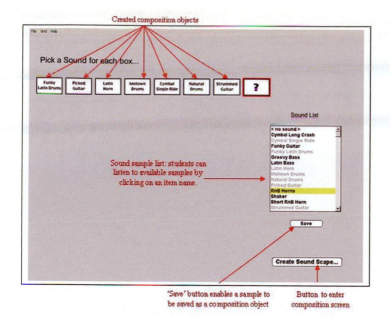

Plate 29 The sample selection interface for the abstract representation prototype

Plate 30 Nancy, on the left of the image uncertain of the boxes

Plate 31 Nancy engaged at level 4

Plate 32 Golden Lycra shape made by Annabelle to enable the children to cluster inside like an egg

Alisha's (age 5:1) double portrait of 'Me and mummy paddling in the sea' (see Plate 8) was always intended to be her mother and herself, although the context was not determined until she had been drawing for 25 minutes. Both her title and extracts from her talk – 'I'm at the seaside …. I live at the seaside, I'm at the seaside now …. I've got the seaside in my head, I remember and I've got the days …. I've got all of them in my head' – confirm that this work was based on her own experience. Her final act was to vigorously dot red marks between the sea and the curved sky as fireworks. Perhaps as a response to a previous conversation regarding the forecast snow, these dots became snow – 'They're not fireworks, they're snow, yeah 'cos you can't put white on the paper, but you can't do white.'

Lowenfeld and Brittain (1947/1987) suggested that some children are trying to work through particular situations and relationships, seeking to understand the feelings they arouse. It is as though they are using the drawing activity as a means of engaging in quality thought which examines and questions the values they encounter in their social and family life. In the following examples both Lucy and Bethanie explored the notion of friendship. Lucy's (age 4:11) narrative showed how unhappy she was when she first started nursery class and how happy she became once she started to make friends: 'I've got loads of friends …. I've got about a hundred friends …. I'm happy at school.' Her drawing 'My Georgina and her friends' (see Plate 9), however, also reflected her feelings toward her older sister Georgina, who she drew in a circle with two friends saying, 'She's got loads of friends and you can't fit them in … she's got hundreds of friends.' Lucy's drawing and narrative were directly related to her school experience, whilst Bethanie's drawing 'Me and my friends at the swimming pool' (as discussed earlier, see Plate 4) started as a discussion about learning to swim – 'I have swimming lessons and I can swim without my armbands …. I'm cleverer than you 'cos I don't need armbands' – but finally became a pool in her garden. After drawing eighteen friends she drew herself isolated at the front, saying:

> Look how many I've done, I'm going to do myself at the bottom cos I'm going to jump in the pool… They're just waiting to – just in the pool, weren't they?… This is at my house and some friends came and wanted to swim at my swimming pool, yea, I got my swimming pool out and I call my friends up to come and play with me.

All of these examples illustrate how inextricable are the visible and the audible to our complete understanding of the experiences being described. In the words of Froebel (1826), 'The word and drawing… belong together inseparably as light and shadow, night and day, soul and body do' (cited in Sutton 1967: 136).

Sources for imaginative stories

The previous section focused upon subject matter derived purely from first-hand experiences, but the narrative accompanying many drawings showed that their content was often supplemented by information gained from secondary sources. The three examples discussed in this section illustrate the way children assimilate knowledge, combining it in a seemingly effortless manner with their first-hand experience, so that both the finished drawing and the narrative extend beyond simple recall into the realms of imaginative story.

The predominance of rainbows in children's drawings reflected not only the 'magic' of their appearance in nature but also the frequency with which they are used in society as trademarks and symbols in advertising, and particularly in young children's television entertainment. Viewing one morning's children's television as part of our research, we found the rainbow symbol was repeated in four different programmes aimed at three to five year olds, including *Storymakers* and *Tweenies* (CBeebies, 22 August 2005), while on another occasion the theme of *Rolie Polie Olie* (Channel 5, 3 July 2005) was 'Always chasing rainbows'. Many children knew the song 'I can sing a rainbow' (lyrics by Currie) and sang the first verse while they drew, using it as a way of remembering and ordering the colours.

Amy's (age 4:11) initial utterances about her drawing 'Treasure on the top of the rainbow' (see Plate 10) focused on determining the correct order of colours, which were perhaps related to this song as she recited 'orange, purple yes … purple, purple and orange and blue … the other colours are? I know … black and brown … orange … white.' Amy's multicoloured rainbow was meticulous in both its concern for detail and factual accuracy, and the precision and care employed in drawing the shapes and filling them in. The first direct reference to her subject was made when adding blue circles on the top of the rainbow as sky, as she said:

> I'm doing a bright blue sky … grey sky … it's not really a grey sky … that means it's gonna rain …. Do you know when it's sunny and rainy what does it make … a rainbow … cos the rain gonna turn into a rainbow …. When I came back from my motor riding I saw some rainbows coming from my house.

Amy's recalled experience, however, turned into fantasy as she recounted a story about herself and her father finding treasure on top of the rainbow: 'I didn't see any treasure cos it was on top of it … my daddy pushed me all the way up to the top and he got the treasure, golden coins …. We shared them out, we got sweeties.' Amy's final reference to her drawing related to the meaning of the circles on the top of the rainbow. She said, 'This is my dad's head, my head, gold money dropping down …. I get all tomatoes, get all colouring on my hand .... I'm going to do these tomatoes, them as strawberries and I'm going to do some green stuff on top.'

Neil's (age 5:3) drawing 'They're my dogs – that's a dogs' home' started with a baseline and a small orange sun in the top left-hand corner as a 'seaside'. This was short lived, however, as his interest turned to animals, ultimately focusing on both his and his family's liking for dogs (see Plate 11). He talked continuously throughout his 55 minutes of concentrated activity, often repeating himself, but clearly signifying his intentions as he progressed.

> Actually I draw some big cow, I gonna do animal, I think I do a dog ... put it in a cage. I like dogs, I got one at me house, I got two at me Nan's and two down house .... I going to look after one when they go on holiday, the little 'softie' dog cos it's staying with us ... and the big dog, the 'barmie' one ... she has loads of fur on him, loads fur ... he got fur on his head and fur everywhere .... I gonna do a cage in it, but that's the hutch where they are puppies, we'll have to do the puppies first.

Neil finally drew twelve dogs, including 'a cute one what's in heaven', and a bath tub in blue for 'me and Mummy [to] wash them'. He contained them, first in a 'pink house' with a 'green chimney' which became a dogs' home – 'They're my dogs, that's a dogs' home' – and ultimately a playground which he coloured in red, pink, purple and grey patches, carefully ensuring that he left some white so as not to obliterate the dogs. 'I done a dogs' home, I just colouring the playground .... I'll leave a bit white.' A blue cross was added 'to tell people it's a dogs' home'.

The final example is by Lauren, whose detailed drawing of 'My family on holiday by the seaside' (as discussed earlier, see Plate 2) included an array of different sized and coloured birds. These added an element of fantasy, and she referred to them as 'mummy birds', 'baby birds' and 'nasty birds' as she wove a story around them.

> these three are twins, they're the nasty ones, that's why they're all twins .... They fight one another, they fight all the little baby birds, they fight all the little ones they fight all over .... I'm just going to draw a cat now, I'm going to draw a cat up there ... scratch, scratch those naughty ones, the cat goes and scratch the nasty birds.

All the examples described in this section might be said to represent timeless subject matter, as although some of the information came from television, earlier generations could have derived similar knowledge from books or from conversations with adults. The powerful combination of talk and drawing in these sessions highlighted another aspect of children's thinking – knowledge as the understanding and sharing of facts. Our research showed children acting as experts by disseminating information.

Heroes and subjects from the media

Today's society offers a wealth of visual stimulation through television, books and advertising, and the comparative affluence of the western world has led to young children owning televisions, videos, computers and computer games. In response to this relatively recent phenomenon the narratives we collected contained frequent references to fictional characters, and the accompanying drawings portrayed scenes of these heroes acting out storylines invented or remembered by the children. Some were so involved in this fantasy world that they sang, shouted, whooped and exploded as they rehearsed their hero's actions. Gardner hypothesised that it is through such drawings that 'the child makes his initial efforts to gain control of his feelings about these powerful themes' (1982: 134). Sharing knowledge about such media characters formed the focus for long and detailed discussions and provided a high level of interaction. Although the influence of the fast-moving cartoons and films, such as *Power Rangers* (Heroes for Kids Ltd), was noticeable, so also was the domination of Disney films such as *Snow White* (Disney Marketing). The transference of films and television programmes on to DVDs has led to a revival of interest in films such as *Peter Pan* and *Star Wars* which can be enjoyed as a family. The case studies that illustrate this section show how narrative and drawing influence each other, providing an informed and powerful social experience.

The film *Peter Pan*, as seen on television, was the subject matter for James's (age 5:4) exciting drawings of pirates. The content of his drawing, 'Pirates, pirate ships and buried treasure', (see Plate 12) was derived from his experience of a wide range of media sources and an informed knowledge and understanding based on long immersion in this aspect of the culture. His enthusiasm for the subject led not only to a sharing of ideas with his partner but to changes in the pitch, tone and volume of his voice as he identified with the characters. While it was impossible to physically act out the scenario portrayed in all its glory, his obvious involvement suggested that he was projecting his ideas on to paper.

> That's the captain pirate ... what about a skull and crossbone? ... how about an eye patch? ... do you know what, the captain, I've done an eye patch on him ... so no one can see it, it would look horrible ... a hole in your eye ... and the eye did fell out.

James's understanding of the pirate culture led him to make a 'treasure map' as a second drawing, which took the form of a path leading to a cross via 'the banana palm trees ... the desert and past the pyramids ... through the crocodile river [and] the tropical rain forest [to] "X" marks the spot' (see Plate 13).

The theme of pirates, romanticised for modern consumption in stories like *Peter Pan* (recreated as film) and children's television programmes such as *Captain Pugwash*, looks back to an unsavoury reality several centuries ago but portrays it through cartoon with light-hearted story lines. Of equal interest, however, and also based on film, was the notion of space travel. *Star Wars* and *Power Rangers* formed the subject matter for a number of drawings. The following example focuses on the release of *Star Wars III – Revenge of the Sith* (Lucas Films, 2005) which completed the *Star Wars* saga. James's (age 6:0) drawing '*Star Wars, The Revenge of the Sith*' (see Figure 5.2) illustrated the final battle in this film, his narrative revealing the extent of his knowledge about the main characters and their weaponry.

> I'm going to do the mask of Darth Vader .... It's Darth Vader and Obi-Wan .... It's a robot on the dark side ... with masks .... Look at that ... those are the things that the gun is shooting and its hitting his lightsabre ... but it hasn't killed him.

Finally James insisted on writing *Star Wars III* to complete the work. 'I'm ready to write, but I don't know how to spell *Star Wars* .... I've finished it, *Star Wars, the Revenge of the Sith*.'

In contrast, the final example relates to the more traditional fairy tale prince and princess characters. Although Caitlyn's (C) interest in *Sleeping Beauty* was aroused by watching the 1959 Disney film on DVD (Kronke Amazon.com), her drawing 'Me and you in the Princess Land' (as discussed earlier; see Plate 5) finally contained a 'magic' ice cream cornet in the sky, the sun, two black bags, a castle, one purple and six orange flowers and Sleeping Beauty flanked by herself on the left and her friend Jay (J) (age 5:3) on the right. Caitlyn first named the figure as 'Princess Rose in a silver cape' who later became Sleeping Beauty.

Figure 5.2 James (age 6:0), '*Star Wars, The Revenge of the Sith*'

A conversation between the two girls helped to determine the heroine's characteristics:

C   'What colour hair, what colour eyes does Sleeping Beauty have, Jay?'
J   'Blue.'
C   'No.'
J   'Brown.'
C   'Uum, I'll think of a nice bright colour – red ... red for a beautiful smile and a nose.'
J   'Princesses can have red eyes in stories, can't she, Mr Coates?'
C   'Sleeping Beauty sometimes has grey clothes you know Jay – black and grey clothes.'
J   'Sometimes they're pink or sometimes you have new clothes.'
C   'New clothes ... cos in the story I got to school one day ...'
J   'She had new clothes didn't she, can you remember? ... She had blue you remember, I can remember.'
C   'Yes! I was only kind of bring Sleeping Beauty book, and I'm gonna bring another .... Princess book here tomorrow .... Of course I've got lots of picture books.'

Caitlyn finally determined the nature of her Sleeping Beauty as 'Sleeping Beauty wears a dress what is grey ... this is Sleeping Beauty with her dress on, her grey dress on ... [it's] me and you in the Princess land ... that's you Jay with the fat body ...'

Our examination of both the drawings and the narratives that form the data for this category suggests that the children related to such media sources in two ways. The first was when the children focused on the fictional characters almost as though they cast themselves in these roles, so they were Darth Vader or a pirate fighting battles and finding treasure. In the second the children participated in the story alongside the fictional characters but retained their own identity.

Conclusions

Our investigation stressed the recording of narrative during the drawing process and highlighted how many children create a unity of the audible and the visible. While pictures often stood as images in their own right, the addition of narrative provided insights into the stories behind them and deepened our understanding of the way children think.

Our experience confirmed that children often talk aloud either to themselves or to their peers as they rehearse the drawing's story or content as it proceeds. Perhaps children have always talked at length and in some depth during the drawing process, but we have found little in the literature to confirm this. Jameson (1968), however, regarded the art of young children as an important attempt to communicate not only with themselves but also with teachers, parents and friends, their subjects relating to both first-hand experience of the world and the world of the imagination. He wrote, 'What he really wants is to talk to himself in pictures. He wants to go for a walk in the park, or go in a boat on the sea, or join the birds, or more likely the jet airliner and fly through the air' (1968: 62).

On the other hand, Spencer in 1854/1929 and Ruskin in 1857/1892 considered subject matter only in relation to the experiences children might have had of people, animals and nature, and objects; and Sully, in 1895, narrowed his discussion to drawings of the human figure and animals, regarding imaginative thinking as ascribing subjects to scribbles and symbolic representations, 'He [the child] means to draw a man or a horse and consequently the formless jumble of lines becomes to his fancy a man or a horse' (1895: 388).

In nineteenth-century England, picture books and pamphlets published specifically for children were numerous. They were mainly illustrated by line drawings, initially as woodcuts and later, as printing technology improved, as sophisticated wood and metal engravings. High-quality colour printing did not become available until the end of the century (Hunt 2009). At best, these drawings reflected the tradition of fine, naturalistic draughtsmanship prevalent at the time as children's book illustrators were inevitably influenced by the prevailing visual culture and their artistic training. Picture books are after all '… sophisticated members of the literary-artistic culture' (Hunt 2009: 10). The drawings, however, were hardly likely to influence the visual expression of young children and inform their subject matter.

The rise of modernism, which came to dominate western visual culture throughout the twentieth century, radically changed both the nature and role of drawing, as it freed artists from the constraints of the academic rules which required anatomical correctness and accurate representation. Paul Klee, the artist most directly informed by children's drawings, is for our purposes the most important in this respect. He best represents those who enabled subsequent generations of artists and illustrators to go beyond accurate representation in a single artistic medium, and make imaginative works which revelled in expressive distortion in a range of mediums. These include such as collage, photography and typography in conjunction with the traditional pencil, pen and ink, watercolour and gouache, their reproduction made possible by photolithographic printing techniques.

The rapid expansion of the media industries after the Second World War, coupled with this freedom to invent, have resulted in a global culture dominated by film and television, as well as illustrated children's books translated into many languages. The animated cartoon film is now a pervasive influence on children. Indeed a glance at any British *Radio Times* reveals a constant diet of mainly cartoon films from Children's CBeebies, CBBC and CITV between 6.00 a.m. and 7.00 p.m.

While many of our children still focused on first-hand experiences as sources for the subjects of their drawings and attendant stories, all of them enthusiastically and actively participated in most aspects of media culture. Some spoke volubly about their expertise, and some based their drawn images on what was to them a compelling landscape of experience. Without doubt, these secondary sources have extended the subjects and themes available for visual expression, and the popularity and range of children's illustrated literature has enhanced children's potential for devising imaginative and informed stories. Present-day communication systems ensure that such influences have the potential to affect the culture of a wide range of social and racial groups in both the developed and the developing world, and it may well be that global research into children's drawings will reveal similar media-based themes.

Our investigation into young children's drawing is ongoing, and continues to highlight the quality thinking which underpins children's visual and verbal expressions. The activities of self-directed drawing and reciprocal talk allow young children to create their own realities and share these imaginative worlds with anyone who has the time to observe and listen. Indeed, we are of the opinion that early years practitioners are missing a vital opportunity to learn about how children think through empathically sharing their worlds and thereby learning more about their ideas and feelings. Observing and listening to children is, after all, vital if we are to achieve one of the most important aims of early childhood education, that of enabling them to grow in confidence and discover their own voice.

References

Books and articles

Anning, A. (2002) 'Conversations around young children's drawings', *Journal of Art and Design Education*, **21**(3), pp. 197–206.

Arnheim, R. (1956) *Art and Visual Perception: A psychology of the creative Eye*, London: Faber & Faber.

Chipp, H. B. (1968) *Theories of Modern Art*, Los Angeles, Calif.: University of California Press.

Coates, E. and Coates, A. (2006) 'Young children talking and drawing', *International Journal of Early Years Education*, **14**(3), pp. 221–41.

Darrell, M. (1972) 'Arthur Rackham', pp. 7–12 in *Once Upon a Time: The fairytale world of Arthur Rackham*, London: Heinemann.

Flam, J. D. (1984) 'Matisse and the Fauves', pp. 211–39 in W. Rubin (ed.), *Primitivism in 20th Century Art: Affinity of the tribal and the modern, Vol. I*, New York: Museum of Modern Art.

Franciscono, M. (1998) 'Paul Klee and children's art', pp. 95–121 in J. Fineberg (ed.), *Discovering Child Art*, Princeton, N.J.: Princeton University Press.

Gaitskell, C. and Hurwitz, A. (1975) *Children and their Art*, 3rd edn., New York: Harcourt Brace Jovanovich.

Gardner, H. (1980) *Artful Scribbles*, New York: Basic Books.

Gardner, H. (1982) *Art, Mind and Brain*, New York: Basic Books.

Gentle, K. (1985) *Children and Art Teaching*, London: Croom Helm.

Gordon, D. E. (1984) 'German expressionism,' pp. 368–403 in W. Rubin (ed.), *Primitivism in 20th Century Art: Affinity of the tribal and the modern, Vol. II*, New York: Museum of Modern Art.

Grohman, W. (1960) *Paul Klee Drawings*, New York: Harry N. Abrams.

Guenther, P. (1989) 'An introduction to the Expressionist movement', in *The Robert Grove Rifkind Center for German Expressionist Studies, German Expressionist Prints and Drawings, Volume I: Essays*, Los Angeles County Museum of Art.

Haftmann, V. (1967) *The Mind and Work of Paul Klee*, New York: Frederick A. Praeger.

Hunt, P. (2009) 'The world in pictures' in D. McCorquordale, S. Hallam and L. Waite (eds), *Illustrated Children's Books*, London: Black Dog.

Jameson, K. (1968) *Pre-school and Infant Art*, London: Studio Vista.

Kellogg, R. (1959) *What Children Scribble and Why*, Palo Alto Calif.: N. P. Publications.

Kellogg, R. (1969) *Analyzing Children's Art*, Palo Alto Calif.: National Books

Kellogg, R. with O'Dell, S. (1967) *The Psychology of Children's Art*, USA: CRM.

Klee, P. (1965) *The Diaries of Paul Klee 1898–1918*, ed. F. Klee, London: Peter Owen.

Lankheit, K. (ed.) (1974) Documentary Edition of Kandinsky, W. and Marc, F. (eds) (1912) *The Blaue Reiter Almanac*, London: Thames and Hudson.

Löwenfeld, V. (1939) *The Nature of Creative Activity*, New York: Harcourt, Brace.

Löwenfeld, V. and Brittain, L. W. (1947/1964) *Creative and Mental Growth*, 4th edn, New York: Macmillan.

Lowenfeld, V. and Brittain, L. W. (1947/1987) *Creative and Mental Growth*, 8th edn, N.J.: Prentice Hall.

Lucie-Smith, E. (1990) *The Thames and Hudson Dictionary of Art Terms*, London: Thames & Hudson.

Luquet, G. H. (1927/2001) *Children's Drawings* (first pub. 1927 as *Le Dessin Enfantin*), trans. A. Costall, London/New York: Free Association Books.

Lynton, N. (1989) *The Story of Modern Art*, 2nd edn, Oxford: Phaidon Press.

Macdonald, S. (1970) *The History and Philosophy of Art Education*, London: University of London Press.

Malraux, A. (1974) 'Foreword', pp. 14–16 in D. Newton (ed.), (1980) *Masterpieces of Primitive Art*, London: Thames & Hudson.

Marsh, J. (1999) 'Teletubby tales: popular culture and media education', pp. 153–74, in J. Marsh and E. Hallet (eds), *Desirable Literacies*, London: Paul Chapman.

Marsh, J. (2005) 'Digikids: young children, popular culture and media', pp. 181–96 in N. Yelland (ed.), *Critical Issues in Early Childhood Education*, Maidenhead: Open University Press.

McMillan, M. (1919) *The Nursery School*, London and Toronto: Dent.

Newton, D. (1980) 'Primitive art – a perspective', pp. 27–47 in D. Newton (ed.), *Masterpieces of Primitive Art*, London: Thames &Hudson.

Partsch, S. (2003) *Klee*, Cologne: Taschen.

Preston, B. (ed.) (2010) *Radio Times*, London: British Broadcasting Corporation.

Rhodes, C. (1994) *Primitivism and Modern Art,* London: Thames & Hudson.

Ring, K. (2006) 'What mothers do: everyday routines and rituals and their impact upon young children's use of drawing for meaning making', *International Journal of Early Years Education,* **14**(1), pp. 63–84.

Rubin, W. (1984) 'Modernist primivitism – an introduction', pp. 1–84 in W. Rubin (ed.), *Primitivism in 20th Century Art, Vol. 1,* New York: Museum of Modern Art.

Ruskin, J. (1892) *The Elements of Drawing,* new edn, Orpington and London: George Allen.

Schmalenbach, W. (1986) *Paul Klee: The Düsseldorf Collection,* Munich: Prestel-Verlag.

Spencer, H. (1854/1929) *Education – Intellectual, Moral and Physical,* The Thinker's Library No. 2, London: Watts.

Spiller, J. (ed.) (1961) *Paul Klee: The thinking eye – the notebooks of Paul Klee,* New York: George Wittenborn.

Steveni, M. (1968) *Art and Education,* London: B. T. Batsford.

Stolnitz, J. (1960) *Aesthetics and Philosophy of Art Criticism: A critical introduction,* Boston, Mass.: Houghton Mifflin.

Sully, J. (1895) *Studies of Childhood,* London: Longman Green.

Sutton, G. (1967) *Artisan or Artist?* Oxford: Pergamon Press.

Thompson, C. (1999) 'Action, autobiography and aesthetic in young children's self-initiated drawings', *Journal of Art and Design Education,* **18**(2), pp. 155–81.

Varnedoe, K. (1984) 'Gauguin', pp. 178–209 in W. Rubin (ed.), *Primitivism in 20th Century Art: Affinity of the tribal and the modern, Vol. II,* New York: Museum of Modern Art.

Vaughan, W. (2005) 'Foreword: Palmer and the revival of art', in M. Butlin (ed.), *Samuel Palmer: The sketchbook of 1824,* London: Thames & Hudson/William Blake Trust.

Viola, W. (1944) *Child Art,* 2nd edn., Bickley: University of London Press.

Wilkinson, S. (1996) 'Is there a seven in your name? Writing in the early years', in D. Whitebread (ed.), *Teaching and Learning in the Early Years,* London: Routledge.

Wilson, F. M. (1921) 'A lecture by Professor Cizek' (pamphlet), London: Children's Art Exhibition Fund.

Other media

'Always chasing rainbows', *Rolie Polie Olie* (2005), Channel 5 television, 3 September.

Currie, J. 'I can sing a rainbow', lyrics available at: http://www.est-lounge.com/songs/song-i-can-sing-a-rainbow.shtml (accessed 17 April 2006).

Disney Princess. Website: http://disney.go.com/princess (accessed 12 November 2010).

Heroes for Kids Ltd. Website: www.heroesforkids.co.uk (accessed 12 November 2010).

Sleeping Beauty (1959) film dir. D. Kronke. Available at: http://disney.go.com/disneyvideos/animatedfilms/sleepingbeauty/ (accessed 12 November 2010).

Star Wars III, Revenge of the Sith (2005) wr. and dir. G. Lucas. DVD cover notes, Lucas Film Ltd, USA: 20th Century Fox.

Storymakers (2005) BBC, CBeebies television, 22 August.

Tweenies (2005) BBC, CBeebies television, 22 August.

Chapter 6

Painting dinosaurs: how a reception class context shapes children's opportunities for creative expression

Jenny Hallam, Helen Lee and P. Mani Das Gupta

The study of children's drawings is well established within developmental psychology and has been an area of interest since the nineteenth century (Coates and Coates 2006). Traditionally, this body of research uses experimental methods to identify and map out key developmental milestones in children's drawing development. Research in this area aims to give a comprehensive insight into drawing development by proposing a general stage theory (Luquet 1927, 2001) and addressing specific aspects of drawing such as the representation of the human figure (Cox 1993). The focus on drawing in most developmental research, however, provides a narrow presentation of artistic expression; children create artwork using diverse media such as paints, pastels, clay and collage. Furthermore, the use of primarily experimental methods means research into the wider social, cultural and educational contexts which shape the creation and interpretation of children's artwork (other than drawing) has been marginalised.

This chapter applies arguments drawn from critical psychology and social constructionism to provide an insight into how children and teachers in an English reception class[1] understand and co-construct art. The focus here is on how an art activity (painting dinosaurs) is introduced to a reception class by their teacher and how a piece of artwork, co-created by a child and the teacher during the class, is interpreted. The methodology employed enables an examination of painting within a familiar context, in which the activity makes sense to the child. Finally, studying children's artistic development in a naturalistic context moves beyond a traditional, individual-based approach by exploring the creation of art in a context which involves a whole class and their teacher. In summation, the chapter investigates the wider educational contexts which shape the development of expression in children's artwork.

Researching the development of expression in children's drawings

Teachers, researchers and educators agree that it is vital for children to receive a good art education (Hargreaves 1989). It is argued that creating art is a valuable experience which enables children to express and explore their ideas (Chapman 1978), develop observational skills (DfES 1978), build upon practical and perceptual skills (NCC 1990), gain confidence and promote feelings of self-worth (O' Connor 2000), and develop creativity and imagination (Arnheim 1989).

Experimental research focusing on the development of expression in children's drawings, however, presents different developmental patterns, which suggest a period of stagnation during the primary school years (five to eleven year olds). Ives (1984) and Jolley, Fenn and Jones (2004) identified a lull in development between the ages of seven to nine and six to nine consecutively. Davis (1997) suggested a slightly different pattern and proposed a U-shaped curve of development. Davis argued that children entering the education system are able to create expressive drawings on a par with those created by adult artists. However, during primary school, children's expressive drawing ability deteriorates and then only picks up again in children identifying themselves as artists during high school (eleven to seventeen year olds).

In line with the majority of research within developmental psychology, the dominant methodology used in drawing research involves asking individual children to complete set drawing tasks in a standardised, experimental context. The quality of the completed drawings is judged by adult raters, trained in a scoring system devised by each researcher, leading to variability in the scales used. For example, Ives's (1984) research required judges to measure the correctness of expression using a Likert scale, while Davis's (1997) research used Likert scales to measure the overall expression and composition. By contrast, raters in Jolley and colleagues' (2004) study used a Likert scale to measure the quality of expression and counted the number of appropriate expressive aspects of the drawing (such as a smiling sun in a happy picture) to measure quantity of expression. Even this brief summary illustrates that the different scales in each study measured different aspects of the drawings. Therefore, the overall evaluation of expression in children's drawings in each study is not truly comparable.

In addition to concerns about the use of rating scales, critical psychologists such as Potter (2000: 35) have challenged the use of an experimental method and an exclusive focus on what he terms the 'output' (drawings) of the 'cognitive system' (the child). Studying individual children in an experimental context results in a neglect of the broader social and educational contexts which work to shape children's artistic growth. Therefore, results from experimentally based research can only offer limited insight into *why* a dip occurs in the development of expression in children's drawings. For example, when reflecting on their research findings, Davis (1997) and Jolley and colleagues (2004) proposed that educational factors could be responsible for this slow period of development. However, this remains speculative because the educational factors put forward by Davis (1997) and Jolley and colleagues (2004) – such as teachers' lack of confidence in teaching art, primary school teachers' lack of art training and limited time spent on art lessons – were not addressed in their research.

Given the importance of artistic development, the reported lull in the development of expression in children's drawings and its possible link to the education system is a cause of concern. It suggests that children receive an inadequate art education which leaves them with a limited ability to visually express their ideas. The research presented in this chapter is based on two premises: first, that expressiveness is not limited to one form of artwork (drawing for example), and second, that children's expressive art may be influenced by the familiar classroom environment in which artistic activity often occurs. This study examines the reported lull in expressive development, broadening the research scope to include painting and examining the creation of art in the classroom. Central concerns are to investigate the educational contexts which shape children's artistic growth, and the educational practices which may contribute to this growth.

The importance of studying educational contexts

The study of educational contexts is informed by the work of Vygotsky, who emphasised the *inextricable* link between the child and the wider contexts which shape their development. Vygotsky (1981: 163) argued that development occurs on two planes: 'first it appears between people as an inter psychological category and then within the child as an intra psychological category'. Hence development is shaped by interactions in which socially constructed forms of knowledge are transferred to and internalised by children. For Vygotsky the zone of proximal development (ZPD) is key in this process. The ZPD is defined as the distance between the child's 'actual developmental level as determined by independent problem solving' and the 'potential development as determined through problem solving under adult guidance or in collaboration with more capable peers' (Vygotsky 1978: 86). Therefore, the ZPD provides the space where children's mental functioning develops through working with a more skilled partner utilising culturally defined psychological tools such as language.

Within the Vygotskian framework children's artistic development is inseparable from the wider contexts it takes place in. This is supported by research which demonstrates that the creation of artwork is socially negotiated (Coates and Coates 2006), influenced by historically specific artistic styles (Wilson and Ligtvoet 1992), and reflects cultural conventions (Elatta 1992). Children cannot be viewed as detached knowers whose biologically driven behaviour can be measured scientifically (Gergen 1994). Instead, general artistic development is socially embedded and enabled through specific cultural and historical conditions. This focus on the wider context makes the classroom a natural starting place for research which aims to investigate children's artistic growth. When children enter the school system they begin to learn what art is about and develop artistic skill through engaging with teacher-led art activities. Therefore, the classroom represents links between individual, society and culture, as it is a place where children work with teachers to learn the skills and art conventions valued by their culture. As such an examination of the co-creation of art in a classroom context addresses the different, interrelated, contextual layers which shape children's artistic growth – from the cultural values used to decide what is 'good' art to specific interactions between teachers and children.

Exploring the creation of art in the classroom

Education in English state-run primary schools is guided by curriculum documents associated with Foundation Stage (three to five years); Key Stage 1 (five to seven years) and Key Stage 2 (seven to eleven years). In the Foundation Stage children work with their teachers to meet the learning requirements outlined in the Early Years Foundation Stage (EYFS) documents. The EYFS documents were developed by a government agency – the Department for Children, Schools and Families – and aim to prepare children for Key Stage 1 by providing a sound basis in key areas of learning and development (personal social and emotional development, communication language and literacy, problem solving reasoning and numeracy, knowledge and understanding of the world, physical development and creative development). The creative development section in these documents encompasses responding to experiences, expressing and communicating ideas, exploring media and materials, creating music and dance, and developing imagination and imaginative play. Once children leave the Foundation stage they enter Key Stage 1, and from this point onwards their learning is shaped by the Art and Design curriculum which outlines attainment targets in exploring and developing ideas, investigating and making art craft and design, evaluating and developing work, and knowledge and understanding.

Hallam, Lee and Das Gupta (2007) argued that three teaching positions are presented in the National Curriculum for Art, those of expert, facilitator and philosopher. They argued that the curriculum gives equal weight to each of these positions, and implies that in order to be successful, teachers must develop an approach which enhances the skills children need to become artists (an expert teaching position), give children freedom to express themselves (a facilitator teaching position), and allow children to develop their aesthetic sensibilities and a knowledge of 'what' art is (a philosopher teaching position). These teaching positions are also presented in the EYFS documents used in the Foundation Stage.

Despite presenting each of these positions the English National Art curriculum does not give much practical advice on how to put these theoretical principles into practice. This is particularly problematic for the majority of primary school teachers who have no formal art training and are not confident in their own artistic skill. Indeed, when speaking about their experiences primary school teachers expressed dissatisfaction with the curriculum documents for art, and suggested that they adopted the position of *either* 'expert' or 'facilitator' when teaching art in the classroom (Hallam, Das Gupta and Lee 2008). Furthermore, it was suggested that a focus on skills in the curriculum encouraged teachers to adopt the position of 'expert' and marginalised the position of 'facilitator' which encourages the development of expression. This disruption between the positions of 'expert', 'facilitator' and 'philosopher' suggests that there is a gap between education policy and practice which could be detrimental to the development of expression in child art. It indicates that a focus on expression and an approach that promotes artistic freedom is being squeezed out of primary school classrooms.

The current study

Introducing a social constructionist framework

In order to explore the proposed gap between educational policy and practice this study brings a social constructionist approach to the study of children's artistic growth. Social constructionist theory builds upon Vygotsky's conceptualisation of the child as a social being, and places an emphasis on broader contextual concerns. Social constructionism also draws attention to the role language plays in constructing human experience and how this experience is mediated historically and culturally (Willig 2009). Thus social constructionists work to 'explicate the processes by which people come to describe, explain and otherwise account for the world (including themselves) in which they live' (Gergen 1985: 266). Rather than trying to uncover the laws that govern human behaviour, social constructionism advocates the study of the discursive practices that are used to construct the world and ourselves. Research conducted within this framework seeks to develop an understanding of how 'objects' are constructed in talk and other forms of text within a specific context.

In contrast to experimental research, a social constructionist framework does not centre on studying the individual child and how their experience of the world is internalised in the form of cognitive change. Instead, the way in which 'individual characteristics are developed, expressed and experienced through the child's participation in social relationships and activities' is the focus of study (Wetherell and Maybin 1996: 247). This emphasis on participatory activities shifts the researcher's gaze from accessing and measuring the internal cognitive state of the child to exploring social interactions and their role in shaping development. Hence, the traditional relationship between context and cognition is inverted. A popular strand of traditional experimentally based research focusing on the development of expression in children's drawings follows what Burman (1994: 114) terms an 'inside out' conception of development. Development is viewed as a largely biological driven process in which children reach milestones at specific ages. In contrast, a social constructionist framework subscribes to Burman's (1994: 114) characterisation of an 'outside in' process where socially negotiated goals are internalised by children. Thus interactions which occur in a given context are seen as constituting cognition and therefore social interaction – not cognitive output – is the focus of study.

Research methods

In line with a social constructionist framework, ethnographic methods were used to collect a range of qualitative data from art classes held in primary schools. Ethnography is a method aligned with interpretivism, and is characterised by researchers locating themselves in the everyday context they are studying (Hammersley 1990). When working in the field researchers use a number of methodological techniques – such as observation, reflexive field diaries, informal conversations and formal interviews – to explore and develop an understanding of people's active experience of the world (Burgess 1984). A major advantage of the ethnographic framework is that it enables immersion in the symbolic world of the classroom and first-hand access to social relations being played out by teachers and children in their own terms (Fielding 1993).

During the ethnographic phase of this research the first author worked as a classroom assistant in reception (ages four to five years), Year 1 (five to six years), Year 4 (eight to nine years) and Year 6 (ten to eleven years) art lessons held in two Staffordshire primary schools. These year groups were chosen on the basis that they represent each of the key stages outlined in the English primary curriculum.

The researcher assisted the teachers participating in the study on one art project which lasted for approximately six weeks. Working as a classroom assistant the researcher helped teachers set up the art materials for the weekly art lesson and worked with children during the class. Observations made during the lesson from the position of participant observer were written up as field notes at the end of the lesson. In addition, video and audio equipment were used to record the last art lesson of the project and photographs were taken of the children's artwork.

At the end of each art project teachers were asked to select six pieces of artwork – two that they considered to be above average, two average and two below average. These pieces of artwork were used to guide a discussion between the teacher and the researcher covering issues such as what they liked/disliked about the work and why the teacher had graded it the way they did. The children's comments about the artwork selected for discussion were then identified from the classroom recordings.

Throughout the ethnographic phase of the research it was observed that teachers in all key stages encouraged the children to create realistic artwork, and emphasised the importance of developing artistic skills. The following case study, which examines the co-creation of art in a reception class art lesson, exemplifies this 'expert' teaching approach. A multidimensional analysis which draws upon reflexive ethnography (Burgess 1984) and different forms of discourse analysis is used to analyse the range of qualitative data collected during a dinosaur project.

Case study: part one

The case study begins with an exploration of a 'carpet time' discussion during which a reception teacher introduced the task of painting dinosaurs to her class. Carpet time is a well established part of the reception children's daily routine in which the children gather around the teacher on the carpet to discuss a learning topic. Observations of 'carpet time' interaction are presented to explore the wider classroom context and then a synthesis approach to discourse analysis is utilised to examine how artwork is co-constructed within this context. This analytic approach incorporates what Edley and Wetherell (1997) term bottom-up and top-down approaches to discourse analysis.

A bottom-up analytic approach focuses on language and the way it is utilised to achieve certain functions such as encouraging a child to use a particular colour in their artwork. Consequently, analysts employing this approach work with naturally occurring talk to investigate and describe the underlying mechanisms of interactions and methods used to accomplish conversational goals (Atkinson and Heritage 1984). Close attention is paid to how linguistic devices such as metaphors are used to construct knowledge. In addition the ways in which turn taking, pauses and interruptions are utilised to manage the interaction are of interest. To enable this type of analysis the 'carpet time' interaction has been transcribed using the conventions of conversation analysis outlined by Wooffitt (2001) (see Appendix).

A top-down approach is informed by the work of Michel Foucault, and attends to how the wider socio-political contexts shape interaction. For Foucault (1969: 49), discourses are 'practices that systematically form the objects of which we speak'. In line with this argument a Foucauldian analysis centres on exploring the 'discursive economy' available in a particular society which shapes and limits peoples' experience and understanding of the world (Willig 2009: 112). Therefore the analytic scope is broadened beyond the immediate interaction. This enables an examination to be carried out of the official educational discourses presented in the curriculum and the ways in which they organise and regulate how teachers approach the teaching of art.

Introducing the art activity

In the following extract, taken from a reception class, the children (four and five years old) had been working on a dinosaur project. Following this theme the teacher started the art lesson by having a discussion with the children about dinosaurs and what they had learned during the project. After this discussion the teacher introduced the art activity, which involved painting pictures of dinosaurs.

When delivering her introduction the teacher created a physical hierarchy by gathering the class around her. The teacher's elevated position mirrors her position in the classroom as someone whom the children literally have to look up to for knowledge. Furthermore, the positioning of the children focuses their attention towards the teacher rather than each other, thereby placing her in a position of control. (See Plate 14 and the Appendix.)

Example I

1. **Teacher**: >What we are going to paint this afternoon?< We are going to
2. think about volcanoe:s an:::d the landscape a little bit and what the earth
3. would look like, what #up#family #down#groups as well. So you might want to have
4. some (1.90) #up#ferny tree::s and you might want to have a family group of
5. dinosaurs (1.20). Perhaps a herd of BI::G lo:ng necked plant eaters (0.76)
6. °keeping their babies safe°. (1.56) What else might we have seen? (0.58)
7. We talked about it very briefly before, (1.10) child one?
8. (0.78)
9. **Child 1**: er::m::: (0.77) the mill (0.96) the mill (1.56) the hundred million
10. trees.
11. (0.73)
12. **Teacher**: Yes >lots and lots of trees.< (0.7) Child 2 (1.56) what did Miss
13. Howard[2] talk to you about last week? (8.96) Child 3?
14. (1.23)
15. **Child 3**: Wh, when, when, when the dinosaurs come out and they are
16. not ready they die:::

17. (0.71)
18. **Teacher**: <u>Yes:::</u> .We did look at some fossils of baby dinosaurs. (0.5) What
19. did the dinosaurs do? (0.71) Did they have live babies like we do? (1.02)
20. Did they lay frog spawn in ponds? (1.08) What did they <u>do?</u> (1.47) Where
21. did the babies come from? (1.08) child 4
22. (1.61)
23. **Child 4**: °From the #up#egg...°
24. **Teacher**: <u>Yes::</u> ((evident excitement in voice)) eggs. You have got a nes:t
25. with <u>eggs</u> in and we found out that they put rotting vegetation over the top
26. to keep them warm and that <u>some</u> of them were (1.18) very, very good
27. mothers. Go on child 5 you are <u>desperate</u> to tell me something
28. (1.2)
29. **Child 5**: We saw a fossilised bone outside.
30. Teacher: Did you? (0.4). Here? That's wonderful. But they did have
31. fossilised eggs and some that had al::ready opened with baby dinosaurs in
32. (0.78) some (1.10) remember we saw the picture of that one holding a
33. fossilised baby dinosaur and it was only as big as a kitten and there would
34. be nests and maiasaura was a <u>very</u>, <u>very</u> good mother she stayed and
35. watched over her: babies and fed them on leaves and berries while they
36. were still in the nest. (0.9) °Don't pick you nose sweetie.° (0.96) So you
37. might want to do something like that but I want a <u>busy</u> <u>scene</u> with a
38. dinosaur family in (0.8) and you have got some little fine brushes to do
39. some nice detailed work, (0.84) <u>careful</u> work (1.73) and some nice:
40. #up#colours. (1.64) Nothing, nothing (0.86) 'cos we don't know what colour the
41. dinosaurs <u>were</u> (0.5) so we have got nothing like a <u>vibrant</u> blue or anything
42. 'cos I would imagine that dinosaurs were probably much the same sort of
43. colour that you get in animals these days although we have no idea 'cos
44. we <u>really</u> don't know.

In this extract the teacher's introduction sets clear boundaries for the class. This is demonstrated in lines 1 to 7 where the teacher introduces concepts that the children are expected to 'think' about in relation to how they will be translated into artwork. The relationship between thinking and creating outlined in this section splits the artistic process into two stages. The first stage centres on planning the composition and the second stage focuses on the production of artwork. In lines 1 to 3, the teacher's statement that 'we are going to think about volcanoes and what the Earth would look like' involves the whole class in the planning stage. The inclusive function of the word 'we' conceptualises the 'thinking' part of the task as a joint activity that will be negotiated through class discussion. This construes cognition and planning the composition of artwork as a shared activity (Middleton and Edwards 1990). In lines 3 to 4 as the production of artwork is discussed this focus shifts as 'we' becomes 'you'. The statement 'you might want to have ferny trees' construes the creation of artwork as an individual endeavour in which collectively generated ideas about 'family groups' (lines 3 to 4) are transferred to the page in the form of 'a family group of dinosaurs' (lines 4 to 5). This section of talk challenges the individualist conceptualisation of 'the child' evidenced in experimental research which sets about studying the internal workings of children in a highly controlled context. Rather than being internally located, thinking and planning are joint activities achieved through social interaction.

Once the teacher establishes the task focus in this opening section of talk – thereby embedding her ideas in what is presented as a joint collaboration – she uses directive questions to give different members of the class the opportunity to share their ideas. This places the teacher firmly in a traditional teaching role. As the 'expert' she requires pupils to follow her instructions and produce the kind of artwork she expects. Indeed, when leading the discussion the teacher utilises the method of elicitation to maintain control of the collective account generated by the class (Edwards and Mercer 1987). The teacher's use of questions such as 'What did Miss Howard talk to you about last week?' (line 9) acts as a series of prompts which shape the focus of the discussion. This creates a teacher-generated list of concepts that can later be incorporated into children's artwork. Therefore, the teacher plays a key role in planning the artwork the children will produce. So in this context, artwork produced during art lessons is less of a reflection of the children's 'inner world' and more of a representation of their understandings of specific task boundaries.

Significantly, prompt questions (such as those presented in lines 6 and 7) are followed by a pause but no response from the children. During the pauses it was observed that children who wished to make a contribution silently raised their hand to gain the teacher's attention rather than directly vocalising a response – this is evidenced in Plate 14, where a child on the left-hand side has their hand raised in the air. The teacher's position of power and privilege is reinforced as she organises turn-taking by choosing who will make a contribution. Upon hearing the children's responses the teacher acknowledges each contribution by incorporating it into her next statement to the class. This performs an important pedagogical function as it evaluates the response and gives the class insight into the 'value' of what has been said (Edwards and Westgate 1994). For example the child's suggestion of 'the hundred million trees' in lines 9 to 10 is barely acknowledged by the teacher's response of 'yes lots and lots of trees' (line 12). Furthermore, the speed of her talk quickly moves the discussion on to someone else who can offer an alternative. In contrast, the suggestion that dinosaurs came 'from the egg' in line 23 fits in with the teacher's agenda of encouraging the class to paint a family group of dinosaurs. This contribution is met with enthusiasm (line 24) and is heavily elaborated on. The teacher talks about dinosaur 'nests' (line 24) and how these would look covered in 'rotting vegetation' (line 25), thereby presenting a composition she would like to see. The depiction of a family scene is linked clearly to the teacher's expectations for the task, as in lines 37 and 38 the teacher asserts 'I want a busy scene with a dinosaur family in.' By presenting her expectations to the class from the first person the teacher suggests that in order for the children's artwork to be successful they must follow her guidelines. The relative positioning of teacher and child works to construe art as an activity where children endeavour to meet the teacher's criteria for what makes good artwork. Therefore, the teacher's use of questions and organising turn-taking serves to elicit information from the children which creates a collective account of dinosaurs that suits her agenda (Middleton and Edwards 1990).

The introduction concludes with the teacher outlining her expectations of good art and good artistic behaviour. From line 38 onwards, when outlining what constitutes successful art the teacher does not enter into a discussion with the class. This indicates that the understanding of what makes good artwork cannot be negotiated. Instead, there are socially agreed rules used by the teacher to decide the merits of artistic expressions. The focus on 'nice detailed work, careful work' in line 39 clearly conveys to the class that realistic work which captures lots of fine detail will be judged as successful. This focus on detail meets the curriculum requirement for teachers to 'teach skills and techniques associated with the things children are doing' (DCSF 2008: 111). Consequently, the presentation of art which is actively negotiated in the classroom is guided by educational goals presented in the curriculum.

In line 41 the theme of realism is extended to the colours used to paint dinosaurs. The teacher advises her class that their palette will not contain 'vibrant blue' because she 'imagines that dinosaurs were much the same colour that you get in animals these days'. The restricted palette alongside the provision of 'fine brushes' which enables the production of 'detailed work' highlights how the tools provided also shape the artwork produced during the lesson. This focus on skills and realism limits children's opportunity to work in an expressive way. The absence of an expressive understanding of art throughout this interaction closes down this conceptualisation of art. Following this, children will strive to produce realistic and not expressive pieces of artwork.

In summation the teacher's role in shaping the artwork created in their lesson occurs on two levels. During the planning stage the teacher guides the class discussion to ensure that her pupils reach a joint understanding of what is expected in the task through collective discussion. Once the children start to produce their artwork the teacher's influence is still evident as they manipulate the classroom environment in terms of the resources made available to children. This encourages the class to produce the kind of work the teacher expects to see.

Case study: part two

The next section examines the ways in which a piece of artwork created during the lesson above was interpreted by the child who created it and the teacher who took the class. The multiple interpretations of the artwork are analysed using thematic decomposition; that is, a close reading which first organises the text into different themes which are then analysed using a social constructionist framework (Marshall, Stenner and Lee 1999; Stenner 1993). Therefore, the following analysis centres on an exploration of coherent themes or stories that run throughout the teacher and child's interpretation of artwork. This focus on studying the ways in which artwork is interpreted signifies an important departure away from traditional experimental methods which aim to objectively quantify the expressive devices present in children's artwork. As such it enables what Wilson (1997) terms a postmodern research approach which recognises that children's art is a 'socially constructed concept' which 'reflects cultural norms' (Wilson 1997: 155).

The benefits of adopting a postmodern approach are twofold. First, it enables an examination of the social and cultural values that shape the interpretation of children's artwork. In line with Vygotskian theory an exploration of the wider cultural contexts is essential as it gives insight into the values that shape children's understandings of art and their artistic development. Second, a focus on exploring interpretation rather than seeking to study art in a uniform and objective manner opens up the possibility for multiple perspectives to be examined. Within experimentally based research children were not allowed to voice their own understanding of their drawings. Instead, drawings completed by children of various ages are scored by adult raters to identify developmental patterns. Therefore, the child's voice and their understandings of their artwork are lost and development is conceptualised in adult terms. A postmodern approach to the study of children's artwork gives the child a voice and opens up the possibility of exploring possible gaps between what children represent and adult interpretation. This exploration of differing interests and experience is important because it puts the child's perspective back into the study of children's artwork, and stimulates debate surrounding the status of child art and the way it is interpreted (Wilson 2000).

Interpreting dinosaur artwork

The following analysis centres on the artwork 'A reception child's painting of a flying dinosaur' (see Plate 15) which was categorised as 'below average' by the teacher.

Extract 2: The child's perspective

1. **Child**: Look at mine.
2. **J.H**:[3] Lovely. What dinosaur have you decided to do?
3. **Child**: It's a flying one moving.
4. **J.H**: Is it a flying one? Wow I don't think I have seen a flying one
5. today on this table yet.
6. **Child**: A flying dinosaur.
7. **J.H**: Yes a lovely pterodactyl.

Extract 3: The teacher's perspective

1. **Teacher**: I would. I expected something more from these two erm.
2. This child particularly he's another one who it depends on what
3. mood he's in. If he is in a good mood you will get something fairly,
4. fairly careful but I think this was just let's do something and then go
5. away which is fair enough because I suppose you are not always in
6. the mood to paint are you?
7. **J.H**: No. I have noticed this …. So I think with this one. I didn't think
8. it was representational but then when he told me about it he said it
9. was a flying dinosaur.
10. **Teacher**: Ahhh.
11. **J.H**: He meant it to be a pterodactyl.
12. **Teacher**: Right.
13. **J.H**: So then it made more sense to me because I thought it looked
14. almost like a sort of human figure.
15. **Teacher**: Well I thought it looked like a *Monsters Inc.* type
16. character.
17. **J.H**: Yes and I was a little confused but he just said to me that it
18. was a pterodactyl so I thought, then I understood what he was
19. doing.
20. **Teacher**: A pterodactyl yes but I still think he could have made a
21. better job of it because we had drawn and talked about and gone
22. on about dinosaurs so much and he is quite capable of producing
23. something that you can recognise.

In Extract 2 an expressive theme dominates as the child conceptualises the depicted dinosaur as a 'flying one moving' (line 3). Exclusive focus on expressive elements of the work rather than representational detail is noteworthy. The artwork is construed as an expression of movement specific to a pterodactyl rather than something that aims to 'realistically' recreate what this dinosaur might look like. It is important to note that this child has not adhered to the strict requirements outlined in the teacher's introduction to create a piece of artwork which depicts a dinosaur family. In order to create a piece of expressive artwork this child has moved beyond the task boundaries and adopted a position of resistance.

In Extract 3, educational and developmental themes shape the teacher's evaluation of the artwork and position the teacher as an educational expert. Indeed, the quality of the artwork is conceptualised first in terms of the teacher's expectations of the child and the extent to which they met task requirements. In line 3 the child is positioned as capable – someone who has the ability to create something 'fairly careful'. This is contrasted with the teacher's conception of the dinosaur artwork as something the child quickly dashed off so they could 'go away' and pursue another activity (lines 4 and 5). Hence the artwork is judged in terms of the disparity between the child's capabilities and what was actually created. The proposed lack of time, effort and skill are used to construe the work as substandard.

In line 15 a second value judgement is introduced as the teacher discusses the extent to which the child met task requirements. Significantly the image is construed as a '*Monsters Inc.* type character' and not a dinosaur. Thus, the child is positioned as someone who has failed to meet the teacher's expectations of painting a dinosaur. The theme of creating artwork which 'realistically' represents dinosaurs continues in line 20 where the teacher concedes that the image is of a 'pterodactyl'. Art lessons are conceptualised as a space which offer children ample time and opportunity to both 'draw' and 'talk about' dinosaurs (line 21). However the teacher's suggestion that the child could have 'made a better job' (lines 20 and 21) implies that the opportunity to develop both drawing skill and ideas is not reflected in their final piece of artwork. The child is construed as a 'capable' student who has failed to meet their full potential of creating 'something that you can recognise' (line 23). Significantly educational expectations focus on the child's ability to create representational artwork. In line with this educational theme, expressive elements of the piece are not discussed. Instead realistic artwork that meets the task requirements is valued and evaluated as good.

The evaluation of this artwork from different perspectives identified a point of tension. The child conceptualised their artwork as an expressive piece, and focused on the message it communicated. In contrast, the teacher's interpretation of the piece was dominated by an educational theme centring on the extent to which the artwork met teacher expectation in terms of meeting task requirements, demonstrating artistic skill, creating representational artwork, and putting time and effort into the artwork. Significantly, in line with this theme, the child's work was not conceptualised as art. Instead, it was viewed and valued as a representation of the child's capabilities. This indicates that, within this educational community, the creation of art is conceptualised as an activity during which children should meet a number of learning requirements outlined in curriculum documents. Meeting learning objectives, developing skills and creating artwork congruent with the child's stage of development are the key to successfully meeting educational goals.

Drawing conclusions

This case study has raised a number of issues for researchers studying children's artwork, centring on the importance of exploring the creation of art in an educational context. Furthermore, it has identified educational issues such as the teacher's active involvement in planning the children's artwork and a focus on creating realistic art which could be detrimental for the development of expression in child art. These issues will now be discussed in turn.

The social construction of artwork

An examination of the creation and interpretation of child art in a classroom context highlighted the importance of studying development in naturalistic contexts. Analysis of a carpet time interaction demonstrated how in this classroom context the teacher actively worked with the children to develop ideas which would later be transferred into the children's artwork. Therefore within this classroom 'understanding is not automatically driven by the forces of nature, but is the result of an active, co-operative enterprise of persons in relationship' (Gergen 1985: 267). This suggests that the act of planning what to paint is not an individual endeavour, but instead it is a dynamic process mediated through joint interactions between teachers and children. This case study highlighted the importance of examining the contexts in which early artwork is produced, and analysing the co-creation of art. Studies of this nature provide more evidence for Edwards and Mercer's (1987) claim that cognition is a social process during which the teacher shapes the planning of artwork. As such, rather than simply providing an educational backdrop for individual development, schooling is taken as a site for formal apprenticeship where children take on the skills and values of their culture through instruction from teachers (Rogoff 1990).

The inextricable link between the wider social, educational and cultural contexts and children's understanding of art evidenced in this case study supports a Vygotskian concept of development. This directly challenges the dominance of an experimental methodology which seeks to create an environment where the child is abstracted from the wider social realm. Neglect of the broader contextual constraints that shape children's artwork within an experimental framework prevents researchers from addressing the complexity of development in the real world. As such this research approach fails to acknowledge that far from being a direct expression of a child's inner world, artwork is instead a cultural artefact created in line with art conventions popularised and taught during a specific time and culture.

The ethnographic methods used in this case study also demonstrated that the wider context plays an integral role in shaping the interpretation of children's artwork. The differing interpretations of the dinosaur artwork put forward by the teacher and the child demonstrated how values specific to different interpretive communities shape the ways in which art is conceptualised. This challenges the assumption that viewing artwork is an objective, straightforward process held within experimental research investigating children's drawing development. In this case study children's artwork was presented as what Newcombe and Hirsch (1984: 62) term a 'cultural medium' – something that presents a 'multiplicity of meanings'. This offers further support for Wilson's (1997) argument that child art is a socially constructed concept which reflects wider cultural norms and values. Furthermore, it highlights a limitation of the current dominance of rating scales within developmental research. The use of such scales in research conducted by Davis (1997), Ives (1984) and Jolley and colleagues (2004) prevented the raters from interpreting artwork by restricting them to quantifying certain aspects of the piece by ticking boxes that best represented their judgement. This severely limits the study of children's artwork by reducing a piece that communicates ideas and concepts to an item that is simply scored.

Subsequently, any deeper meaning the artwork may hold is lost, as rating systems cannot explore the relationship between viewer and artwork. Hence, developmental research would benefit from including an exploration of context and interpretation to approaches that simply apply a scoring system to artwork. A move towards a postmodern framework would enable developmental researchers to embrace diversity and explore the values drawn upon to evaluate children's artwork. Moreover this approach would enable raters to read the 'text' of the artwork and respond in a way that they see fit, rather than focusing on elements of the artwork that researchers consider to be salient.

Educational concerns

Shifting the research focus from an experimental context into the classroom enabled an investigation into educational practices which could be detrimental to the development of expression in children's artwork. Throughout this case study the ways in which the teacher presented the art activity and interpreted the dinosaur painting limited children's opportunity to create expressive art in various ways. To begin with, when introducing the art activity to the class this teacher worked from the position of 'expert' and used the method of elicitation to maintain control of the interaction. During the introduction, dominance of a skills-based art discourse, combined with the teacher's position of expert, offered the children little scope to negotiate a more expressive, personally meaningful conceptualisation of art. This may have restricted children's ability to express themselves freely, as the children of the class were left in no doubt that they were required to create artwork that met the teacher's strict criteria of painting a realistic, family group of dinosaurs. A focus on realism and skills was also evident in the teacher's evaluation of a piece of artwork created during the lesson. This focus led to a piece of spontaneous, expressive artwork being positioned as undesirable by the teacher because it did not meet the task requirements. Consequently, the children in this class were taught that successful artwork recreates reality, and expressive art was marginalised.

Exclusive use of the 'expert' teaching position and a focus on skills, as evidenced in this case study, has important implications for educational policy and practice. First, it offers support for the proposed gap between the curriculum requirement for teachers to develop an approach that balances the positions of 'expert', 'facilitator' and 'philosopher', and teaching practice (Hallam et al. 2008). The absence of 'facilitator' and 'philosopher' teaching positions observed in this case study limited children's opportunity to engage in free expression and enter into discussion about what makes good art. However, it is important to note that the teacher's focus on skills and therefore the position of expert was closely linked to learning objectives outlined in the EYFS curriculum documents. Meeting the objectives for art outlined in these documents is a specific concern for teachers. Therefore, when working in the classroom, teaching practice is shaped and constrained by the learning requirements stipulated in the curriculum. This suggests that despite acknowledging the importance of a balanced teaching approach, curriculum-based art projects largely focus on skill development (Jolley 2010).

Given the extensive use of a skill-based art discourse and the exclusive use of an 'expert' teaching approach evidenced in this case study, it is unsurprising that research has tended to find that expression in art does not flourish during the primary school years. However, action can be taken to support a more balanced approach to art that would encourage rather than inhibit expression in artwork.

Ways forward

This study suggests that, in order to improve art education, changes need to be implemented to give teachers the support they need to adopt a balanced teaching approach in the classroom.

Such change could begin during teacher training. Gibson (2003) argues that after completing teacher training – which incorporates two units dedicated to the visual arts – Australian student teachers felt confident in their ability to teach art. This contrasts sharply with research conducted by Clement (1994), which reported that the majority of English primary school teachers felt their teacher training did not adequately prepare them to teach art effectively. Therefore, the first step in supporting art in schools is to address teacher training to ensure that upon completing their postgraduate certificate in education – a year-long course for university graduates who want to train as teachers – trainee teachers are equipped with the skills required to teach art confidently.

Furthermore, the importance of expression and creativity in art, and practical advice on how to develop a teaching approach that incorporates the positions of 'expert', 'facilitator' and 'philosopher' would be beneficial. This focus could also inform continuing professional development for primary school teachers. In response to requests made by the teachers who took part in this research for further in-house training, art workshops were held at both of the schools involved. During these workshops teachers collaborated with a professional artist to develop their skills and reflect on their approach to teaching art. Positive feedback collected during the workshops indicated that teachers had been introduced to new ways of understanding art, gained insight into the issues children face when participating in art lessons, and learned of the benefits that art has to offer.

Policy change could also continue to support the development of expression in children's artwork. Stronger links are needed between the teaching positions presented in the EYFS documents and curriculum-based art projects. Curriculum documents could be developed to offer clear and practical advice on how to adopt a balanced teaching position rather than simply outlining the requirement to incorporate the positions of 'expert', 'facilitator' and 'philosopher' into teaching practice. Furthermore, the current bias towards skill development could be countered with the introduction of art projects that centre on expression. In addition to this all curriculum-based art projects would include practical support on how to develop skills, promote expression and develop an understanding of aesthetics. This move would help to counter the current bias towards skill development. Changes in the curriculum and the continued delivery of art workshops would give the practical support and help some teachers need to present a balanced view of art in the classroom that creates a space for expression.

Appendix: Jefferson style transcription conventions

(0.5)	Numbers in brackets refer to pauses in tenths of seconds
:	Indicate and extension of the preceding vowel sound. The

	more colons there are, the greater the extent of the stretching.
(( ))	A description enclosed in a double bracket indicates a nonverbal activity.
	<u>Red</u> underlining (reproduced here in black) indicates stress or emphasis on the speech.
=	Indicates continuous talk between speakers.
#up##down#	Indicates marked rising or falling in speech intonation.
o	Degree signs enclose talk that is lower in volume than surrounding talk.
><	Greater than and less than signs enclose speech which is noticeably faster than the surrounding talk.
BIG	With the exception of proper nouns, capital letters indicate speech that is noticeably louder than that surrounding it.
[	Indicates overlapping talk.

Notes

1 In England reception classes include four and five year olds, and are the first step into formal schooling.
2 To protect participant identity this is a pseudonym.
3 The researcher, Jenny Hallam.

References

Arnheim, R. (1989) *Thoughts on Art Education,* Los Angeles, Calif.: Getty Center for Education in the Arts.

Atkinson, J. and Heritage, J. (eds) (1984) *Structures of Social Action. Studies in conversation analysis,* Cambridge: Cambridge University Press.

Burgess, R. (1984) *In the Field: An introduction to field research,* London: Routledge.

Burman, E. (1994) *Deconstructing Developmental Psychology,* London: Routledge.

Chapman, L. (1978) *Approaches to Art in Education,* New York: Harcourt Brace Jovanovich.

Clement, R. (1994) 'The classroom reality of drawing', in D. Thistlewood (ed.), *Drawing and Development,* Harlow, Essex: Longman/NSEAD.

Coates, E. and Coates, A. (2006) 'Young children talking and drawing', *International Journal of Early Years Education,* **14**(3), pp. 221–41.

Cox, M. (1993) *Children's Drawings of the Human Figure,* Hove: Lawrence Erlbaum Associates.

Davis, J. (1997) 'Drawings demise: U shaped development in graphic symbolization', *Studies in Art Education,* **38**, pp. 132–57.

Department for Children, Schools and Families (DCSF) (2008) *Early Years Practice Guidance,* London: DCSF.

Department of Education and Science (DfES) (1978) *Art in Junior Education,* London: HMSO; reproduced in A. Rowlands and M. Cox (2001) 'Steiner education and young artists: a comparison of drawing ability in Steiner, Montessori and traditional schools', *Paideo*, 24 December.

Edley, N. and Wetherell, M. (1997) 'Jockeying for position: the construction of masculine identities', *Discourse and Society*, **8**(2), pp. 203–17.

Edwards, D. and Mercer, N. (1987) *Common Knowledge: The development of understanding in the classroom*, London: Routledge.

Edwards, D. and Westgate, D. (1994) *Investigating Classroom Talk*, 2nd edn, London: Falmer.

Elatta, T. (1992) 'Sudanese graphic imagery: a survey for art education', cited in D. Thistlewood (ed.), *Drawing Research and Development*, Harlow, Essex: Longman/ NSEAD.

Fielding, N. (1993) 'Ethnography', in N. Gilbert (ed.), *Researching Social Life*, London: Sage.

Foucault, M. (1969) *The Archaeology of Knowledge*, London: Tavistock.

Gergen, K. (1985) 'The social constructionist movement in modern psychology', *American Psychologist*, **40**, pp. 266–75.

Gergen, K. (1994) *Realities and relationships: soundings in social constructionsm*, Cambridge, Mass.: Harvard University Press.

Gibson, R. (2003) 'Learning to be an art educator: student teachers' attitudes to art and art education', *International Journal of Art and Design Education*, **22**(1), pp. 111–20.

Hallam, J., Das Gupta, M. and Lee, H. (2008) 'An exploration of primary school teachers' understanding of art and the place of art in the primary school curriculum', *Curriculum Journal*, **19**(4).

Hallam, J., Lee, H. and Das Gupta, M. (2007) 'An analysis of the presentation of art in the British primary school curriculum and its implications for teaching', *International Journal of Art and Design Education*, **26**(2), pp. 206–14.

Hammersley, M. (1990) *Reading Ethnographic Research: A critical guide*, New York: Longman.

Hargreaves, D. (1989) *Children and the Arts*, Oxford: Oxford University Press.

Ives, S. (1984) 'The development of expressivity in drawing', *British Journal of Educational Psychology*, **54**, pp. 152–9.

Jolley, R. P. (2010) *Children and Pictures: Drawing and understanding*, Chichester: Wiley-Blackwell.

Jolley, R. P., Fenn, K. and Jones, L. (2004) 'The development of children's expressive drawing', *British Journal of Developmental Psychology*, **22**, pp. 545–67.

Luquet, G. (1927) *Le Dessin Enfantin*, Paris: Alcan.

Luquet, G. (2001) *Children's Drawings (Le Dessin Enfantin)*, trans. A. Costall, London: Free Association Books.

Marshall, H., Stenner, P. and Lee, H. (1999) 'Young people's accounts of personal relationships in a multi-cultural East London environment: questions of community, diversity and inequality', *Journal of Community and Applied Psychology*, **9**, pp. 155–71.

Middleton, D. and Edwards, D. (1990) *Collective Remembering*, London: Sage.

National Curriculum Council (NCC) (1990) 'The arts 5–16: practice and innovation: Harlow and Boyd', reproduced in A. Rowlands and M. Cox (2001) 'Steiner education and young artists: a comparison of drawing ability in Steiner, Montessori and traditional schools', *Paideo*, 24 December,.

Newcombe, H. and Hirsch, P. (1984) 'Television as a cultural forum: implications for research', pp. 58–73 in W. Rowland and B. Watkins (eds), *Interpreting Television: Current perspectives,* Beverly Hills, Calif.: Sage.

O'Connor, M. (2000) 'The creative tension which stifles children', *Independent* supplement, 18 May 2000, reproduced as pp. 8–9 in A. Rowlands and M. Cox, (2001) 'Steiner education and young artists: a comparison of drawing ability in Steiner, Montessori and traditional schools', *Paideo,* 24 December.

Potter, J. (2000) 'Post-cognitive psychology', *Theory and Psychology,* **10**(1), pp. 31–7.

Rogoff, B. (1990) *Apprenticeship in Thinking: Cognitive development in a social context,* New York: Oxford University Press.

Stenner, P. (1993) 'Discoursing jealously', in E. Burman and I. Parker (eds), *Discourse Analytic Research Repertoires and Readings of Text,* London: Routledge.

Vygotsky, L. (1978) *Mind and Society: The development of higher psychological processes,* Cambridge, Mass: Harvard University Press.

Vygotsky, L. (1981) 'The development of higher forms of attention in children', in J. Wetsch (ed.), *The Concept of Activity in Soviet Psychology,* Armonk, N.Y.: Sharpe.

Wetherell, M. and Maybin, J. (1996) 'The distributed self: a social constructionist perspective', in R. Stevens (ed.), *Understanding the Self,* London: Sage.

Willig, C. (2009) *Introducing Qualitative Research in Psychology: Adventures in theory and method,* 2nd edn, Maidenhead: Open University Press.

Wilson, B. (1997) 'Types of child art and alternative development accounts: interpreting the interpreters', *Human Development,* **40**, pp. 155–68.

Wilson, B. (2000) 'The Vilnius Conference and the future of child art: a philosophical agenda', in L. Lindström (ed.), *The Cultural Context: Comparative studies of art education and children's drawings,* Stockholm: Stockholm Institute of Educational Press.

Wilson, B. and Ligtvoet, J. (1992) 'Across time and cultures: stylistic changes in the drawings of Dutch children', in D. Thistlewood (ed.), *Drawing Research and Development,* Essex: Longman.

Wooffitt, R. (2001) 'A socially organised basis for displays of cognition: procedural orientation to evidential turns in psychic-sitter interaction', *British Journal of Social Psychology,* **40**, pp. 545–63.

Chapter 7

Diversifying discourse: the influence of visual culture on children's perception and creation of art

Marie Fulková and Teresa M. Tipton

Introduction

> Education is not conceived of independently of those educated. At the very most, one may speak of a pedagogy of sharing, which is cooperative in nature.
>
> (Tochon 2001: 10)

Under the influence of diverse genres of visual digital culture, young children experience the world as a media-rich web of interconnected, living relationships that flow between many different kinds of worlds, events, and spaces. Fields of experience move within and through actual, fictive and virtual spaces that are animated, digitized, televised, computerized, and conceptualized in and through their daily 'lived' experiences. While the interaction of artistic and socio-cultural practices as research is a fairly recent area of examination, young children can be observed to have already integrated their experiential realms and developed their own notational codes through symbolic and imaginative languages. Yet, in spite of the non-linear milieu of their daily experience, the curriculum for young children in art and cultural education unfolds hierarchically according to identified grade-level outcomes aligned to teach the elements and principles of art and assessed to developmentally appropriate standards.

In this chapter, we examine how the experiences and influence of visual culture in the contemporary context demand a reframing of the interpretation of children's art beyond the developmental perspectives of analyses of mark-making. Visual culture in this sense includes all forms of visuality and their contexts of origination (Hernández 2000), and includes schoolbooks, storybooks, television, digital media, interactive gaming, films, clubs, toys, the Internet, and advertising aimed at young children. Coding and expectations conditioned by popular culture also include social practices such as shopping, friendships, sports, music, social networking, virtual reality games, and 'fandom' with movie stars, which are predominant in the frames of reference of western school-age children (Fulková and Tipton 2008).

We argue that influences from popular and visual culture, especially those drawn from television, advertising, the Internet, and media, cannot be separated from other forms of culture (Fulková and Tipton 2008; Tipton 2008a). Thus, all kinds of visual experience become constitutive elements in mental schema as images (Gombrich 1960). Contextually then, we frame our research by asking how these elements of visual culture impact on the development and perception of young children and their art if these are primary influences in their lives.

We approach this query from two levels. The first is to re-examine and redefine a primary interpretive approach used in studying images produced by children so as to establish another context for analysis through discourses. Interpreting children's signs in art as discourses shifts the meaning of representation from 'reality' to one of communication (Fulková and Tipton 2008). By broadening the view of young children's visual representation, our work will also be relevant pedagogically for the design, instruction, and assessment of the art and cultural education activities offered to children.

Second, drawing on the first level above, we critically frame an instructional query concerned with identifying the suggested implications for practice and teacher training of our approach to interpreting children's signs. Here, we use a narrative approach to examine a cross-cultural case study as the context to ground a semiotic visual analysis within the methodology of participatory qualitative research.

Across various cultural backgrounds and experiences, young children are increasingly leaving primary care environments to attend pre-school programs, and their educational development is beginning before they enter public school. Internationally, a range of strategies and approaches guide the delivery of early childhood programs, yet the underlying educational structure tends to be teacher-led and offers directed activities. In western cultures, art activities in early years programs typically introduce and encourage young children to explore and use a variety of materials and visual arts methods. There is an emphasis on developing perceptual and creative abilities and increasing production skills. In addition, these activities are framed by 'culturally transmitted knowledge' such as recognizing the works of famous artists and engaging in the crafts of national traditions. As these programs also tend to be product-oriented, arts and crafts activities often include the creation of holiday-inspired crafts and gifts, completing pre-designed worksheets and coloring sheets, and creative projects for topic-based work. When visual culture appears in early years art and cultural education, it is generally treated in terms of topics derived from popular culture trends and artifacts (Tipton 2008a).

In relation to this situation, theoretical and practical pedagogies that prepare teachers to work with young children artistically generally emphasize the analysis of artistic expressive language (Lowenfeld 1947). Personal and artistic development for the young child is generally interpreted through families of signs that unfold representationally (Eisner 1976/2002; Arnheim 1969/1997). In turn, the theoretical underpinnings of teacher training programs emphasize curricula for understanding that develop 'age-appropriate' motifs and patterns typed to the growth of 'realistic' representations. Universal stage theories have influenced the design and delivery of curriculum materials aimed at developmentally appropriate arts instruction. Thus, instruction leads children developmentally through sequential stages in drawing and painting as defined by stage theorists (Kellogg 1970; Taunton and Colbert 1984, 2000; Hart, Burt, and Charlesworth 1997). At the same time, however, the undirected appearance of popular culture representations such as gaming characters and cartoon figures or symbols in children's iconography often complicates the developmental framework used by teachers to assess art achievement.

The stage theory of development is increasingly being reinforced by the content of computer programs teaching art education concepts through interactive software. The most popular software programs for young children schematize characters and objects according to an age-appropriate framework of cognitive development, and support a mimesis of the representational schema they have programmed. Programs such as Creativity Express, for example, designed to entertain as well as to teach, schematize famous works of art as cartoon images the child interacts with through animated characters.[1] Without experiencing the opportunity to engage with the unfolding of one's own schema and imagery, mimesis of prefabricated schemas can supplant or overwrite a child's own innate process of schema development. Motifs derived from commercially produced materials repeat notational systems using signs and symbols so that these become codes associated with various socio-cultural practices, for example the current use of animated smiley faces as a shorthand for emotions.

As schools and nations are increasingly specifying standards and outcomes for visual art through sequentially based strands, themes, and content, there is a prevailing attitude that 'The arts communicate through non-discursive means using a visual, musical and dramatic vocabulary that is expressive, cultural and symbolic' (Bamford 2006: 35). While we support this statement's intention, the emphasis here, however, dichotomizes discourse to a literacy framework that favors a conventional interpretation of written and spoken language. Our position is that there are various forms of language including non-verbal, kinesthetic, auditory, interpersonal, and artistic ones, and they are all discursive. Yet visuality remains a neglected language whose literacy has yet to be fully integrated educationally.

We support literacy as Freire (1970) meant it, as the ability to use codes and conventions of various languages, inclusive of visual ones. Developing multi-literacies however, is undermined by schooling practices that are driven by assessment standards that tie achievement to the operations of logic and reason. Thus, national curricula increasingly narrow the meaning of literacy to written and spoken language, eliminating the symbolic discursive languages of the child. Our research extends the meaning of language as discourses to include discursive levels. Discursive levels are revealed at a reflective, meta-cognitive level, by inquiring into the interaction between making and speaking about one's own artwork and the artwork of others. Even young children are able to reflect, and their reflection reveals the inseparable inter-visuality of lived experience.

Child development and theory in art

Analysis of drawings and paintings produced by children usually occurs when adults examine the art itself, often without the context it was produced in, and without the inclusion of other languages the child may have used when creating. Theoretical postulates about child art tend to universalize formative relationships between families of signs and symbol patterns. Child art was treated as an object produced by a subject and then analyzed 'objectively,' influencing the development of taxonomies and typologies, accentuating children's autonomy and respect towards a child as an expressive individual. The child as author of their own work is a relatively new concept, and relationally depends on how the child is treated pedagogically and discursively.

Children's drawing appeared as an object of study in the field of developmental cognitive psychology and the theory of art education until the 1980s. Developmental stages of children's art and typologies that emerged out of these confluences were designed to support objective analysis, and were understood as stable and universally valid processes and facts. What all models analyzing children's art through stages of development have in common from this period is the use of resemblance to denote 'realistic' figurative code. The confusion between 'realism' as a style of art and 'reality' has been accompanied by the historical and ambiguous association of appearance as a simulacrum or mirror image of visual reality (Nochlin 1971/1990: 13–14). The influence of realism in thinking, perception, and behavior can be seen as part of a stylistic as well as a historical movement to create 'objective' investigation of the external world (Nochlin 1971/1990: 17).

During the 1980s, the introduction of art as a disciplinary subject instead of an expressive one placed an emphasis on teaching children the skills and techniques related to the development and interpretation of artistic products within the disciplines of art (history, production, criticism, and aesthetics). By contrast, furthering the interpretation that meaning is framed and negotiated, Culler (1988) suggested that the use of signs is determined by various discursive practices, values, institutional settings, and semiotic mechanisms. Analyzing drawing as a social practice with children thus can be differentiated from analysis of drawing as a product (Pearson 2001).

In the 1990s, the discipline-based model gave way to a postmodern one of interdisciplinary visualities. Discussing the act of drawing in relation to the original context of its appearance extends the discourse from identification to how drawing practice is socially constituted and framed. Cox (2000: 119) argues that the particular developmental pattern in western children's drawings has not always been the same and is not universal, even leaving out individual differences and cultural variations. In her cross-cultural research on representations of the human figure, for example, Cox (2000: 127) found that head and torso shapes are represented in different ways in different societies. Her research concludes that young children accommodate their representations to the style predominant in their culture (2000: 132). Freedman speaks of this process as educating identity:

> The effects of images shape an individual's self-concept, even in the ways they shape the notion of individualism. Individuals appropriate characteristics of visual representations, adopting these representations as a description of himself/herself.
>
> (Freedman 2003: 2)

The premises of the Enlightenment-Romantic era conceptions of art, however, act as barriers to a transdisciplinary perspective, as art is seen as a specific area of creation that surpasses the sphere of everyday life, and as the psycho-pathographic projection of the personality into visual imagery. Both of these conceptions are still manifest in the interpretation of children's art today. In addition, the influence of Piaget's theory of cognitive development from the 1960s remains a formative component of preparatory curriculum for early childhood teachers, even though many have questioned his description of the sequential aspects of the development of reasoning and cognition. In the same manner, equating realism in art as reality continues to constrain an emerging reconceptualization of what and how images are produced and function.

What is difficult about refuting these discourses, as Darras suggests (2000: 23), is that their frame of reference appears as a universally accepted way of representation. Less analyzed, from our point of view, are the material and non-material discourses that the western, interpretive model of child art precludes. Asking what impact institutionalized schooling practices have on the expected development of children and their art, examines the reflexivity between structure and content of particular schema that are acceptable and those that are eliminated. A particularly universalized example of this is the motif of a 'sun' that occupies the upper right or left of a young child's drawings, or a floating 'rainbow,' both of which usually appear along with a line across the bottom of a page to signify a picture with a 'ground.' They appear through mimesis after being introduced in contexts other than their own. Yet these motifs do not usually appear in drawings by children who have not previously seen them in colouring books, media, or other teachers and children producing them, as Tipton found in rural parts of the Amazon in Brazil (field notes, 21 July 2009). Our research supports findings that reinforcing the mimesis of mass-produced schema can arrest the young child's own sign system and schema development. On the other hand, the interaction of the various sign systems from visual culture can develop innovative schematic and symbolic languages in the child (Tipton 2008a).

According to Wilson (2000: 244), there is also a need to examine the role of the teacher in both the literal and figurative creation of child art, and to ask why it is that some things that children create become art and others do not. This question recognizes that there are other languages children use, some of which are characteristically performative in nature:

> When it comes to childhood images and art-like activities we have hardly begun to consider the interpretation of images from different perspectives – from the vantage point of the child, the teacher, the empirical researcher, the semiotician, the postmodern philosopher.
>
> (Wilson 2000: 243)

As we argue, it is possible to approach the topic of children's drawings from yet another perspective, where drawings themselves can be seen as coded, interdisciplinary discourses with their own narratives and interrelated systems. According to Gee (2004: 39), discourses are distinctive ways people talk, read, write, think, believe, value, act, and interact. Discourse is not just a way of using words, but as a way of using deeds, objects, tools, and so forth, to enact a certain sort of socially situated identity:

> Discourses recruit specific social languages (way with words) and cultural models (taken-for-granted stories), which in turn encourage people to construct certain sorts of situated meanings – that is, encourage them to read context in given ways.
>
> (Gee 2004: 40–1)

For our purposes, discourse also includes the context and space within which it is constituted (Fulková and Tipton 2008).

Semiotic play and the re-presentation of meaning

Matthews (2003: 49) traces the way in which pre-verbal gestures on the part of a developing child serve as a set of strategies by which objects and spaces are investigated, as well as serving as a kind of language by which other representations are later based.

Tipton's observational notes from a longitudinal study of Czech boy, Rajko at age twenty-two months support his work:

> Rajko takes a marker, one by one from a pile to the right of a large sheet of smooth, white paper (18 x 30 in). Holding the marker as an extension of what his hand can do, first back and forth, then on top of one another, straight lines, then erratic, circular, partial lines, partial circular shapes interrupting, folding over themselves, a total body movement from the right side of the paper to the left. Larger and longer than his own body, he nevertheless moved his body through the space of the paper, marking and selecting one color on top of another. Then asking for help ('pomoc') to open and close the marker's lids. Requesting glue and help to take a fallen shard of pine needles from the indoor tree and put it on the paper, his selection of objects and their use is both deliberate and experimental. The experience of experimentation unfolds in the different movements and their corresponding lines, from which the child stops, looks, and says, 'hezký' (good, nice). At this point, there is no clear distinction between marking on materials other than paper (self, clothes, wooden floorboards) which were discouraged and directed back to the paper. The boundary of experimentation is fluid and open. It is the adult which conditions the child's response to a prescribed container or routine.
>
> (Tipton, field notes, 28 March 2005)

Tipton's own reflection on this observation follows:

> Is this movement between child and paper also a dance of exploration of space in which the body moves and how? ...the guide's challenge is to present choice while steering selections in a safe environment where the freedom to explore choice is given time, energy, space and material to engage and enact.
>
> (Tipton, field notes, 28 March 2005)

The drawing is one form of documentation which includes the observational notes of the teacher as researcher (Katz and Chard 2000). Examining Rajko's transposition through autopoiesis, that is, as an act of self-creation, sheds light on how self-organizing systems create change through processes of communication and influence the development of emergent, new configurations of complexity (Luhman 1990/2002). Autopoiesis is the self-creational operation mechanism by which the growing child learns how to interact with objects, people, and spaces.[2] This self-organizing development is non-linear and is in some ways uncategorizable. Ten months later, this observation of Rajko was documented:

'Teresa is flying over the sea,' Rajko says as he draws and paints at the table. His hands move across the paper like his colored pencil did, gesturing a movement that he has already conceptualized. Red, black and blue paint is the sky, he says, indicating pools of color painted over multicolored pencil lines. When he mentions that I am flying, in contrast, his hand moves in a straight line across the picture plane. Later a thunderstorm comes and washes away all of the colors, he says. How would we have known what the picture meant to him if he didn't share it before it disappeared?

(Tipton, field notes, 5 January 2006)

Exploring the interaction between tool, body, movement, imagining, and conceptualization by drawing and painting is a process that is well represented by the concept of autopoiesis. Autopoiesis implies that each individual constructs information according to their own unique pattern of codes, structures, laws, and preferences. The recognition of the unpredictable nature of this combination is to factor in the influence of both synchronicity and disruption when planning for or designing art and cultural activities for young children. It means that as a part of the structure and function of experiential relationships, the design must accommodate one's interaction with oneself, interaction with others, with social factors and the cultural context.

Matthews (2003) supports Bruce's (1991) and Allott's (2001) view of the importance and role of play in the development of all forms of representation. Further, forms of symbolization and representation, including speech and drawing, may be based upon babies' body actions that can be considered their own dynamic language (Matthews 2003: 89). This mechanism can be seen working perfectly if one looks at the plethora of baby videos on the Internet of infants watching MTV videos and rhythmically copying the dance moves, as filmed by parents. Is it no less apparent that prefabricated and mass-produced images are likely to be mimicked and internalized as the child's own when they encounter systems of manufactured representations such as those on clothes, in colouring books, cartoons, DVDs, toys, television, and educational materials?

On the other hand, the introduction of instructional materials to copy or color in can also be seen as an unnatural imposition of schema over the development of the child's own (see Plate 16). This is apparent by the time the child is in pre-school and kindergarten, when the first negative creativity responses, such as 'I can't draw,' appear in speech and behavior. In these situations, the distinction between child-initiated and teacher-led art has already begun and is being patterned.

Methodology of the case study: transcoding cultural spaces

Constructivism, critical reflection, and dialogic communication become important pedagogical methods for identifying and using discourses that may operate beyond the two-dimensional framework of analyzing traditional visual images based on dichotomies (Fulková and Tipton 2008; Tipton 2003). Dialogic methods transform the didactics of passively looking 'at' something, to an interactive mode of pedagogy. Dialogue, as the passing of meaning between two or more people, assists in the transformation of 'self-talk' into reflections on actions that form the basis of meta-cognition. Meta-cognition is an essential skill for revealing the meaning-making structure underneath interpretations given by students (Tipton 2008b). Meta-cognition is a skill that is nurtured when one is able to reflect upon observations of experience.

In pedagogical terms, attending to the semiological relationships through which the young child is experiencing the world assists in an understanding of how art both develops and is narrated within an unfolding system of language depiction. Art as language depiction happens on two levels – on the level of art creation and on the level of communication. This is a simultaneous gestalt that appears as an integrated process where the meaning is created about these functions and through them. By exploring the interaction of this process, an active reflection about the work's meaning unfolds. This is a process of experimentation and novelty as well as an exploration of structure and containment.

Research conducted with pre-school and young primary children, inside and outside classroom settings from the Czech Republic, provided the following examples from twelve children, seven boys and five girls between four and five years old.[3] As part of the original research design, two participating women teachers of European descent were given a full set of curriculum materials and themes. They in turn selected six themes for the children to use, and changed one of them (from 'My favorite character' (in a story) to 'My hero'). They let children choose what they wanted to draw in the other five themes: Create a family shield or flag, My things (I like), At my place, My territory, and Stranger. For the theme Stranger, we found that the notion of a 'stranger' was a new concept for the children. They could, however, differentiate between people they recognized and people they did not recognize. Before starting the project, the teachers read the story 'Rapunzel,' which was later found to influence some drawings of 'My hero.' Some images were cut out of magazines and were available to use with colored markers and supplies from the school. For our purposes, we used letters for the children's names.

Some of the students conceptualized 'Stranger' as an animal, such as a lion, snake, or a hybrid being with multiple legs. Child V created an image with five multicolored suns; three of them had smiling faces and two did not. V's explanation was, 'Pink and green suns are strangers and the others are not' (see Plate 17).

For the theme 'At my place,' we can see images referring to situations in and out of the home such as Child A's picture of a visit to a swimming pool with his father, which he called 'Crazy water' (but he did not want to talk about it). Child T drew a toy and explained that he was the 'owner of the castle.'

The sheets of paper Child B used for drawing become his personal symbolic space. This space was filled with a number of signs and symbols that create and are created by dynamic narratives. He wanted to direct the result of his efforts, and was not pleased with teacher direction or control. We could see that he took his concept of a 'Stranger' from a mixture of popular movies for children and the story 'Jack and the beanstalk,' in combination with impressions about his father's absence from his life. Because of the complexity of his sign and symbol systems, we focused our analysis on his work as an example of 'transcoding' or the intersection of cultural idioms:

> Transcoding or transduction is the manner in which one milieu serves as the basis for another, or conversely is established atop another milieu, dissipates in it or is constituted in it.
>
> (Deleuze and Guattari 1987/2005: 313)

Transcoding occurs between and across diverse contexts and sign systems, and is illustrative of border crossing between visual culture and social environments, (Fulková, Tipton and Ishikawa 2009). Take for example Child B's interaction about his drawing 'The stranger,' where a particular sequence appears to be a combination of dream imagery and a movie story.

R:[4] 'What is a stranger?'

B: 'Somebody you don't know. I made a giant big so you can't see him. I have a movie of a giant at home.'

R: *Mickey and the Magic Beans?*

B: 'What I wanted to say it was in that movie, there were some things, should I tell it now?'

R: 'It's up to you.'

B: 'It's a talking hand. It's just pretending.'

R: 'How does it work?'

B: 'There are lots of many guys that make the actions work.'

R: 'I can't see the rest of him, what does he look like?'

B: (without answering) 'There's a guy with the green face who tells the story. There's a guy who looks like a guy who makes a story. Jiminy Cricket is the guy, he does eat a little bit of the ice cream. I don't know that part, I'll think about it when we talk.'

R: 'What's going on in this picture?'

B: 'He knows, he does look like a guy, a normal guy that is in a movie that I don't know, I think.'

R: 'What's he wearing?'

B: 'T-shirt, shirt, and uh, that's all.'

R: 'Do you know what he looks like?'

B: 'No.'

R: 'Is that why he is a stranger?'

B: 'That's why he steps on the snake. The snake wakes up and bites him on the foot. His shoe is in the castle, and he can't wake up, the snake fell asleep again. And then he did bite his hands, and then he got another Ouchy.'

R: 'Why is the snake this color?'

B: 'I wanted to have it like this. I wanted it to look like the same movie. T and A.'

R: 'Why T and A?'

B: 'T like dog, and A like Anacan. He's part of this part (pointing to another drawing).'

R: 'Those pictures are connected?'

B: 'Yes, because of this part (A). I keep changing my mind so it doesn't matter.'

The gestalt of B's mind has its own laws. The individual behaves differently according to the way tensions between the perception of self and the environment are working. Child B did not always remember what he did or thought before that present moment, and constructed a new 'memory' instead. While appearing finite to adults, the drawing continues to exert its imaginative power within the playful imagination of B. The creative act is always in process of creating itself, and the drawing itself is its expression.

This means that there is not a stable 'vocabulary' of fixed meanings or signs that we may simply refer to, other than from a particular snapshot of a moment, which has been temporarily, or artificially, isolated and separated. As Kristeva comments:

> [Sign] is a part of a specific structure of meaning [*combinatoire*] and in that sense it is *correlative*: its meaning is the result of an interaction with other signs.
>
> (Kristeva 1986a: 72)

Discursive intervisuality

We can take into account at least four kinds of discursive layers in interpretation. First, there is the socio-cultural environment of the child. Next is the context of the majority culture, or more precisely the cultural treatment of images (cultural interface), then the context of the environment in which the picture was created (for instance, there is a difference between pictures made at school or at home), and finally the context of the author (including the type of background, gender, habitus, and their position).

In the interpretation we offer here, we will deal with neither taxonomy nor a hierarchy of signs. We use the terms 'signs' and 'symbols' as expressing the functions of children's mark-making, such as referring, substituting, and representation, while the process of denotation is open and infinitely unanswerable. Both Cox (2000) and Darras (2000: 22) suggest that images and the sign systems associated with them should be interpreted as repertoires of communication favored by their culture of origin. 'This milieu is particularly open, plural, interactive, polyphonic, dialogic, and ephemeral' (Darras 2000: 22).

While discourse has traditionally been tied to the modality of speech, the space and system of its formation has been characterized by Foucault (1972) as an unstable field of all kinds of *énoncés*. *Énoncés* are formations of 'statements' that can be constituted through other non-written sign systems, such as gestures, scribbles, drawings, body language, and dress, as well as non-verbal codes and languages (Gee 2004; Fulková and Tipton 2008). Considering 'mark-making' in terms of these various forms of discourse shifts the model of its interpretation from that of object identification to that of inter-actional and inter-relational identification.

Thus, the main material for our research is related as an array of *énoncés* (Foucault 1972). These include comments, interviews, images, artifacts and objects of everyday use, artistic and other manifestations of symbolic orders. Foucault, whose use of the word 'discourse' asserted the concept of power and space as expression, enables us to understand works of art (both visual and linguistic representations) as discursive within the social domain.

By shifting science discourse from its positivist designations of 'truth' to that of 'tool,' it is possible to compare scientific and humanist discourses not as models but as metaphors for different kinds of knowing (Hosek and Freeman 2001: 510). Looking at the 'reality as representation' conundrum through a neurodynamic lens can shed new light on what is nearly universally accepted as a representational paradigm of the 'visual brain' (Myin 2000: 45). Under the influence of contemporary neuroscience two different theories of perception and visuality have emerged (Zeki 1993; Myin 2000). One ties an understanding of visual processing to representational theories that relate a replication of an external reality to an internal one. Another non-representational one posits an active engagement with the environment.

> Two concepts dominate this research: the notion of pathways or modules, and the notion of representation. These two concepts ground the hope for a deep connection between the representational science of vision and the art of visually representing.
>
> (Myin 2000: 43)

Starring in *Star Wars*

We return to the example of Child B to illustrate how his mark-making can be interpreted in the light of the arguments presented above. In our study, B responded to all themes with completed drawings, and commented on them together with the researcher and his teacher. B is a four and a half year old boy in a bilingual family (American English and Czech). His parents are separated and he lives with his mother. His father visits the family approximately once a month and they often phone each other. B often talks about his father, and many interpretations of his drawings relate to him.

B's artworks are full of signs that have the form of individual experimentation with sign creation, which B was pleased to interpret. Part of the videotaped dialogue follows between the boy, a teacher, and a researcher, who asked him questions about his drawings, beginning with 'My favorite character (My hero)' (see Plate 18).

R: 'What do these lines mean?'
B: 'They are bad guys there.'
R: 'What is the green bit here?'
B: 'His handle. I can't draw him, but he looks like a farmer. He said he would be a good guy, a Jedi, but he wasn't. He has this part on his head (gesturing as if a long, single spike is there).'
R: 'What does it mean?'
B: 'That is his friend. That means he is a good guy. That X means he can't win when he is old. That means it is a video number two. This means that when he is mad, that is 'his part' (pointing to a furrow on his own brow). That is where he thinks where to get to his mom. That is when he couldn't sleep. There is one in the last part of the ten part, there was a kind of animal and he was a good guy and he had a rifle.'
R: 'Chewbacca?'
B: 'There was another one. A guy who didn't want to eat Luke Skywalker; he couldn't get up because his feet were in ice. The force means that he was strong. They put the guys in warm water.'

[We can note at this point that the boy's description in the video diverged from the drawings because of the questions his teacher asked.]

Not only do these signs not need assessment and verification by adults, but explaining, searching, and creating meaning does not exist outside the structure where communication about and with the image occurs.

B's narrative includes references to media images, characters, and events from film, video games, commercials, and cartoons. Looking at the means that B uses to create the form of symbolic relational space, into which we, through communication with B, are conjoined and integrated, the drawings all possess one principal trait in common: most of the signs that he uses are not of iconic character but they are abstract signs, whose meanings are to be unwrapped only by other signs with commentary or interpretative signs. As Kristeva elaborates:

> [Sign] does not refer to a single unique reality, but evokes a collection of associated images and ideas. While remaining expressive, it none the less tends to distance itself from its supporting transcendental basis (it may be called 'arbitrary').
>
> (Kristeva 1986b: 72)

When letter and number characters are used in images, the meaning is formed on the floating boundary between cultural standardization and personal use. Young children often change or 'correct' meanings according to the context, associations, the need of the metaphor that is just being created as it is being spoken, and the need for a child's own version of an original narrative. Berger speaks of this when he writes,

> One is taught to oppose the real to the imaginary, as though the first were always at hand and the second distant, far away. This opposition is false. Events are always to hand. But the coherence of these events – which is what one means by reality – is an imaginative construction.
>
> (Berger 1984: 72–3)

B's narrative appears to be formed from inspiration arising from previous experience, memories, daily events, unexpected happenings in his environment, and unfiltered information coming within the perceptual field from outside sources, and together these are transformed into a new version of themselves. The visual expression of the images is so dynamic in space and narrative through the complex constellations of signs and their references to experiences with film images and stories, that they evoke further exploration into the personal semiotic system from which they originated.

Identity as co-constructive virtualities

Affecting B's narrative and bringing the 'representation as reality' model into further question are influences from digital media technologies. Historically, the correlation between realism and representation is problematic because the image is viewed iconically 'as itself' instead of as a sign-symbol that 'represents.' According to Kristeva (1981/1999), a semiotic reading of a pictorial representation should be examined not only through its figurative code, which structures configured elements and the modus referred to, but also through its 'discourse,' as this is where the figurative code and its representational meaning are constituted. Through discourse, the image becomes a 'text' and the image's assumed 'reality of representation' is subverted. Images and texts become multilingual narrative spaces where signifiers and meanings arise and cross. Again, a rethinking of the standardized language of children's drawings is also implied by this analysis.

Virtualized embodiment has led to an uncoupling of formerly linearly conceived materiality and its concomitant but slower, evolutionary patterning, into a new kind of presence – the instantaneous and real-time telepresence of the '24/7' camera switched on, observed, and commented on by unperceived, virtual and 'real' observers. The mind interacts experientially with these different simulated, recorded, and telecast environments, not just by 'gaming' inside prefabricated corridors of interactive software programs, but by pushing previously constituted borders of the known into frontiers of new intelligence. For the young child between two and three years old, the distinction between fantasy and real-time telepresence of reality-watching television, for instance, is indistinguishable (Barr and Hayne 1997; Jaglom and Gardner 1981).

The influence of visual culture challenges not only 'representation as reality' as a dominant system of interpretation, but also the interpretation of images through multiple modes of representation, and predictably punctures this system's assumed structure. For this reason, a semiotic system of interpretation reflects upon relationships between signs, meanings, and context rather than fixing meanings to signs.

Extending the analysis further, Kristeva adds a third process, that of transposition as the passage from one sign-system to another (1986b: 111). Transposition can be seen as the underlying mechanism the child uses when they draw and paint. Transposition can also be seen as the way in which visuality itself is constituted and experienced in the contemporary context. Visual culture in this context is less about content than it is about developing a relationship to how the influence of contemporary visuality constitutes thinking, perception, and behavior.

> The multiple sites for intersection and interpretation and the way they are codified into the languages of recognition, constitute the cultural space for our 'reading' of children's artwork. Considering these processes of 'becoming-a-text' of the artwork, we can see that the pictorial representation does not represent a reality but a 'simulacrum-between-the world-and-language.'
>
> (Kristeva 1981/1999: 310)

> le code proprement pictural est dans un rapport étroit avec le langage qui le constitue, et la représentation pictuale se réfère donc au réseau de la langue, qui émane du simulacre représenté par le code pictural, mais le dissout en le dépassant.
>
> (Kristeva 1981/1999: 310)[5]

Deterritoralizing my things

Starting with Kristeva's 'figurative code,' we examined B's work in relation to its discursive layers. B's short crossed lines mean direction, allowed or also forbidden, when 'something is not possible,' signified also by the letter 'X.' B indicated this in narrative as well, commenting 'The spacecraft cannot fly down,' and 'He cannot win, he is old.' In his drawings, spirals are used to indicate concrete people and objects, as well as abstract concepts (such as 'brain and thinking'). Sharp, strong zigzags are often used to express abstract phenomena, for example thinking, worries, plot, and dynamism of the action. Lines closing ovals, or irregular circles around a sign of enclosure, function as a restriction of the space, or represent a concrete fence. Circles also mean people. There are no complete human figures, only a sign for legs, which appeared twice with a fictive continuation outside of the sheet. B atypically positions the plot of the narrative inherent to the image between the 'legs' (vertical lines), the space where other children often put the 'body.'

The layout of the space, on the other hand, points to the deep-rooted conception of a 'picture' in western culture, where since the European Renaissance; a framework has been established as a 'window' through which a segment of 'reality' can be seen. It shows the influence of the 'cultural interface' (cultural treatment of image) with learned conventions of 'reading' two-dimensional, rectangular images, as well as the influence of education, and the influence of the contemporary, visual environment in which the child has grown up.

Commonly asked questions like 'What is it?' and 'What have you drawn?' are often posed to children about their art from adults, as the expectation is that some of the elements will be 'unrecognizable.' Such questioning reveals the (western) cultural response to pictorial representation, or in other words, to a picture as iconic. But B complicates the cultural interface by inventing and using his own language, with its vocabulary of 'abstract' signs which adults could misinterpret as 'scribbles.' It reminds us pedagogically that we need to question the 'natural' notion of 'representation' as 'reality' that can be named or identified. B's drawings and his accompanying narratives and explanations also complicate the classical interpretation of children's art, as these refer to the dynamism of the filmic images and narratives of the *Star Wars* series that reach across the space of his various images and that connect them together. His drawings and visual competencies come from the moving image and from the complex semiotic structure of the visible fictions existing within his visual culture. B constitutes his own languages and at the same time enacts these within his own narrative and virtual imagination.

Symbolic world-mapping

For the second context, B distinguishes several parallel 'realities,' symbolic areas, filled with characters and plots: in other words, the space of the image, the space of the film fiction, and the space of his life's reality, to which he, as well as the interpretation of his pictorial signs, belongs. We can also say that B simultaneously verifies three (or more) versions of the world: it is interesting that the child considers the space of all the images to be a common space for all, and at the same time, as separable. One of these spaces was created by an intertextual directive B gave to the teacher to write down exactly what he said into his image.

B could choose which image to start with, so he selected 'My favorite character.' Then he matched, in a specific order, his other drawings and pictures to this image. He often mentioned the name Obi-Wan Kenobi (he obviously likes the rhythmical element of this expression and repetition of vowels, which rhyme). He told the film story in detail, deducing the plot from his interpretation of individual signs and the relationships that symbolized the character and the selected scenes from his story. He often quoted the dialogues of the main film characters. He went on to reflect on the qualities of 'good and bad guy,' and moved to the picture of 'Stranger,' an entrance to another film story. This image evoked an inter-textual reconfiguration of the folk story 'Jack and the beanstalk,' through the Walt Disney cartoon version, *Mickey and the beanstalk*, with Mickey Mouse as Jack.

The symbolism of the animals that B chose (bull and tiger, in the topic 'My things') represented force, speed, wildness, and perseverance. By means of signs, which support and reinforce the interpretation, the boy created an environment for these animals. The bull was fast and 'cool enough.' As for the speed, the boy compared the bull to a motorbike, in which he finally seemed to be more interested. His collage from magazines in the school supports the narrative. 'This is a (Jedi) rocket, which I want to buy; my Dad wants to buy it for me.' This attitude exemplifies his previously formed cultural relations (buy it) and value preferences (I want it).

It seems that naming exerts a special, magical quality for this boy. The tiger, which for the boy shares an attribute of a hero, a policeman, is supposed to listen to his orders: 'He will be untamed, but I know his name.' The bull is supposed to 'understand,' too. B chooses a relational web of symbols of power, order, and justice. The image of the tiger was linked to his last chosen picture, which depicted family symbols. B talked about a coat of arms that his family has: 'There is a tiger on it, but I can't draw a tiger.' Several times he simultaneously connected the interpretation of two pictures, only to explain later that he 'was just joking, it wasn't true.' A few times he even changed the interpretation of the signs and offered a new version. He presented himself changing his mind as a 'good joke,' a very effective way of leading a conversation, perhaps demonstrating that he was comfortable and familiar speaking with adults and engaging their attention through storytelling.

This analysis of B's work has implications for pedagogical practice, and suggests the need to shift the current emphasis of looking for specific forms of visual language development. Instead there is a need to emphasize the consideration of how children experiment with various syntaxes and imaginative structures that allow them to move between fictive virtualities, everyday experience, and intervisual narratives.

Virtually real

B has mastered all the plots and characters of all the episodes from the *Star Wars* film series; he knows the characters' names and qualities, and their roles in the stories. With the help of these characters of modern mythology, this boy conceptualizes, recognizes, and creates good and evil, lies, fighting, defeat, and victory. In his versions of the world, where a metaphor is a constituting element, there are policemen, guns, Grandma, giant, snake, *Star Wars* characters, a coat of arms, rocket, Daddy, tiger, bull, ice-cream and beer, all in an interconnected relational dynamic. Plate 19 and its accompanying discourse illustrate this very clearly:

R: '"Your territory, your place." Can you tell us about it?'
B: 'This side is my daddy and this I forgot to draw a line here. I wanted to make another A here for A giant.'
R: 'What did you want to show us? Are these two connected too?'
B: 'Yes, because other guys do it like this.'
R: 'What does 'this' mean?'
B: 'That means that they have pistols. That is the color of his pants.'
R: 'Why didn't you draw his face?'
B: 'Because it wasn't a long paper. Dad lives in America but he comes to visit.'
R: 'Do you talk to him on the phone a lot?'
B: 'No, because then I would be crazy and wouldn't even sleep.'
R: 'Why did you put this kind of ship inside a picture with your daddy?'
B: 'So when you don't want to play any more than you can take some toys with you.'

For B, metaphoric messages are often created as part of a changeable game of meanings – accidental clusters of lines and dots often tempted the boy to match these verbally with more visual meanings. The seeming tumult is arranged into mutual relations in a symbolic order of good and evil, force and speed, and admiration for the omnipresent authority of (the absent) father who ensures justice, order, and law. The female element appears only as a remark about the mother of the film character who 'could not sleep worrying about her,' and in the image, 'My things,' where there is food in the middle and above the tiger (separated by a green, closed line), a sign he interpreted as 'for my Grandma in America.' His first name, placed three times in the picture (and several times as the initial B), confirms the presence and ownership of a self-confident and communicative author (see Plate 20).

The boy's drawings significantly manifest cultural influences, which coincide with his fascination with *Star Wars*. The first episode of *Star Wars* was made in the 1970s. It coincided with a time when the military systems for fighting in space were being developed, and the media took over a number of its metaphors. Just like the first videogame from the 1970s, *Star Wars* remains a compelling, contemporary mythological narrative together with its movie remake, fandom, and websites. Roland Barthes foresaw this phenomenon when he wrote:

> In passing from history to nature, myth acts economically: it abolishes the complexity of human acts, it gives them the simplicity of essences, it does away with all dialectics, with any surpassing beyond what is immediately visible, it organizes a world which is without contradictions, because it is without depth, a world wide open and wallowing in the evident, it establishes a blissful clarity: things appear to mean something by themselves
>
> (Barthes 1972/2000): 129)

Given the rich complexity of his narratives, it can been seen that the primary influences in B's stories come from popular films, computers, and the cultural habitus of his family. But without further ethnographic work with the family members directly, we cannot depict the character of this habitus. Both Hodge and Tripp (1986) and Giles (2003:139–40), however, offer evidence for a causal link between watching television and the variety of discursive and narrative forms that children are able to apply to different situations without having to create them in their daily lives. There is also evidence that for young children, television stimulates the development of knowledge structures of the world that set up expectations about cause and effect.

B's drawings and their interpretation offer a representative example of how popular cultural output infiltrates the art and cognition of children. Here, the influences of new myths are particularly interesting, with their shifts in meanings, the way that fragments of the stories move through time and space, and their new assemblage and use in the present-day culture. Educationally, these influences can be tracked by the appearance and use of characters and narratives from popular movies, video games, Internet sites, the latest electronic 'toys,' and virtual reality gaming. Whereas it was once common that children understood 'Leonardo' and 'Raphael' as animated turtles endowed with special attributes, these characters have been superseded by today's version of 'Hado,' and other popular culture characters and social networking video games that now appear in the drawings of primary children.

Conclusion: implications for school practice

> The world is a web of interdependent living communities, not a department store.
>
> (Manes 1995: 88)

Children's discourses about their art may be increasingly encouraged, but as a tool for understanding semiotic knowledge, these discourses are methodologically undervalued. Children's drawing is a form of social communication. Drawings are not solely products, they are also complex notational processes that represent many kinds of languages. Within a rapidly changing menu of research modalities and methods, children as authors of their own work participate in these discourses as well.

Children from different cultural backgrounds, subcultures, or habitus seem to prefer completely different narratives, and use an entirely different expressive arsenal of visual signs which constitute a wide array of visual languages. The manner of 'reading' pictures from previous historical and social periods has changed into one that mimics film production, and needs a completely different description and use. Fragments of cultural layers form 'shorts,' or sequences of fictional worlds where the meaning of signs is fluid and they are no longer solely mnemonic. A child's mark-making is virtualized through narrative while narrative is concomitantly virtualized.

This interface is relational. It is a way of expressing feelings, systematizing thoughts, and experiencing one's existence. From the pedagogical point of view, the cultural interface is closely connected to how visuality is experienced and taught. The whole process of exploring how meaning arises may not be a new concept. But educationally, its dialogic aspects are not given pedagogical preference. In this sense, considering artistic behaviors (whether these are accompanied by writing and oral language) as dialogic, as autopoeisis and as mimesis, means that instruction is directed away from the control of a facilitator or teacher. As Kristeva (1986a) comments, mimetic behaviors function not solely for copying, but for individualizing the mirroring process. This is the place where young children start their journey of learning.

The autonomy of the individual can be compromised, even undermined by the imposition of predefined knowing. Our research calls instead for engagement with and development of willful choices through collaborative learning processes in order to cultivate negotiation and reconciliation across different learning systems and modalities. Engaging student/

teachers in the theoretical and practical exploration of how cultural and mental models of the world are formed and become an interface through which they interact personally, situationally, and culturally may come to be a necessary component of teacher education training programs that aim to develop critical thinking about today's 'moving visuality.'

As today's competencies in visuality are mostly gained outside the school in the world of visual communications and visual production (Fulková, Straker, and Jaros 2004), we should also realize our own preferences for particular visual representations, and deliberately broaden our tolerance towards new and unverified 'languages' of visuality, by drawing on the way contemporary art handles these languages.

Images from software, videogames, school worksheets, activity books, and textbooks invisibly mediate persuasive messages and themes, which challenge educators to reconsider their possible negative judgments of quality and aesthetic preference. Responding to this challenge would allow them to engage fully with the informational realm they and the children they teach belong to, which embodies forms of the world as they are experienced and perceived today. When we diversify discourse in this way, what we learn is that the material challenge, in combination with the material of fantasy, play, and daydreams, and the multi-faceted dimensions of re-presenting visuality, can lead to the generation of metaphor, story, myth, and simulations through creative play.

Celebrating and spreading diversity in the cultural sphere, our work highlights the importance of cultivating respect for a variety of visual languages as an antidote to the downturn of global systems in transformation. Children's visual art can then tell us a lot: not about a specific children's world, but about various versions of the world, which all people together share in creating.

Revisiting the development of art as apprenticeship could shift the instructional paradigm away from predetermined outcomes to an outcome that is supportive of the child's own learning process. This could place the 'child-in-residence' alongside the company of artists and practitioners who make their own art, not just alongside artists-in-residence in schools. In this way, visual culture could become an organizing perspective. Visual culture then, should not be understood as simply the content of imagery, but as a process of interacting and giving the young child choices. Pedagogy that is formulated on guiding children solely towards predefined questions and outcomes subverts the unfolding of the process of discovery, and can fail to allow novelty to surprise us. The heart of the creative urge can be opened instead, where the unknown, the unexpected, and the unpredictable come together through and by our own actions, volition, and tools,.

And should it not be the prerogative of every child to claim their own mind, its tributaries and eddies, to find inside themselves their own stagnant or vapid pools, their own torrents of impassioned waters, and to follow these where they lead, not always being led, but following and making their own way as they go, as they choose, sharing in the company of others? Towards this vision, may we diversify our practices and discourses about and with young children and their art.

Notes

1 See http://www.madcaplogic.com/ for a demonstration of Creativity Express, a software program for children created by former Disney animators. Instructional materials for teachers working with young children today follow the trend of interactive media by using brightly colored mass-produced motifs and cartoon characters as a part of educational worksheets and materials.
2 Autopoeisis, from a Greek term, relates to a systems concept used for denoting an inherent tendency of an organism to self-organize in response to its environment (Fulková, Tipton, and Ishikawa, 2009). Adapted from biology, autopoeisis encompasses more than organization and growth. It refers to a network of processes of interaction within oneself, and the reciprocity that occurs between production and destruction during change. An innate movement for regeneration referred to as self-organization can be used to reference psychosocial development as well. See an original idea of this function in Maturana and Varela (1980).
3 The case study is taken from a research project conducted in 2001 in conjunction with the Institut Pedagogicko-psychologického Poradenství CR (anglicky) and the Czech Ministry of Education, called Exploring the Specific Aspects of the Education of Children from Different Minority Groups in the Czech Republic. This part of the study focused on bilingual families whose parents work for foreign companies, and children who attend nursery schools where English is the main language of education.
4 R is the researcher; B is Child B.
5 'The pictorial code is closely connected with language which constitutes the code; and the pictorial representation is thus related to the net of language system, which stems from the simulacrum represented by the code of the image; however, by overlapping this code it is at the same time decomposing it' (our translation).

References

Allott, R. (2001) *The Natural Origin of Language: Vision, action, language*, Knebworth: Able Publishing.

Arnheim, R. (1969/1997) *Visual Thinking*, Berkeley, Calif.: University of California Press.

Bamford, A. (2006) *The WOW Factor: Global research compendium on the impact of the arts in education*, New York: Waxmann Münster.

Barr, R. and Hayne, H. (1997) 'Developmental changes in imitation from television during infancy,' *Child Development*, **70**, pp. 1067–81.

Barthes, R. (1972/2000) *Mythologies*, trans. A. Lavers, London: Vintage.

Berger, J. (1984) *And Our Faces, My Heart, Brief as Photos*, New York: Vintage.

Bruce, T. (1991) *Time to Play in Early Childhood Education*, London: Hodder & Stoughton.

Cox, M. (1992) *Children's Drawings*, Harmondsworth: Penguin.

Cox, M. (2000) 'Children's drawings of the human figure in different cultures,' pp. 119–34 in L. Lindström (ed.), *The Cultural Context: Comparative studies of art education and children's drawings*, Stockholm Library of Curriculum Studies, Vol. 7, Stockholm: Stockholm Institute of Education Press.

Culler, I. (1988) *Framing the Sign: Criticism and its institutions*, Norman, Okla.: University of Oklahoma Press.

Darras, B. (2000) 'Repertoires of imagery and the production of visual signs: a semio-cognitive approach and case study,' pp. 21–45 in L. Lindström (ed.), *The Cultural Context. Comparative studies of art education and children's drawings*, Stockholm: Stockholm Institute of Education Press (HLS Förlag).

Deleuze, G. and Guattari, F. (1987/2005) *A thousand plateaus: Capitalism and schizophrenia*, trans. B. Massumi, Minneapolis, Minn.: University of Minnesota Press.

Eisner, E. (1976/2002) 'What we know about children's art- what we need to know,' in E. Eisner (ed.), *The Arts, Human Development and Education*, Berkeley, Calif: McCutchan.

Foucault, M. (1972) *Archaeology of Knowledge and the Discourse on Language*, trans. A. M. Sheridan Smith, New York: Pantheon.

Freedman, K. (2003) *Teaching Visual Culture: Curriculum, aesthetics and the social life of art*, New York: Teachers College Press.

Freire, P. (1970) *Pedagogy of the Oppressed*, New York: Continuum.

Fulková, M., Straker, A., and Jaros, M. (2004) 'The empirical spectator and gallery education,' *International Journal of Art and Design Education*, **23**(1), pp. 4–15.

Fulková, M. and Tipton, T. (2008) 'A (con)text for new discourse as semiotic praxis,' *International Journal of Art and Design Education*, **27**(1), pp. 27–42.

Fulková, M., Tipton, T., and Ishikawa, M. (2009) 'Through the eyes of a stray dog: encounters with the other,' *International Journal of Education Through Art*, 5 (2 and 3, December), pp. 111–28.

Gee, J. (2004) 'Discourse analysis: what makes it critical?' pp. 39–41 in R. Rogers (ed.), *An Introduction to Critical Discourse Analysis in Education*, N.J.: Lawrence Erlbaum Associates.

Giles, D. (2003) *Media Psychology*, N.J.: Lawrence Erlbaum Associates.

Gombrich, E. (1960) *Art and Illusion: A study in the psychology of pictorial representation*, Princeton, N.J.: Princeton University Press.

Hart, C., Burt, D., and Charlesworth, R. (1997) *Integrated Curriculum and Developmentally Appropriate Practice: Birth to age eight*, Albany, N.Y.: State University of New York Press.

Hayles, N. K. (2003) 'Virtual bodies and flickering signifiers,' pp. 497–506 in A. Jones (ed.), *Feminism and Visual Culture Reader*, London: Routledge.

Hernández, F. (2000) *Educación y Cultura Visual*, Barcelona: Octaedro.

Hodge, R. and Tripp, D. (1986) *Children and Television: A semiotic approach*, Cambridge: Polity.

Hosek, J. and Freeman, W. (2001) 'Osmetic ontogenesis, or olfaction becomes you: the neurodynamic, intentional self and its affinities with the Foucaultian/ Butlerian subject,' *Configurations*, **9**, pp. 509–42.

Jaglom, L. and Gardner. H. (1981) 'The preschool television viewer as anthropologist,' pp. 9–30 in H. Kelly and H. Gardner (eds), *Viewing Children Through Television: New directions in child development 13*, San Francisco, Calif.: Jossey-Bass.

Katz, L. and Chard, S. (2000) *Engaging Children's Minds*, 2nd edn, Norwood, N.J.: Ablex.

Kellogg, R. (1970) *Analyzing Children's Art*, Australia: McGraw-Hill Education.

Kristeva, J. (1981/1999) *Le langage, cet inconnu*, Paris: Éditions du Seuil, quoted and trans. from the Czech edition, *Slovo, dialog, roman*, trans. J. Fulka, p. 44, Prague: Sofis.

Kristeva, J. (1986a) 'From symbol to sign,' pp. 62–73 in T. Moi (ed.), *The Kristeva Reader*, Oxford: Basil Blackwell.

Kristeva, J. (1986b) 'Revolution in poetic language,' pp. 90–136 in T. Moi (ed.), *The Kristeva Reader*, Oxford: Basil Blackwell.

Lewin, K. (1951) *Field Theory in Social Science: Selected theoretical papers*, ed. D. Cartwright, New York: Harper & Row.

Lowenfeld, V. (1947) *Creative and Mental Growth*, New York: Macmillan.

Luhman, N. (1990/2002) *Paradigm Lost: Über die ethische Reflexion der Moral*, Frankfurt am Main: Suhrkampf Verlag. Czech edition: *Láska jako vášen: Paradigm lost* (2002, trans. M. Petrícek), Prague: Prostor.

Manes, C. (1995) 'Making art about centipedes,' in S. Gablik (ed.), *Conversations Before the End of Time*, New York: Thames & Hudson.

Matthews, J. (2003) *Drawing and Painting: Children and visual representation*, 2nd edn, London: Paul Chapman.

Maturana, H. and Varela, F. (1980) *Autopoiesis and Cognition: The realization of the living*, Dordrecht: Reidel.

Myin, E. (2000) 'Two sciences of perception and visual art,' *Journal of Consciousness Studies*, **7** (8–9), pp. 43–55.

Nochlin, L. (1971/1990) *Realism*, London: Penguin.

Pearson, P. (2001) 'Towards a theory of children's drawing as social practice,' *Studies in Art Education*, **42**(4), pp. 348–65.

Taunton, M. and Colbert, C. (1984) 'Artistic and aesthetic development: considerations for early childhood educators,' *Childhood Education*, 61(1), pp. 55–63.

Taunton, M. and Colbert, C. (2000) 'Art in the early childhood classroom: authentic experiences and extended dialogues,' pp. 67–76 in N. Yelland (ed.), *Promoting Meaningful Learning: Innovations in education early childhood professionals*, Washington DC: National Association for the Education of Young Children.

Tipton, T. (2003) 'Teaching visual culture through semiosis: beyond postmodern paradigms in art education,' in *A Critical Context: Art and design education on the edge* (with CD-Rom), University of Central England, School of Art and Design Education: Cascade Publications.

Tipton, T. (2005, 2006, 2009) Unpublished set of field notes.

Tipton, T. (2008a) *Teaching Visual Culture Through Semiosis: Transforming postmodern paradigms in art education*, Dissertation, Charles University, Prague.

Tipton, T. (2008b) 'Myths of certainty: Interruptions into the nature of learning and meaning,' in *Verejnost A Kouzlo Vizuality: Rozvoy Teoretických Základu Výtvarná Výchovy A Otázky Kulturního Vzdelávání. Symposium Ceské sekce INSEA*, Brno: Masarykova Univerzita.

Tochon, F. (2001) 'Education research: new avenues for video pedagogy and feedback in teacher education,' *International Journal of Applied Semiotics*, **2**(1–2), pp. 9–28.

Wilson, B. (2000) 'The Vilnius conference and the future of child art: a philosophical agenda,' pp. 237–46 in L. Lindström (ed.), *The Cultural Context: Comparative studies of art education and children's drawings*, Stockholm: Stockholm Institute of Education Press (HLS Förlag).

Zeki, S. (1993) *A Vision of the Brain*, Oxford: Blackwell.

Chapter 8

Meaning, mediation and mythology

Susan Wright

From a very early age, children seem instinctively to want to make marks on any available surface, be it the steamy windows of a car, the surface of sand or a blank piece of paper. They do so with great ease and considerable enjoyment, and in the process, explore concepts and discover meaning. Mark-making is a fundamental form of creativity and expression, and is a key precursor to learning sign-making in other forms, such as written words or numbers. Drawing and other art media provide young children with opportunities to share their inner worlds, often more effectively than if communicating through other forms.

In this chapter, I would like to discuss how imagination and creativity are mental capacities that are evoked, stimulated and developed through drawing. Children's drawings involve the depiction of content through graphic and body-based action, while talking about aspects of their artworks and the processes of their creation through a free-form type of narrative. While dialoguing with the materials of art, children discover the power of signs and develop fluid thought processes and skills that equip them to be active creators.

Through the act of drawing, children generate mental images and depict these through configurational[1] signs, shape imaginative narratives, and use gesture and expressive vocalisms[2] to enhance and extend their meaning. These are highly important cognitive and affective processes for young children's development. However, if such processes are not valued in school and culture, and if there is no provision for their development, they typically begin to atrophy later in childhood. Ironically, while pushing children to perform 'academically' in the early stages of schooling, we underestimate them 'intellectually'. Children lose out on the challenges offered through visual thinking and creativity. And as adults, we miss out on naturalistic entry points to learn more about the child, and to learn 'with' them.

Through art, children engage in imaginative play and actively 'construct' their current and expanding understanding of themselves and their worlds, rather than simply becoming the passive recipients of knowledge. The act of drawing becomes an instrument through which children's processes are played out – they can visualise as well as articulate, depict as well as describe. The child's representations of people, places, objects and events are 'told' through 'graphic action' – mark-making that depicts ideas and feelings on paper in real time.

Through such 'graphic telling' or 'visual narrative', children 'conceive' the world, rather than merely render it. Thompson (2002: 190) notes that authentic learning such as this is fuelled by inner passion, which provides its own motivation. It creates a venue that pushes children outside of themselves while connecting new learning to old. Thompson adds that art provides an entry point and a structuring form for children to have a voice and for others to hear that voice: 'A student without a voice is unknown and unknowable' (Thompson 2002: 191).

Giving voice to children through art should be one of the core businesses of early childhood education. Providing children with opportunities to compose through visual narratives complements beliefs about children's right to play (United Nations 1989). Because art is a fundamental means for surfacing the meaning-making and creative competence of young children, it should take prominence in children's learning, knowing, representing and communicating.

Children find 'composing' through art an appealing process, perhaps because it is not strictly rule-bound and hence they feel at liberty to improvise structures. While composing, children develop a repertoire of marks – a 'grammar' of communication – and refine these through practice. By making an object of their own contemplation, they create a symbolic world by manipulating signs and concepts.

Composing: using signs, refining reality

Our representational practices serve a basic human need – to explore and understand the world in meaningful ways, no matter which medium is used to do so (Danesi 2007). Art gives shape to formless ideas. It allows us to create a symbolic world and to 'shape and reshape, revise and revision' (Abbs 2003: 13) our growing awareness of ourselves and the worlds in which we live. Art helps us place our objects, our activities and ourselves in a larger existential framework, through a different way of understanding. This provides a powerful mechanism for reaching the deepest, richest, most abstract aspects of our existence. As Rabiger (2008: 129) states, 'to make fiction is to propose reality'. The process can engender a sense of freedom, release, fulfilment and wholeness because it connects with deep levels of symbol, meaning and emotion.

Dewey (1934/1988) describes thinking in symbols as one of the most sophisticated modes of thought. The human child is endowed with symbol-making propensities and ingenuity to use the system of drawing to manipulate images and concepts and to go beyond reality as immediate experience. Through this process, children join with others who share a culture, who share the same 'imaginative universe' or 'worlds of possibility' (Dyson 1993: 23). This capacity is at its peak in early childhood.

Drawing involves more than simply forming images; it is equated with the capacity to think and to feel. Young children's drawings open a window into their realities and how they shape these. As Cox (2005: 124) notes, the constructive process of drawing helps children to 'purposefully bring shape and order to their experience, and in so doing, their drawing activity is actively defining reality, rather than passively reflecting a "given" reality'. Through drawing and talking, children come to not only 'know' reality, they 'create' it.

Hence, a fundamental component of the work of early childhood educators is to understand a child's drawing in relation to their ideas, actions and feelings. How we may interpret and possibly build upon this in our interactions with young children is an important consideration. One approach is through the application of principles derived from the multidisciplinary field of semiotics. Semiotics assigns much weight to creativity and human inventiveness as factors that shape evolution (Danesi 2007). As an approach to communication, semiotics foregrounds how meaning is not passively absorbed, but arises through the active process of sign creation and interpretation.

In a broad sense, a sign is anything that communicates meaning and 'stands for something else in some way' (Danesi 2007: 29). Signs can take many forms. They can be words, images, sounds, gestures, touch, odours, flavours, acts or objects (Chandler 2002). But signs have no intrinsic meaning in and of themselves. They become signs when we invest them with meaning – when we interpret the sign as 'standing for' or representing something other than itself.

When children draw, they use many 'integrated' signs such as marks on paper, words, gestures, descriptive action, expressive gesticulations, facial expression, dramatisation and vocalisms. Many authors have discussed how talk, drawing and movement are parallel and mutually transformative processes that enrich and inform each other (e.g. Dyson 1986, 1990, 2003; Kendrick and McKay 2004; Kress 1997; Matthews 2004; Short, Kauffman and Kahn 2000; Thompson 1995; Wright 2005, 2007a, 2010). As Linqvist (2001: 8) so eloquently describes this, 'Children draw pictures and tell a story at the same time; they act a role and create their lines as they go along.'

The integration of drawing, talking and role playing becomes what Chandler (2002: 3) calls an 'assemblage of signs', or what Goodman (1976, 1984) referred to as a form of integrated 'languages'. Children are 'playing with the process of signing' which is 'a constructive process of thinking in action' (Cox 2005: 123). They selectively and frequently move from one mode to another – between visual, verbal, physical – to represent and represent what they know most effectively. They may choose to draw it, or to tell it, or to show it through their bodies or to combine these modes. This is a discourse using the 'mixed-media' of image-making, language and graphic and physical action. Through this discourse, children become authors of an integrated text, using a range of voices of communication.

So we must view children's drawings, combined with their spontaneous running narrative and non-verbal communication, as a single multimodal act. The meaning is constituted by its total effect and understood as a complete whole: as a macro event or a macro sign. As such, the artwork-narrative in its entirety is a 'semiotic unit' which carries a larger, unified message. Hence, the component parts of the text cannot be considered one at a time, but instead must be seen as elements of a holistic, single form. Indeed one element, such as a word, cannot be detached from the accompanying graphic mark or physical gesture without impairing the overall meaning of the text. The verbal, graphic and gestural components blend like pieces of a jigsaw puzzle, like voices in a choir.

Yet art is a loosely structured text compared with 'tight-structured' linear texts such as numbers in the decimal system, equations and written language. This is because the elements of art have so many potential relationships. The range of possibilities of signifying meaning through visual elements, such the choice of colour, the use of texture, shape or line, the distance between objects, or the placement of content within a pictorial plane, is virtually infinite.

So we must note the child's use of art elements in relation to words, gesticulations, dramatic vocalisation, pauses or hesitations, and how art elements are combined with language and movement to carry meaning. The work of the visual semiotician Roland Barthes (1973, 1977) provides a useful framework for looking at layers of meaning within texts. At the 'surface level', what is denoted (that is, the literal message) is depicted through content such as people, places, objects and events; at the 'deep level', meaning is connoted (that is, there is a symbolic message), which addresses broader, abstract concepts, ideas and values, such as 'love', 'friendship' or 'justice'. Such concepts are understood as culturally shared meanings (Barthes 1977) and are communicated in visual forms through association.

For instance, in Plate 21 the artist (a boy, age 8.2) denoted pollution through smoke coming out of the airplane, car and electricity plants and acid rain falling from the cloud. The artwork's message functioned through the contrasting of two parks, both with a waterfall and trees. The healthy park on the left is outlined in blue and has blue water and green trees; the unhealthy park on the right is outlined in black and has black water and trees without foliage. There are people and several birds in the healthy park, but there are none in the unhealthy park except one dying bird. The young artist metaphorically described this as 'But over here, that bird's kicking out now that its nest's gone. It can't survive over here, 'cause the trees … some of the trees here are getting cut down.'

Connotative associations with concepts of polluted/unpolluted and preservation/destruction are reflected in what the artwork's people, places, objects and events stand for, which are elaborated in the artist's descriptions:

> I'm going to put a sign there to say that they're [parks, nature] going to be gone …. We're not looking after it. And it's mainly our fault, not the animals'. Humans have been cutting down trees, and um … looting … taking other people's treasures, 'cause they've worked hard all their life to keep the parks a long time. They wanted that [non-polluted park] … but the government didn't listen … and, now it's that [polluted park] …. There is a lot of air pollution, noise pollution and [water] pollution that is making us feel not that good about ourselves.

Connotation is also communicated through aesthetic form, through techniques such as:

- the placement of the two parks in 'the far distance'
- the framing of the two parks with billowing circles, which are metaphorically similar to the cartoon device of 'thought balloons', thus implying a type of reflection on the topic of pollution-destruction
- the contrasting colours of these two frames and the associations of blue with pure, clean water and healthiness, and black with polluted, dirty water and death
- the outline of the dying bird on the right-hand side, which is not coloured in purple like the birds on the left-hand side
- the slumping, foliage-less trees on the right-hand side compared with the strong, upright trees on the left with their dense, healthy foliage.

This artist's combination of visual and verbal content interactively presented his message, through both denotation and connotation. Such crossing over of modes is what makes visual narrative such a powerful medium for children's communication of ideas and expression of feelings.

Visual narratives: configurational signs, causal schemes

Golomb describes children's representational forms as being the outcome of a 'dialogue among the hand, the eye, and the urge to symbolize reality' (1988: 234). Similarly, Vygotsky describes drawing as a kind of 'graphic speech' (Dyson 1982). Yet one cannot overlook the narrative aspects as compelling features of children's meaning-making while drawing.

The work of Bruner (1986), Egan (1999) and Gardner (1983) gives us a more detailed understanding of the function of narrative as a method of thinking, of sharing experience and of assigning meaning. Children and adults alike use narrative as a means of constructing their interior worlds (Goodman in Bruner 1986). The images, messages and insights in these worlds help us to see through the eyes of the creator.

The fantasy-filled narratives concocted by young children seek out the rhythms and patterns of the story form. Yet the content and structure of young children's narratives are often different in important ways from that which typically engages adults (Egan 1988). Structurally, a visual narrative is a spontaneous unfolding of content that moves in and out of loose themes – in whatever order these may evolve. This looseness of structure is associated with the openness of the 'configurational signs' (Arnheim 1969, 1974) that are used in the medium of drawing. Configurational signs are ever-changing. They offer an open invitation to be altered, for children to elaborate upon their forms. Children, for instance, readily add clothing and design features to a drawn figure, depict the person in a different position to show sitting, standing, walking, running or other action, or attach whoosh lines to show that the person is moving quickly through space. Hence, the non-standard nature of configurational signs encourages the invention of new visual forms.

Likewise, the running narrative that accompanies a child's drawing is evolving and open to alteration. It responsively 'mirrors' or accompanies the loose structure of configurational signs. Delightfully, it often includes vocalisms and is accompanied with facial expressions and body-based communication. These and graphic action do the 'talking' of the characters and their experiences as the child depicts, describes, locates, relocates and plays out the plot. At times the child may be one step ahead of us, explaining the meaning of what has just been drawn while simultaneously drawing a new concept (Wright 2007a, 2007b). Likewise, the child may return to previous images to elaborate on ideas with graphic or gestural detail, or extend the narrative in relation to these new concepts.

The plot or theme evolves similarly to how content develops during children's play. This is akin to Egan's (1988) description of how causal schemes determine the organisation of narratives. Egan elaborates that such schemes are 'ordered in sequence by causality' as the plot unfolds, which is determined by 'affective connections' (1988: 11), such as 'these events cause these emotions in people which cause them to do these things which cause these results, and so on' (1988: 24). Ultimately, the overall unit is coherently built, where one scene follows another, taking their places in a larger affective pattern.

The narrative associated with Plate 21 is an example of this, where the artist started with the aeroplane and car to set the context of a polluted, busy world.

There'll be lots of cars, trucks and motorcycles ... noise pollution. And a lot of our seas won't be as nice as they are now. Because ... of ... us ... because whenever we get more buildings, we start not caring about what we already had.

After describing the two parks and how humans have destroyed nature and the government did not pay attention to this, the artist concluded with:

It won't be a nice place to live, if this did happen. There's two people walking here [healthy park]. But there's none here [dead park]. Because they wouldn't want to go here. On this side, they'd come back, but [not] over here.

Such causal-based evolution of plot is an authentic kind of participation for the child, and a concrete form through which we can observe the workings of the child's imagination and the role of imagery in their thinking. Drawing serves as direct documentation of the diverse concepts that children apply to their personal experiences, to more fully grasp their worlds. Indeed, drawing is more than something the child can inhabit or get inside of – it is something the child 'is'.

A blank page can 'become' anything. The infinite possibilities of configurational signs and causal schemes liberate children to construct and re-construct visual arrangements on the page and to 'speak' through the medium of graphic, narrative and embodied communication. Thus, children enter into an interpretive space where they can 'tell themselves about themselves' (Geertz 1971: 26). To be present in that space is to witness the internal worlds that children investigate through art.

Art as a mediating tool

Social constructionist/constructivist pedagogies and socio-cultural perspectives have increased our understanding of how childhood is culturally and historically constructed. Stimulated by the work of Vygotsky (1962, 1967) and Bruner (1996), there is increasing interest in exploring how children's artefacts, such as drawings, are mediating tools for children to create meaning. Drawings provide a naturalistic way to witness children's creative meaning making, because the source of the content emerges from the child's own thoughts, feelings and imagination.

By 'tuning into' (Trevarthen 1995) children's unique forms of representing, and observing what the child actually 'does' when drawing, we can often sustain and extend their interest and involvement. Our presence serves as a form of facilitation. The drawing-sharing experience becomes a 'joint involvement episode' (Schaffer 1992). This requires adult empathy with, first, the reciprocity that occurs between the child and the materials, and second, the reciprocity between the child and us.

At times simply observing, or perhaps commenting in general (such as 'Um-hum' or 'I see') without further elaboration can be adequate to sustain the experience. At other times, we may be interested in finding out more or obtaining a better understanding of what the child is doing. Techniques we might use to go deeper include seeking clarification, using reflective and nudging probes or out-loud thinking (Wright 2010). Yet sensitive, open-ended responses should aim to 'surface' the voice of the child rather than 'lead' it, while also allowing for stretches of silent engagement with the materials without the need to fill the gaps with conversation or questions.

Particularly when a child is engaging in fantasy-based drawing, going with the flow of their thinking will require the adult to 'suspend disbelief' and enter this imaginary world. In such cases, we serve as a type of playmate with the child, and our comments and questions may become a catalyst that enriches the child's play. Our role may be similar to dramatic improvisation, where the interaction becomes relational, interactive, negotiated. This may facilitate and protract the experience, and consequently, the play might be more recursive that if the child were playing alone. During fantasy-based drawing, a child is immersed in an otherworldly state of mind. Hence, we need to recognise the intimate, internalised way the child sustains belief in their characters, settings and actions while in this mind frame.

Rich understandings of the artwork and the creator can arise when we observe the child's various verbal, visual, spatial and bodily-kinaesthetic forms of representation as they unfold. We can come to understand the child's meaning by attending to the graphic 'strategies' that the child uses, the artist's communicative 'intentions', and the 'purposes' and 'functions' of their artwork (Wright 2010). When we search for both the reason and the meaning of the child's work, our attention centres on how the 'features' of the artwork are ascribed aesthetic, intellectual and emotional significance. The aim is to make sense of the meanings of the child's words, images and actions in relation to the text's content and form – how the component parts are combined to make up the whole. Hence, a related aim is to understand the child's 'agency' within the work and the embodied way in which the child communicates their message.

Voice: agency and embodiment

Similarly to how one identifies with characters in a film or novel, children put themselves 'in other people's shoes' when creating fictional characters and plots. This is fantasy-based play on paper, inspired by a blend of personal events, popular media (often fiction) and world events (non-fiction). Children are liberated to draw and tell not only who they are, but also who they would like to be. Thus, art plays a part in the constitution of the self.

Children accept the premise that their work functions as fiction and are comfortable playing with this illusion. As in dramatic play, children use multiple voices and take on many roles as they depict the figures and events within their texts. Hence, they may choose to 'be' all of the characters and can imagine participating in all of the events. This gives each character a form, a type of being. Each is 'enacted' (spoken for) and 'narrated' (spoken about) as the artist moves between characters and events. At times, the same character may 'play' more than one event, and these may be depicted in different spaces on the page. In this sense, each of the characters and events assumes some element of the author's fictional self, similar to how a child, during play, shifts in and out of various roles and events (for instance, 'I'll be the teacher... OK, now I'm the student').

A key component of such engagement is the somatic nature of children's representation. Somatic knowing involves exchanges between the psyche (mind), the soma (body) (Ross 2000) and the 'soul' (Best 2000a, 2000b). When playing, for instance, a child mimics the whooshing sounds of an airplane while gesturing a toy plane's flight-path. The coordination of voicing and gesturing allows the child to 'be' the plane through sound and movement through space. Similarly, while drawing, children often 'play' the characters and embody the events within their artworks.

Children empathise with or imagine themselves in each of the character's positions (or in the position of their drawn animals or inanimate objects). This ability to intuit what that person, animal or object is feeling is a fundamental feature of the arts. In addition to empathy, all forms of representation involve some kind of play or playfulness. Through playfulness, children are exploring ideas somatically. Indeed, in art and other forms of competence that require physical skill (such as acting, sport, playing a musical instrument) there is a dominance of the somatic over the cerebral (Callery 2001). Knowledge is grasped through body-based engagement, through the 'thinking body'.

When drawing, children perform perceptual experiments in their minds and probe their emotions through felt responses to images. Indeed, the dramatic scenes in children's artworks may not always be depicted through spatial or pictorial means. Instead, they may be shown through gesture (as in mime) or through expressive vocalisms (as in radio drama). Gestural representation (Wolf and Davis Perry 1988) or action representation (Matthews 1999) is one of the earliest systems that children employ to symbolise certain movements and events. Bhroin (2007) provides an example of this, where a preschool child seemed to relive a storm as he drew a picture, making banging noises with his crayon. These noises were reminiscent of the sound of hailstones, and the child commented, 'That's the snow coming down from the sky and that's all the cracking on the ground and the stones' (Bhroin 2007: 14).

Barber (2008: 3) describes integrated visual-spatial-kinaesthetic expression such as this as 'a means of direct metaphorical communication'. It is a way of becoming somatically involved via the materials of the drawing medium, and by 'investing these materials with (or discovering within them) the capacity to physically embody the self'. Barber provides an excellent description of this from an adult artist's perspective:

> Just as a skilled and experienced violinist unconsciously presses down, draws, and eases up with the bow in a fully, physically engaged sensitivity to the emotional potency of sound, the artist presses, lifts, and draws the charcoal across and into the page in a visually traced re-experience of the act of touch.
>
> (Barber 2008: 12–13)

A similar somatic expression was demonstrated by a boy (age 6.4) when depicting the sun setting on the left-hand side of the page, then rising on the right-hand side (opposite sides of the world) and then rising again on the left-hand side. This aspect of the artwork, described in greater detail in Wright (2010) (and see Plate 22), functioned as a fade-out and fade-in of daylight. Densely scribbled vertical black lines on the left were used to block out the sun and to make the sky night. Out of this darkness, multiple horizontal lines, starting from the left, change gradually to a single broken line on the right to depict a lessening of darkness into lightness, as in a sunrise. The decrease in intensity of pen stroke is similar to how an orchestral conductor's baton movement gently releases at the end of a phrase. However, instead of demonstrating the emotional potency of sound, the boy's pen stroke configures darkness-to-lightness.

This example, and the incident of the child 'banging' snow marks onto the paper, illustrate how emotional content may be embodied in its 'formal' qualities (in other words graphic, gestural, auditory). Children also show direct, iconic[3] links between perception and embodiment when, for instance, they draw whoosh lines following a moving object, dots or dashes to show the trajectory of a bouncing ball, gesture to mimic the pathway of the movement of an animal across the page, or use word balloons to voice a figure (Wright 2010).

Such physical-spatial-visual interplays often include accompanying vocalisms. 'Vocalisms', which also are iconic signs, include for instance an increase or decrease in the rate or volume of speech during vocal delivery in order to convey urgency, or the opposite, placidity. For example (Wright 2010), one child drew a squiggly line below a figure, while simultaneously saying 'Aaaahhhh' (which decreased in volume and descended in pitch) and gestured downward, to show that a person was falling.

Similarly, 'repeated words' may be used to accompany a child's role play on the page, such as saying 'step, step, step' while mimicking walking up the stairs of a drawn house using their fingers on the page; accentuate some aspect of the child's narrative to give more impact, such as 'He's got great big sleeves. Fat, fat, fat, fat sleeves'; or emphasise a graphic action, such as when colouring the ceiling of the hospital ('colour, colour, colour').

An alternative form of linguistic communication that children use to add expressive value is onomatopoeia – a vocal imitation of the sound associated with something or its action. Onomatopoeia is similar to sound effects on radio drama. For instance, a girl (age 6.7), while describing a mousetrap said, 'and we put some cheese on it, and the mouse runs in, and eats it, and then it goes 'plff' [accompanied by a gesture simulating the rapid slamming of the trap's jaws]! And they're dead. Chops 'em in half.'

Fading in a sunrise and using the 'sound effect' of 'plff' while slamming a mousetrap are examples of somatic forms of expression which may be influenced by children's exposure to media such as film and computer games. Children's frequent experience of a variety of texts may be having an increasing influence on the way they engage with drawing (Wright 2010).

Intertextuality: analogies to other texts

Young children's enacted experiences on paper involve layers of visual action and running narrative working in harmony, simultaneously. Because drawing generally is a solo effort, the child becomes a 'cast of one', simultaneously taking on multiple roles – artist, scripter, narrator, performer, director, audience, critic – and can select when and how to play with all the available 'voices' and how to develop the plot, layer the action and alter the scenery.

The content of such playful encounters seems to be embedded in the themes of a collective youth culture, and may follow some of the conventions of popular media. Indeed, with the extensive exposure that today's children have to a range of texts, such as films, comic books, computer games and TV/DVD, it is not surprising that these texts provide contexts for children to create their own, new texts while drawing. The boundaries between various genres today are quite fluid and are becoming increasingly blurred. Intertextuality[4] appeals to children and adults alike because it taps into our world of lived experience and engages us in 'surrogate emotional experiences' where 'we can temporarily become braver, funnier, stronger, angrier, more beautiful, more vulnerable, or more beset with danger and tragedy' (Rabiger 2008: 175).

It is not difficult to identify instances within children's artworks where the popular media seems to have influenced their thinking and visual narratives. Similar to how a film maker might draw upon myths and legends as a starting point, children either unconsciously or consciously tap into popular culture. Yet, although children may 'borrow' from other texts, each depiction carries a personal imprint where the child infuses their own meaning about the content and how to depict it. This can help children re-vision their own ideas and see life through an alternative prism.

From ancient oral storytelling, to nineteenth-century action-adventure stories for children, to current-day comics, cartoons and cinema, much of popular genre has been rooted in mythical themes (such as heroes battling against evil) and fantasy (such as fairies). Palmer (1986) and Sutton-Smith (1995) have discussed how young children seem to be drawn to such universal themes, which are deeply embedded in children's folk culture. Such themes provide a safe place for children to come to terms with their hopes, fears, wishes and concerns. While borrowing from these themes, children make their own artworks and can grapple with ideas and emotions symbolically. This might include struggles between good and bad, powerful and powerless or cruelty and kindness, which may be resolved through victory or righteousness (cf. Dyson 1997; Golomb 2004; Wilson and Wilson 1977, 1979).

While drawing constructs such as these, the child can shape the fate of the characters and the determinants of power, and select the 'best' methods for playing out particular thoughts and feelings. As they construct content on paper, layers of substance and relationships begin to emerge, which stimulates certain types of problem-solving. The textual features of children's visual narrative include (Wright 2010):

- characters with signifying functions (such as postures, expressions, gestures), linked to their roles, personal qualities, behaviours, goals, speech, actions and subtexts
- objects, places, settings, times, sceneries and décors and associations with these
- structure and flow of information, articulated in space and time (such as themes, plot, events and sequences), which generally is multilinear and integrated
- aesthetic decisions in relation to matters such as:
  - light (day/night) and colour (bright/dull)
  - sound (telling the content; using expressive vocalisms and onomatopoeia; using speech balloons to 'audiate' the characters)
  - action (gesture and iconic devices such as whoosh lines to 'animate' the work)
  - time (compression, flashbacks and flashforwards), such as cutting between scenes (as in the example of fading in the sunrise)
  - space (front/behind, close/distant, above/below), orientational metaphors (vertical/horizontal axes), size differentiations and foci (for example close-ups, or in the distance).

These features are incorporated in children's 'thought-in-action episodes' which evolve in bits and pieces in relation to what the child's imagination suggests, and may change as the child simultaneously 'edits' the visual narrative. For instance, within one drawing episode, the child may return to graphic content to elaborate ideas through visual, verbal or gestural detail, which may expand the theme. This revisiting of ideas provides opportunities to build the plot thread and to add coherence between plot points. Hence, the compositional development is an ongoing process of revision.

The textual space is one in which the child can plan, enact and examine worlds from the inside. Such imaginary worlds can be played and replayed, which empowers the child to make choices about coherence and disruption (Dyson 1997; Sutton-Smith 1995), about power and powerlessness, security and danger, cleverness and stupidity, good and evil and a range of other issues. Indeed, the themes of children's work often connote underlying 'ideologies' such as bravery, honesty, courage, security and hope. This often involves playing out of binary 'oppositions' such as dominance-submission, real-imaginary or natural-supernatural.

Binaries: mythology and imagination

Binary oppositions are young children's first logical operation (Lévi-Strauss 1966), and help children categorise and generate order out of complex human experience (Jakobson and Halle 1956). For thousands of years, in societies around the world, binaries have been used in representational practices, such as oral storytelling, to help people understand constructs such as good-evil, self-other, subject-object, masculine-feminine, light-dark, body-mind, positive-negative, nature-history, sacred-profane, heaven-hell (Danesi 2007). Historically, binaries have been reflected in the myths, legends, folklore and fairy tales that were passed down from generation to generation (Bettelheim 1976; Lévi-Strauss 1969).

Today, the textual features of popular media, such as H*arry Potter* and *Lord of the Rings*, continue to be based on powerful conflicts between good and evil, security and danger, courage and cowardice, hope and despair. Likewise, children explore similar binaries when they draw. Binaries lend a hand to children's development of 'abstract' thought and personalised 'theories' about the real world in relation to their imaginary ones. Imagination is a fascinating feature of children's thinking, which accounts for their easy engagement with both fantasy and exotic real-life content.

Fantasy-based content may lead to the use of mediating concepts and the development of exotic characters which are both human and other (such as aliens or fairies) or natural creatures that use language, wear clothes and have emotions (Egan 1999). But characters such as these do not only make for a gripping story, they serve a deeper, more fundamental role in children's cognitive and moral development.

One boy (age 8.5), for instance, depicted a world in which aliens and humans cohabited in the year 5000 (Wright 2005, 2007a, 2007b). He embraced good plot-development techniques by establishing subtexts where characters' values were illustrated in their behaviours and through tensions between their inner and outer worlds. This is illustrated in an excerpt below, where humans are onboard a spaceship, controlled by aliens, which is:

> powered by some sort of thing from humans, either fear, scared or surprise. And they keep humans onboard and make them scared, so they mostly do it surprise. So they surprise them and all of those things help control it. And right now they are on a case and chasing a police alien, but [he's] a smuggler [of] drugs. He is pretending he is a police man, but he has forgotten that police men can go to jail for drug smuggling. They've got 50 humans on board the ship and are making them surprised. They are so good they are going faster and can catch up.

As illustrated here, and as Egan points out, 'young children have no difficulty being engaged by the weirdest creatures in the most exotic locales' (1999: 41). This boy's use of quasi-human figures offered him opportunities to polarise between real and fantasy worlds. His narrative made a suggestive resemblance between events and characters with another, more abstract level of meaning. Such ideas were shown through his description of the humans onboard being given 'fear or surprise' to 'power' the spaceship and make it fly faster. Although the young artist did not use abstract terms explicitly, his concept of psychic energy was tied to 'affective abstraction'.

When children work within a mythical plane, their plots act as a frame in which they can enact their sense of life's causes and effects such as this, with imaginative dabs of fanciful ideas thrown in. Children push beyond the boundaries of realism, where their dialectical worlds become organised around moral imperatives, and where heroes with great courage, strength and bravery are celebrated for upholding human ideals such as honesty and justice. Modern-day children and adults, like their ancestors, 'need heroic stories to subconsciously "make things right" in human affairs, at least in the realm of the imagination' (Danesi 2007: 125). Through their visual narratives, children can associate with the confidence, ingenuity, strength or whatever of their heroic characters, and can transcend the hero's constraints, arising triumphantly.

Hence, an effective artwork, like a good film, can lead children to experience new conditions, to expand their minds and hearts. Children, like adults, have a desire to experience, if only temporarily, the world of others. This is why drawing is such a powerful medium. Young artists can project into the characters' predicaments, and multiple perspectives arise because 'each character sees differently' (Rabiger 2008: 178).

Summary and conclusions

When children draw, they learn how to differentiate the meanings of separate signs and to see connections between them. For instance, they will make a mark, describe it in words and demonstrate their ideas through movement or gesture. This inter-relationship between language, image and action becomes articulated within the overall text to carry meaning. Indeed, children effortlessly weave between words, images, touch, gesture, vocalisms, onomatopoeia and dramatisation, where the content of one sign is mapped onto the expressive plane of another (Siegel 1995).

Young children's processes of learning the graphic features of drawing takes place in parallel with the process of learning letters, words and numerical symbols. Yet, the 'inter-related' way in which children learn these symbol systems can often be overlooked. In schools, child-centred explorations of mark-making begin to lose ground as the cultural expectation for children to develop numeracy and literacy skills starts to take precedence. Numbers and words begin to assume a privileged status. This is because there is an assumption that thinking is primarily linguistic and numeric, that forming letters and numbers is a 'higher level' ability (Anning and Ring 2004) and that 'skill in reading and writing is a precondition for all meaningful learning' (Gross 1973: 202).

However, drawing and the ensuing talk between children or between adults and children supports the evolution of later writing (Dyson 1993). Drawing is a key precursor to learning sign-making in other forms. Indeed, children's competence in the linguistic mode occurs in parallel with and often is 'built upon' knowledge and skills acquired through graphic-narrative-embodied communication. This position is supported by Thompson (2002: 193), who argues that literacy grows out of non-verbal contexts of play and physical activities, such as the arts. Thompson elaborates that 'rarely acknowledged, the whole language movement's most fundamental tenets rest on the longstanding practice of good art education' and that schools should 'see art education as the model for teaching in all of our disciplines' (2002: 194).

The act of drawing does not function simply to support other forms of learning. Instead, drawing offers a medium for children to think visually and creatively, and an avenue for them to illustrate their competences. Drawing involves more than simply forming images – it is equated with the capacity to think. Hence, it is highly significant as an aesthetic, creative and cognitive meaning-making medium in its own right. Through drawing, children do not only come to know reality, they create it.

Contrary to the 'folk' belief that drawing serves only occupational, expressive or recreational purposes, and hence should take a subservient role to that of 'literacy' and the teaching of what children do not yet know, I am arguing that drawing surfaces what children already know, what they are grappling with and what they are motivated to explore further. This is because drawing is a self-motivated mediating tool for children to develop a repertoire of marks and a 'grammar' of visual, symbolic communication through the manipulation of signs and concepts. The depiction of imaginary worlds while dialoguing with the materials through a free-form type of narrative is akin to play – it 'lets in more meaning' (Pahl and Rowsell 2005: 43) than the more conventional methods of teaching and learning.

Through art, children can drill down to an abstract level of thinking and express sophisticated meaning, the depth of which can often surprise and move us. Sometimes children's ideas stem from popular culture, which provides a safe context for them to create their own fantasy texts – they can temporarily re-vision life through an alternative prism and experience surrogate emotions. This can help them come to terms with their hopes, fears, wishes and concerns, and explore underlying ideologies such as bravery, honesty, courage and security. Children are liberated to draw and tell not only who they are, but also who they would like to be. Thus, art plays a part in the constitution of the self.

There is no doubt that finding time to listen to children's visual narratives may be challenging in teachers' busy schedules, but it is time well spent. Visual narratives offer an opportunity to sit with children, to notice the worlds they create, and to savour and preserve the wonders they are discovering. By doing so, teachers develop professional knowledge about how children's thinking and knowing develops, and can 'ponder on their work and their interactions with children' (Nutbrown 2006: 23). A common mantra in early childhood education is to 'start where the child is' and to build the curriculum and pedagogy around this. A serious interest in children's semiotic dispositions and their sign-making processes and messages can lead to pedagogies, curricula and momentous projects that evolve from and are matched with the potentials and abilities of the child.

Such an approach is different from the common literacy-centric practice in schools of simply asking children to tell or write a story to accompany their already completed artworks. This is because the content of post hoc stories does not capture the 'form' in which the holistic text was composed. It is isolated from the child's real-time 'playing on paper' within the composition's interpretive space, and the associated narrative, gestural and emotional undertones and connotations that accompany this. Hence, ideally we should aim to schedule time to witness individual children's holistic composition, and capture the 'soul' of their in situ facial expressions, vocalisations, dramatisations, gestural enactment and personal engagement with the creative act of meaning-making. Such multi-modal texts can never be repeated exactly the same again. Like good jazz improvisations, they are spontaneous and situated in the moment. As Egan (1999: 19) writes, 'the living word' of young children is not like the distanced and cooled word of the written text or the type of learning that often takes place in traditional, literacy-oriented school curricula.

Hence, when we have the privilege of witnessing children's 'live' acts of representation, we grasp the unfolding of signs within the creators' overall shaping of the text. By watching the graphic depiction, listening to the narrative and noting the gestures and expressive vocalisms of the child, we come closer to understanding the holistic meaning-making act. The work is a composition in progress, building layer upon layer of characterization, settings, frames of movement and integrated scenes. There may be many shifts between fiction and non-fiction, and between graphic, narrative and embodied modes as the artwork's purposes and functions evolve.

Thus, our attention to the child's 'authorial intentions', and how the features of the drawing-telling 'function', are key components for understanding the child's meaning. This provides an entry point and a structuring form for children to have a voice and for us to hear and celebrate that voice. This should be the essence of education.

Notes

1 Configurational signs are similar to their natural referents – a child's drawn tree, for instance, resembles what they see in nature.
2 Vocalisms are emphases through change in pitch, volume or speed of speech.
3 Iconic signs resemble the objects and actions to which they refer, either directly or metaphorically.
4 Blurring of boundaries, called *intertextuality*, credits audiences with the necessary experience to understand that one text is alluding to other texts (Chandler 2007: 200), as in animated films.

References

Abbs, P. (2003) *Against the Flow: Education, the arts and postmodern culture*, London: Routledge Falmer.

Anning, A. and Ring, K. (2004) *Making Sense of Children's Drawings*, Berkshire: Open University Press.

Arnheim, R. (1969) *Visual Thinking*, Berkeley, Calif.: University of California Press.

Arnheim, R. (1974) *Art and Visual Perception*, Berkeley, Calif.: University of California Press.

Barber, D. (2008) 'Somaesthetic awareness and artistic practice: a review essay' (of R. Shusterman (2008) *Body Consciousness: A philosophy of mindfulness and somaesthetics*, Cambridge, New York: Cambridge University Press), *International Journal of Education and the Arts*, 9(1). Available at http://www.ijea.org/v9r1, (accessed 8 December 2008).

Barthes, R. (1973) *Mythologies*, London: Fontana.

Barthes, R. (1977) *Image–Music–Text*, London: Fontana.

Best, J. (2000a) 'Arts, words, intellect, emotion. Part 1: toward artistic mindedness', *Arts Education Policy Review*, 102(6), pp. 3–11.

Best, J. (2000b) 'Arts, words, intellect, emotion. Part 2: toward artistic mindedness', *Arts Education Policy Review*, **102**(10), pp. 2–10.

Bettelheim, B. (1976) *The Uses of Enchantment*, London: Random House/New York: Vintage.

Bhroin, M. N. (2007) '"A slice of life": the interrelationships among art, play and the "real" life of the young child', *International Journal of Education and the Arts*, **8**(16). Available at: http://www.ijea.org/v8n16/ (accessed 10 December 2008).

Bruner, J. (1986) *Actual Minds, Possible Worlds*, Cambridge, Mass.: Harvard University Press.

Bruner, J. (1996) *The Culture of Education*, Cambridge, Mass.: Harvard University Press.

Callery, D. (2001) *Through the Body: A practical guide to physical theatre*, New York: Routledge.

Chandler, D. (2002) *Semiotics: The basics*, London: Routledge.

Chandler, D. (2007) *Semiotics: The basics*, 2nd edn., Abingdon: Routledge.

Cox, S. (2005) 'Intention and meaning in young children's drawing', *Journal of Art and Design Education*, **24**(2), pp. 115–25.

Danesi, M. (2007) *The Quest for Meaning: A guide to semiotic theory and practice*, Toronto: University of Toronto Press.

Dewey, J. (1934, 1988) *Art as Experience*, New York: Perigee Books.

Dyson, A. H. (1982) 'The emergence of visible language: interrelationships between drawing and early writing', *Visible Language*, **6**, pp 360–81.

Dyson, A. H. (1986) 'The imaginary worlds of childhood: a multimedia presentation', *Language Arts*, **63**, pp. 779–808.

Dyson, A. H. (1990) 'Symbol makers, symbol weavers: how children link play, pictures, and print', *Young Children*, **45**(2), pp. 50–7.

Dyson, A. H. (1993) 'From prop to mediator: the changing role of written language in children's symbolic repertoires', pp. 21–41 in B. Spodek and O. N. Sarachio (eds), *Yearbook in Early Childhood Education: Language and literacy in early childhood education, Vol. 4*, New York: Teachers College Press.

Dyson, A. H. (1997) *Writing Superheroes: Contemporary childhood, popular culture, and classroom literacy*, New York: Teachers College Press.

Dyson, A. H. (2003) '"Welcome to the jam", popular culture, school literacy, and the making of childhoods', *Harvard Educational Review*, **73**(3), pp. 323–61. Available at: http://www.edreview.org/harvard03/2003/fa03/f03dyson/htm (accessed 2 December 2004).

Egan, K. (1988) *Primary Understanding: Education in early childhood*, New York/London: Routledge.

Egan, K. (1999) *Children's Minds, Talking Rabbits and Clockwork Oranges: Essays on education*, New York: Teachers College Press.

Gardner, H. (1983) *Frames of Mind: The theory of multiple intelligence*, New York: Basic Books.

Geertz, C. (1971) *Myth, Symbol, and Culture*, New York: Norton.

Golomb, C. (1988) 'Symbolic inventions and transformations in child art', pp. 222–36 in K. Egan and D. Nadaner (eds), *Imagination and Education*, Milton Keynes: Open University Press.

Golomb, C. (2004) *The Child's Creation of a Pictorial World*, 2nd edn, London: Lawrence Erlbaum.

Goodman, N. (1976) *Languages of Art*, London: Oxford University Press.

Goodman, N. (1984) *Of Mind and Other Matters*, Boston, Mass.: Harvard University Press.

Gross, L. P. (1973) 'Art as the communication of competence', paper presented at a Symposium on Communication and the Individual in Contemporary Society. Available at: http://www.ucalgary.ca/~rseiler/grosslp.htm (accessed 20 March 2007).

Jakobson, R. and Halle, M. (1956) *Fundamentals of Language*, The Hague: Mouton.

Kendrick, M. and McKay, R. (2004) 'Drawings as an alternative way of understanding young children's constructions of literacy', *Journal of Early Childhood Literacy*, 4(1), pp. 109–27.

Kress, G. (1997) *Before Writing: Rethinking the paths to literacy*, London: Routledge.

Lévi-Strauss, C. (1966) *The Savage Mind*, Chicago, Ill.: University of Chicago Press.

Lévi-Strauss, C. (1969) *The Raw and the Cooked*, New York: Harper & Row.

Linqvist, G. (2001) 'When small children play: how adults dramatise and children create meaning', *Early Years*, 21(1), pp. 7–14.

Matthews, J. (1999) *Helping Children to Draw and Paint in Early Childhood*, London: Hodder & Stoughton.

Matthews, J. (2004) 'The art of infancy', pp. 253–298 in A. Kindler, E. Eisner and M. Day (eds), *Learning in the Visual Arts: Handbook of research and policy in art education*, Canada: University of British Columbia.

Nutbrown, C. (2006) *Threads of Thinking*, 3rd edn, London: Sage.

Pahl, K. and Rowsell, J. (2005) *Literacy and Education: Understanding the new literacy studies in the classroom*, London: Paul Chapman.

Palmer, P. (1986) *The Lively Audience: A study of children around the TV set*, Sydney: Allyn & Unwin.

Rabiger, M. (2008) *Directing: Film Techniques and Aesthetics*, 4th edn, Burlington, Mass.: Focal Press.

Ross, J. (2000) 'Arts education in the information ages: a new place for somatic wisdom', *Arts Education Review*, 101(6), pp. 27–32.

Schaffer, H. R. (1992) 'Joint involvement episodes as contexts for cognitive development', in H. McGurk (ed.), *Childhood and Social Development: Contemporary perspectives*, Hove: Lawrence Erlbaum.

Short, K. G., Kauffman, G. and Kahn, L. H. (2000) '"I just need to draw": responding to literature across multiple sign systems', *The Reading Teacher*, 54(2), pp. 160–72.

Siegel, M. (1995) 'More than words: the generative power of transmediation for learning', *Canadian Journal of Education*, 20, pp. 455–75.

Sutton-Smith, B. (1995) 'Play as performance, rhetoric, and metaphor', *Play and Culture*, 2, pp. 189–92.

Thompson, C. H. (1995) '"What shall I draw today?" Sketchbooks in early childhood', *Art Education*, 48(5), pp. 6–11.

Thompson, D. K. (2002) 'Early childhood literacy education, wakefulness, and the arts', pp. 185–194 in L. Bresler and C. M. Thompson (eds), *The Arts in Children's Lives*, Netherlands: Kluwer Academic.

Trevarthen, C. (1995) 'The child's need to learn a culture', *Children in Society*, 9(1), pp. 5–19.

United Nations (1989) *Convention on the Rights of the Child*. Available at: http://www. unicef.org/crc (accessed 6 January 2008).

Vygotsky, L. (1962) *Thought and Language*, Cambridge, Mass.: MIT Press.

Vygotsky, L. (1967) 'Play and its role in the mental development of the child', *Soviet Psychology*, **5**(3), pp. 6–18. Reproduced as pp. 537–54 in J. S. Bruner, A. Jolly and K. Sylva (eds) (1978) *Play: Its role in development and evolution*, Harmondsworth: Penguin.

Wilson, B. and Wilson, M. (1977) 'An iconoclastic view of the imagery sources in the drawings of young people', *Art Education*, **30**, pp. 4–12.

Wilson, B. and Wilson, M. (1979) 'Children's story drawings: reinventing worlds', *School Arts*, **78**(8), pp. 6–11.

Wolf, D. and Davis Perry, M. (1988) 'From endpoints to repertoires: some new conclusions about drawing development', *Journal of Aesthetic Education*, **22**(1), pp. 17–34.

Wright, S. (2005) 'Children's multimodal meaning-making through drawing and storytelling', *Teachers College Record*, 15 September. Available at: http://www.tcrecord.org (ID no: 12175).

Wright, S. (2007a) 'Graphic-narrative play: authoring through multiple texts and fluid structures', *International Journal of Education and the Arts*, **8**(8), pp. 1–27.

Wright, S. (2007b) 'Young children's meaning-making through drawing and 'telling': analogies to filmic textual features', *Australian Journal of Early Childhood*, **32**(4), pp. 37–48.

Wright, S. (2010) *Understanding Creativity in Early Childhood: Meaning-making and children's drawings*, London: Sage.

Chapter 9

Children's creativity with time, space and intensity: foundations for the temporal arts

Susan Young

If asked how many senses we have, most people in Western European and North American societies would answer five: sight, hearing, touch, taste and smell. And it is generally agreed that of these five senses, the visual dominates (Pink 2006). This domination of the visual results in a tendency to stand back and look at the world, in a detached way, and to fix and objectify what we see. A good example of this is the long-standing tradition in early years practice of observing children and noting their behaviour. We also use visual analogies to extend into understanding, saying, for example, 'I see' when we understand. These analogies emphasise the strength of the visual in our thinking. However, recently there has been increased interest, introduced through the work of anthropologists, in cultures where different sensory categories, different sensory priorities and different forms of sensory integration seem to prevail (Classen 1993). Geurts, for example, spent time with the Anlo-Ewe people in southeastern Ghana and came to understand that for these people it was the sense of proprioception, the internal sense of bodily awareness and balance that was dominant and infiltrated deeply into their culture (Geurts 2003). Proprioception and its partner kinaesthesia are senses not usually mentioned in the list of five.

Recognising that sensory categories, and how we prioritise them, are not universal givens but are culturally constructed can lead us to acknowledge how these constructions carry certain limitations and, from this, to imagine alternatives. If the kinaesthetic embodied senses, including touch, had a more dominant place in our sensory orientation to the world, then awareness of our own physicality and how we relate physically to others might play a more prominent role. Likewise, if the sense of hearing took a more dominant position alongside the visual, then the immediacy and contact of sound and listening might be stronger. And all these senses, kinaesthesia, touch and hearing are associated with closeness and immediacy, with relating to others, in marked contrast with the separation and detachment that tends to be the result of a primarily visual orientation to the world.

So what do these two introductory paragraphs tell us that is of central importance for the chapter that follows, concerned as it is with children's creativity with time, space and intensity? Its importance is twofold. First, we become more alert to the fact that aural and embodied experience can tend to be neglected in preference for the visual; something that has serious implications for the conceptualising, valuing, interpreting and planning of creative activity in educational contexts. One aim of this chapter is to explain this version of creativity and to encourage reconsideration of the way creativity tends to be conceptualised. A more expansive view of creativity is required. Second, a focus on aural and embodied experience reminds us that these are the sensory experiences that are most concerned with close and intimate contact and expressive communication between people. A second aim of this chapter is to propose that expressive, non-verbal communication is a generative resource for creative activity. The non-verbal communication between infants and their caregivers has been extensively researched over the last thirty years. The understanding, explanations and theories arising from this field of research can, I suggest, provide an understanding of some of the generative resources for creative activity on which children draw. Theoretical frameworks for understanding children's artistic and creative activity have tended, in much research and practice, to be drawn from adult activity, taking these endpoints as yardsticks against which to look retrospectively and assess the competence of children. So, to take one example, young children's improvised music is often analysed according to criteria of rhythm and melody that are conventional to western art music: that is music descending from the classical tradition which uses written staff notation. But if we genuinely wish to understand children's creative activity on their terms, then it makes little sense to interpret their work against criteria drawn from adult arts practice and every sense to interpret their activity from precursors in earliest childhood.

This next example illustrates both aims of the chapter. It is drawn from a study of everyday home life among two year olds (Young and Gillen 2010). From this study we obtained a video recording of an Italian mother sitting in the kitchen of her apartment with her daughter on her knee and playing a simple lap game. The game involves a short, made-up rhyme of simple repeated words in which she holds her daughter Beatrice's hands, rocking her back and forth three times and at the climax pretending to let her go. Beatrice tips back but is safely caught in her mother's firm, two-handed grasp behind her shoulders. Her mother emphasises the thrill of the momentary loss of balance with a quiet, vocalised shudder. Beatrice asks for the rhyme game to be repeated. It is repeated, with more intensity this time. And again, a third time, tipping back even further to increase the excitement that accompanies the danger of falling. The simple rule of 'again but a bit more' often underpins children's game sequences, extended through repetition with variation. The final turn arouses Beatrice to a pitch of squealing excitement. The mother decides enough is enough and calms Beatrice down by distracting her attention to a hair slide. This little game encapsulates much that will be explored in this chapter: playing with the sense of balance, bodily contact and touch, rhythmic movement and timing, vocalisations, intimacy, emotion, trust, and the repetitive form of a game that rises to a pitch of excitement and then calms. The game is, in a way, a small improvised art form, a dance, a piece of music, a little narrative with a temporal structure that is emotionally satisfying to both and strengthens their bond.

Essentially this lap-game is non-linguistic and relies on embodied sensory modes of contact, interaction and communication. Although Beatrice's mother chants some simple words, they are just part of the whole blended multi-modal mix, more important for their rhythmic etching in sound of the movement than for their denotional meaning. Donald (1991), theorising the evolution of culture and cognition, has proposed that humans appear to possess a level of cognitive competence that is non-linguistic. This he terms 'mimetic culture', and he suggests it is rooted in inter-sensory, gestural and dance-like use of the body. Since Donald further suggests that mimetic acts by their very nature 'inherently possess the potential to communicate' (1991: 114), then to describe the lap game played by Beatrice and her mother as 'mimetic' seems apt.

In educational practice what tends to predominate is not the non-linguistic 'mimetic culture' but a visual culture which leans on observation and focuses on the static, concrete world (Bresler 2004). It results in versions of creativity that similarly focus on the object world in material or imagined form and are concerned with forms of thought and dispassionate, cerebral ideas that can be fixed in time and space. Aural and bodily creativity, as expressed in mimetic acts, with their immediacy, their capacity to draw in others, their fluidity in time and space, leaves no visible trace on paper or in materials. The invisible aural and embodied world – dynamic and articulated in time/space relationships – receives less attention.

Donald's mimetic culture has many similarities with a form of understanding Egan terms 'somatic' (1997). Somatic understanding, according to Egan, is prelinguistic and:

> deliver[s] a distinctively human "take" on the world prior to, and subsequently underlying later language developments. That is, for all our later cognitive development, we remain creatures whose understanding of the world is profoundly shaped by our particular kind of bodies and senses.
>
> (Egan 2003: 30)

There are expectations that children will talk about their experiences, crystallising ideas in language terms, and extend their thinking by collaborating through language. 'Mimetic' or 'somatic culture', whichever of these two closely related terms we select, provide something outside and beyond language, something foundational. Not foundational in the sense of being a prior stage that is superseded by language, but foundational in the sense of being a basic generative resource for creative imaginations; and, moreover, not just in individual experience but in the wider cultural context. As Egan puts it, 'a basic element of [that] wider cultural context for modern humans is the persistence within the architecture of our minds of a prelinguistic somatic understanding or mimetic culture' (1997: 170).

As this chapter continues three more examples ground and illustrate the discussion. This work is all taken from early years practice but the broader ideas and propositions that I draw from the examples are widely applicable to all ages. These three examples, together with the example already given of the lap-game, are taken from four separate and very different research projects, united by their focus on young children and time-based arts of music, theatre and creative play. As each example arrives it expands the scope of the chapter and opens out another area for discussion, while at the same time contributing to the main theme of creativity as rooted in non-verbal, embodied expressivity which I argue is a fount of the temporal arts.

The first study of the three focused on young children of three to four years old playing spontaneously on educational percussion instruments in a nursery setting in London, UK (Young 2000). The children were free to come and go to the music area and initiate play with the instruments. Although at the start of the project I was interested in how the children played with the instruments individually, the study increasingly became involved in the role of adult as play partner. It found, perhaps not surprisingly, that if the adult joins in with playing on the children's terms in imitative turn-taking, the music play episodes developed in imaginative and interesting ways. The next project was commissioned by a theatre company based in Edinburgh, Scotland who were developing theatre for under three year olds (Young and Powers 2009). As researchers we studied how the early exploratory theatre pieces engaged the children and from these analyses, suggested ways in which the theatre team of actor, musician, designer and dancer might develop their work. A final project explored approaches to working in creative play in children's centres serving majority Muslim communities in four cities in the United Kingdom (Young and Street 2010). The project started with an interview study of eighty-six Muslim women from diverse ethnic backgrounds, mostly carried out by women from within their own communities, in which we enquired about their own perspectives on playing with their children and asked some more specific questions to gather their views on aspects of creative arts areas such as music, visual arts and dance.

As a brief aside, before the next example, one of the challenges of writing about children's creative, time-based activity is the clumsiness of attempting to describe mimetic activity in words. I face a dilemma. If I leave out the detail then I risk superficiality and not conveying what is most important, but the descriptive detail risks clogging up the reading with words. What is more, the words then need to be re-imagined by the reader, not simply as a visualisation, but by animating and sensing the movement sympathetically and auralising the sounds.

Making music

The purpose in presenting this next example is to illustrate the theme of rhythmic, communicative activity first illustrated in the lap-game and transferred now to play with musical instruments (Young 2000). Manu has just turned four and is sitting on the nursery floor, by the side of a wooden xylophone holding two beaters, one in each hand. He is joined by Linda, the nursery teacher, who sits at the xylophone directly opposite him. She also takes up two beaters, one in each hand. Manu plays one clean strike on the xylophone and then looks up at Linda. Linda, looking continuously at Manu, plays a single strike in response. He replies with one more strike, looking down at the xylophone to play and back up at Linda afterwards. He thus coordinates his gaze between looking at the instrument to play and at Linda to maintain contact. This turn-taking of single sounds continues for a little longer. Manu changes to a very slow slide of the beater across the keys producing an almost inaudible glissando sound from the xylophone. He quietly vocalises as he makes this sound. Linda watches and listens carefully and when he has finished, lifting his beater slowly and deliberately from the xylophone, she plays a matching glissando, matching in dynamic, in pace, in the number of keys it slides over. Manu watches her beater intently and then looks back up at Linda. She waits. He then introduces a new idea, a slow, steady-beat tapping with one hand on one key; eight strikes in total, each time the beater arcing up and down above the keys in an exact same pace to produce the regularity of sounds. He then changes hands (a beater held in each hand) attempting to do the same pattern with his other hand. He struggles a little to play with the same exactness of pace and volume using his non-dominant hand. Again, Linda has watched and listened and responds with an imitation of his idea. Manu takes his turn when she has finished. He returns to the glissando idea, but this time concludes it with a small sequence of taps. At that point, a child calls them both from across the room. Manu looks around. Interrupted, he drops the beater and joins the other child.

Such a simple sequence was typical of many that began to evolve in the nursery where the study was being carried out (Young 2000, 2005a). We were interested in how, if an adult participates as play-partner in children's self-initiated play with instruments, it resulted in changes to the way they played. The usual educational practice is to leave children to their own devices, born of the belief that free, playful exploration is the source of creativity and adults should not intervene. The study included comparisons of children's play with instruments with or without an adult play-partner to confirm the differences. Linda, a practitioner of long experience, was following a simple protocol to imitate the children's play with the xylophone, and never to initiate. Far from playing randomly and somewhat sporadically as they characteristically did when playing alone, the children's playing with a partner started to evolve around sequences of structural ideas. In this example, the partner was an adult practitioner, but as partnered play was modelled, the children also started to play with one another, producing similar rhythmic successions (Young 2008).

From this study, we concluded that the desire to connect with others, the affirmation of being listened to and played with, stimulated the generation of expressive playing ideas that could maintain the musical interaction. A well-judged balance of repetition with variation was engaging and sustaining. The simple one-strike turn-taking at the start of their playing together enabled each to match and time to the other and settle into the collaboration. Had this first phase continued for too long, interest would have waned. Manu changed to a new idea. Later the linking together of two ideas – the glissando with the regular tapping idea – ensured coherence with novelty. From the music-making of all twenty-six children in the nursery we could distil common processes of repeating ideas, sequencing, chaining, varying them and combining.

Creativity in its broadest sense across all temporal arts activity rests on introducing novelty in the form of a new idea while remaining consistent with what has come before. The balance of variation with repetition over time has to be well judged however. Just as in the Italian lap-game, variations introduce interest, can generate anticipation and thus sustain the play. But too much variation would result in a loss of continuity. Importantly, these music-making processes emerged in partnered play rather than individual play. From this study I proposed that the interpersonal dimension, the desire to make and sustain sociable contact through non-verbal means, through sound and gesture, is a source of music-making ideas (Young 2003b, 2005a).

There is another key point to add. Only through recognising Manu's intention to make a genuinely musical event could we begin to understand children's unconventionally expressed music in a more profound way, and avoid dismissing their play as mere noise, as 'messing about', and risking an underestimation of the abilities of their time-based, musical thinking. Receiving children's performance activity, whatever the medium, as intentionally creative legitimates it. The important message to carry over in to practice is that if we want to understand the nature of children's creative expression we need to recognise, respect and receive their intentions as legitimate, and accord their performances the same status we accord to those of adults.

These structural processes emerging and identified from the partnered music play in the nursery have their counterparts in music, dance and improvised theatre made at all ages and in culturally diverse forms (Sawyer 2006). An initial period to settle in to playing, moving or story-telling together will precede the first exposition of an idea that is relatively straightforward, to be followed by newer ideas in balances of innovation and repetition appropriate to the genre, its style, the occasion, the participants and so on. At root, the human need to engage with others, to interact and share pleasure with them, as we saw in the little lap-game at the start of the chapter as well as Manu's music-making with Linda, is a motivational force for the creation of ideas in time-based arts.

Conventional conceptions of creativity, particularly those arising from the practices of western performance arts in music or theatre, have tended to be individualistic, solitary and cerebral – emphasising detachment – and as such to downplay the social, communicative and embodied nature of these art forms (Blacking 1989; Sawyer 2006).

An approach to music-making with young children as improvisatory play-partnering goes against the grain of usual practice. In educational settings music is typically a large-group performance activity, dominated by song-singing, in which an adult leads and guides the activity and the children participate in a conforming and regulated way (Young 2003a, 2005b). There is little or no room for children to make their own contribution. A revised conception of music with young children as a collaborative music-making process places the adult as a musically playful partner, who listens, observes in an embodied, empathetic way and takes up their musical ideas, assisting children to weave them into music-making events. Teaching is transformed as it takes on a more open-ended, improvisational and dialogical quality.

Achieving that improvisational and dialogical quality calls for receptivity and responsiveness – the reciprocity it requires – to be conveyed through all our senses, including bodily empathy. Linda watched Manu with that continuous gaze which is characteristic of adults working with younger children, not to observe in an objective way, but to gather in the gamut of expressed body language and its tenor, timing and dynamic, blended with the sounds made on the xylophone. Recently there has been an increased emphasis on the importance of children's voices and listening to children in English educational and other contexts (Clark and Moss 2001). While this is valuable and can relate to listening to children as creative makers, its translation into practice tends to emphasise listening to children talking, rather than 'listening' in the sense of being openly receptive with all senses to non-linguistic, mimetic activity (Young 1996). A dialogical pedagogy for expressive performance arts calls for educators to engage in joint exchanges with children where they feel and actively engage with the sympathetic response that the child's actions and feelings invite.

Important too, in Manu's example, are the affordances of the instrument (including the beaters) in enabling certain forms of expressive playing –

and likewise constraining others (Young 2000). As the study progressed we found that the xylophone, with its flat surface of wooden playing keys, offered a sufficient range of possibilities for the children to be musically inventive. It was not an ideal instrument, but it sufficed. Notice too that the children had two beaters, one in each hand. Two-handed play immediately increased the possibilities for playing movements. Simple shake and tap percussion instruments, which are the usual clutter for music in educational settings, are too limited to engender interesting play and betray limited expectations of children as music-makers. There are, similarly, instruments that would be too complex, offering overwhelming options, or where children's attention would be diverted to the technical demands of producing sounds at the expense of the interpersonal dimension. Improvising music with instruments demands this balance and blend of movement as skill-technique to produce sound and movement as gestural with communicatively expressive intent. In this way, the morphology of instruments and its contribution to inventiveness is an interesting and important dimension of creativity to consider. Certain potentials for creativity inhere in the instruments, not just in the child's body and mind.

Here conceptions of creativity in music-making with instruments can be further expanded, beyond the idea of two-way interaction between two players, to a conception of the process as a three-way interaction between adult, child and sound-making object. Indeed, the expansion can continue to embrace others in groups, other objects in interesting and more complex networks of interaction and engagement. In other forms of time-based artistic activity such as dance, song, story-telling or theatre there may be no central or obvious object making up the three-way process as in music; yet objects, playthings, furniture or even just the available space, the room, still enable and constrain. In the example drawn from the theatre project that follows we will see how small gestural, non-verbal events, ripe with inferred meaning, evolved around certain everyday items such as a banana or a set of keys.

There is one final interesting element of the study to report. We carried out a very simple test (Young 2000, 2003b). The nursery teacher who was familiar to the children positioned herself at the xylophone ready to play for two half-hour periods on two different days, and I, as a trained musician unfamiliar to the children, did exactly the same. This occurred during the free play periods in the nursery when the children could initiate play with a range of different activities on offer. We carefully recorded the number of children and the length of time that they remained playing on the xylophone. Not only did the nursery teacher receive more play partners than me, the play was sustained for longer, quite considerably longer in many instances. My musical training enabled me to respond with more accuracy, and with more musically interesting and expressive improvisations. The video recordings show this to be the case, with the nursery teacher often mistiming a response, offering less well-matched or unrhythmic versions. From this very simple test it might appear that familiarity, the quality of the relationship between adult and child is a factor in the length and quality of the improvisation. It implied that a communicative relationship is more satisfying than conventional musical quality; conventional, that is, in terms of the usual parameters of western art music which prizes certain forms of sonic accuracy. If musical quality were judged on the expressive, communicative quality of the play within the small sphere of adult–child, then the nursery teacher's play is likely to have been of higher quality in 'communicative musicality' terms to the children (Malloch 2000). These propositions gather weight from the studies of adult–infant interaction in the first year to which we turn next.

Theoretical framework

There are two main theoretical axes that underpin this chapter. One axis is concerned with sensory coordination and integration, and continues the theme of multisensorality which unifies all senses without emphasising some at the expense of others. The other axis is concerned with expressive communication and continues that theme, arguing that the temporal arts are rooted in the sociability and intimacy that from birth bonds babies with their caregivers and, indeed, fosters close human relationships at whatever age. The two themes and their theoretical axes interconnect and relate tightly, and here they are separated only to reflect the different fields of research that have given rise to them and to assist with explanation.

In the 1980s there was a surge of interest in the competences of newborn babies. There was a tendency previously to think of babies as unthinking and unfeeling, but studies of babies started to reveal fascinating abilities and these, in turn, led to attempts to decipher what mechanisms might underpin these abilities. For example, in a now well-known simple test, Meltzoff and Moore (1985) found that if an adult puts out their tongue, the newborn is able to imitate that movement by also putting out their tongue in response. This study and many other ingenious experiments with newborns and very young babies provided evidence to support an explanation of this imitation as based on perception that is unified and intermodal (e.g. Meltzoff 1986) – that is, the visual, auditory, proprioceptive and oral information are coordinated and articulated as one. There are variations on the explanations for the imitative capabilities of newborns and the very young (see Zeedyk 2006), but broadly they are thought to reside in some sort of multisensorial process by which the senses are not operating separately but as one perceptual unit. As brain imaging techniques developed in the mid-1990s and could be applied without risk or discomfort to babies, a group of experiments by neuroscientists reported the discovery of mirror-neurons that were activated not only by the person performing actions but by those witnessing (Gallese, Keysers and Rizzollatti 2002). These inherent mirroring properties not only help to explain the mechanisms of imitation among newborns but also may hold some keys to empathetic kinaesthetic experience (Berrol 2006).

These findings challenged the prevailing idea that the senses are discrete (Meltzoff and Moore 1985) and that sensory impressions only become coordinated and connected through active, concrete experience, primarily motor action. This view originates in Piagetian thinking (Piaget 1953), and its continuing influence explains why exploratory experience with materials is still such a strong component of early childhood educational practice. Inter-modal perception, on the other hand, implies some kind of integratory process that allows all the sensory modes to interact and work in synchrony (Spelke 1976). Indeed, the synaesthesia experienced by some people, the remarkable stories of people who hear colours, or taste food as tactile shapes and textures, may be exceptional examples but seem to confirm sensory integration (Cytowic 1989).

This leads to various speculative ideas which are interesting for the possible insights they offer. One theory is that synaesthesia is caused by sensory modes that fail to disengage and differentiate as children mature (Meltzoff 1986). It suggests that sensory impressions do not need to be increasingly built up and connected to one another, but instead reduce and mould to the surrounding cultural context. So, to follow the argument through, children become more sensorily articulated in keeping with cultural environments and their culturally constructed sensory categories. Babies and young children of the Anlo-Ewe become more attuned to a culture orientated by sensitivity to the body. In contrast, in typical western cultures, children may become more attuned and sensorily articulated to the visual, static and disembodied. Babies in industrialised countries, for example, are typically placed apart in rigid carry-seats and cots, away from the near-constant human contact that many babies experience (Gottlieb 2004). Much of what we take for granted and natural about our bodies is instead evidence of the power of specific environments to shape our physicality. The idea that then follows is that far from needing to help children to progress from uncoordinated sensory experience to increasingly coordinated and integrated sensory experience, the opposite may be the case. Education may need to enhance the already integrated nature of children's experience of the world, and look closely at its own processes to avoid separating out or neglecting sensory experience, particularly bodily experience.

Timing

It was not only the babies' perceptual abilities that aroused interest among these researchers making new discoveries of what babies could do, but also the interaction between babies and their caregivers that occupied their attention. As research within the field of adult–infant communication developed, from micro-analyses of video-recodings of interaction researchers began to discover regular patterns of timing underpinning the communicative behaviours between infant and caregiver (Condon and Sander 1974; Trevarthen 1977; Tronick 1982). Typically, baby and mother settle in to a synchronous turn-taking pattern of mimetic behaviours – small gestures, vocalisations, facial expressions, touches – in which the length of each turn and the small pause between turns is exactly timed. Indeed, the successful timing of their turns and the establishment of this shared rhythmic framework (Fogel 1977, 1993) appear to be fundamental to communication. Finding that shared timing can easily be disturbed if mothers are suffering from postnatal depression or even cultural displacement, if they were recent immigrants (heralding briefly the final example that I mention in this chapter), and finding that the babies become quickly upset and bewildered by their mothers' lack of rhythmic attunement, seems to confirm that well-matched timing is essential (Gratier 1999). Looking back to the lap-game and music play, both relied on synchronous timing achieved through the rhythmic exchange of vocalisations, gesture, bodily movement, facial expressions and, in the music game, sounds made with the xylophone. As evidence of these timing patterns accumulated, Malloch (2000) went so far as to suggest that forms of timing represent core biological structures of human functioning. If we accept such a fundamental premise, then it is a small step to suggest that forms of timing represent a core structure of children's creative activity.

'Vitality contours'

Forms of well-matched timing may be essential, but they are not enough to explain the nature of communication. Stern's studies of mother–infant interaction focused on the expressive and emotional qualities of the exchanges, encapsulating these in the term 'vitality contours' (Stern 1985). The idea of vitality contours suggests that we can 'read' the emotional dynamic in different modes of experience. So, for example, a sweeping gesture of the arm, a vocalised 'whooo...sh', a glissando heard on a xylophone, a small surge of emotion, the movement of a wave, a gust of wind can all be experienced as having a matching contour in duration and intensity, and have a matching expressive quality. Although each of those small events is experienced in a different mode – felt, seen, heard – nevertheless we can 'read' them as dynamically matching and expressive of a similar feeling. In both the lap-game and the music play, the sounds, the movements, the touch, what was seen, were not experienced as separate modes, but as unified, multi-modal experience that was meaningful and expressive.

The value of Stern's work is to draw attention not only to the unified multi-modal nature of mother–infant interaction but also to its dynamic quality, and this in turn, importantly, imbues it with emotionality and its communicative potency (see also Zeedyk 2006). Stern criticised the usual simple classification of feelings as 'happy, sad, excited' and so on, saying that they were static and not genuinely how we experience emotions as flowing through time and contoured by rises and falls in intensity. He suggested that emotions might be best captured by kinetic terms such as 'fading, exploding, bursting, pulsing, wavering' (Stern 1993). Pavlicevic (1997), working in music therapy, has coined the useful term 'dynamic feeling forms' to describe the expressive contours she perceives in the musical improvisations of her therapeutic work and that are indicative to her of the emotions expressed by her therapy clients. Returning momentarily to think about educational practice, Stern's criticisms of the simplification of feeling states can be applied here too. All too often children are asked to identify their experience in terms of these simple, static feeling states, which seem impoverished in relation to the dynamic expressivity of their own creative activities and imaginations.

The processes of unified and intermodal perception, the idea of vitality contours, even the synaesthesia I mentioned briefly, belong to a group of basic-level processes in which salient features from sources of experience slip easily and fluidly from one mode or medium to another. These processes allow us to tune in to others on a non-verbal level, and are essential to communication and intimacy with others. When Manu played with Linda, his music play was quite closely tied in to the turn-taking structures of interaction, which I am suggesting he would have absorbed from being successfully parented as a baby. The precursors of his music-making lie in the sociable experiences of his babyhood and earlier childhood. I propose this as an illuminating theoretical framework to explain early improvisatory activity in music – and indeed not just music, but across the full range of time-based creative activity such as dance and theatre. But it then raises the question of how these basic-level processes and the rhythmic and contoured interactive structures they give rise to can be imaginatively projected into these time-based media and start to rise up and detach from their low-level origins (see Shore 1996 for an interesting discussion on this question). For unless we can untangle that process, we are at a loss for how to design educational experiences that mediate between the children's own improvisatory proclivities in time-based media of music, dance, theatre and the cultural forms of these arts.

Possible answers seem to lie in theories of metaphor, of which there are several (see Seitz 1997). One that I find fruitful is Johnson's (1987) theory of transformation, in which he suggests that bodily experience, what we sense and know in an embodied way, can rise up and be imaginatively projected into more abstract levels. Johnson arrives at his conclusions from philosophical analysis of linguistic structure. So, to give one of Johnson's examples from many, we walk upright and experience the world in a kind of 'top to bottom' way, and so project this intuitive understanding of verticality on much else that we conceptualise about our world and how we talk about it. Johnson proposes that multi-sources of experiential information – motor, emotional, sensory activity and interactions with both the social and material world – combine in a rich mix of experience that becomes translated and projected into other media. So a schema of verticality is not just a geometric, 'up-down' structure, but is fused with dynamic 'ups and downs' of emotional experience derived from interactions with others. Beatrice's physical experience of sitting upright on her mother's lap is reinforced by the tipping and play with balance, but imbued too with the emotional intensity engendered by the game with her mother. Johnson, like Egan, Donald and Bruner, the other theorists I refer to at different points in this chapter, is mainly concerned with the embodied origins of language. Nevertheless their theorisings of processes that underpin language offer insights that are transferable to creative, non-verbal processes. What I find valuable about Johnson's theory of metaphoric transformation is its holism, by that I mean its infusion of emotional experience into motor and sensory experience and its inclusion of interaction with people, things, indeed the whole environment as engendering that experience.

How might that process of projection and redescription happen? For Johnson, and others interested in metaphor (Seitz 1997), metaphoric thinking involves the making of a connecting relationship between two different things, often in two different modes. To create the connecting relationship some qualities are shared across both modes – the timing and contour of a sweep of the arm, for example, matches the timing and contour of the xylophone sound that it makes. But at the same time some other qualities are transformed. The sound, although equivalent in certain basic-level and salient features to the movement, is also clearly different from the movement and is a transformation. The dynamic feeling form of both sound and movement are experienced as the same, but the movement is transformed in to an aural counterpart. Children need to learn to recognise what is the same and what has changed. Egan (1997, 2003), with a specific interest in children's learning, emphasises the importance of metaphor and how it facilitates cross-modal transformations in young children's thinking process. For Egan, somatic thinking and metaphor provide cognitive tools that can drive children's imaginative thinking.

Games

Picking up the thread of adult–infant interaction again, around the age of three or four months adult–infant interactions begin to extend into longer and more complex bouts of playful communicative behaviour. The lap-game was a continuation of this play well in to the second year. These games quickly become established around relatively small things in small moments. A tickling game may involve movement, kinaesthetic awareness, touch and just a little vocalising. Certain parameters, kinds of rules evolve, and these govern the timing, the intensity, the vitality contours of the games and the weighting of the modalities in which they occur. Once established by the pair, the clusters of playful behaviour which make up the game can be endlessly varied in playful sequences. Elaboration is designed to raise interest and hold attention. The repetitions start to set up anticipations which accumulate to points of climax and then resolve. Inferring and anticipating what might come next is a source of considerable pleasure for all involved.

Bruner (1983, 1990) discovered that very quickly in game-playing, the baby or very young child can predict and anticipate the next moves. Their communicative moves are woven in to the unfolding sequence and are meaningful in terms of their game-embedded role; they can pick up meaning from what has gone before and also suggest meaning for what might follow. Awareness of the intentions and meaning of others, as in the universal game 'Peep-bo', emerges from the multi-modal animations of the game. For Bruner this was evidence that game playing provides the foundation on which infants develop a form of rudimentary symbolic play. Led by his interest in verbal communication, Bruner proposed that exchanges of meaning in game-playing can lead to language development. Language development aside, the game-playing format, as unfolding events ripen with non-verbal, inferential meaning, can provide a basis for other forms of time-based improvisation, in drama, music or dance.

The overall game structure has forms of coherence that hold it together over time, as one structure made up of phrased parts. Together they arrive as some kind of conclusion or climax through the build-up of tension and then resolution of that tension. They are, in that way then, a kind of narrative – not narrative in the sense most commonly associated with the term of words and story, but of mimetic narratives that unfold over time, through a sequence of small events that convey meaning. To summarise thus far, the small exchanges between babies and adults develop and extend to longer sequences or games and the temporal, embodied, emotionally dynamic, communicative processes that underpin them then rise up through metaphorical transformation as the structural narratives that drive creative activity and fuel its emotional energy.

Joint engagement

We return to adult–infant interaction a final time to incorporate one more idea. At first, play objects distract and take the baby's attention away from other people. They may switch between looking at a plaything and then at people. But later they can coordinate play with a thing with an adult, and also incorporate the plaything into extended games. It was just this kind of three-way game play that provided the underlying structure for the music play between Manu and Linda, in which a sound-maker, the xylophone, was the plaything. 'Three-way play' has been noticed by several researchers and named differently by each, but Moore and Dunham (1995), reviewing the field as whole, settled on the term 'joint engagement' to embrace them all. The plaything incorporated into shared play carries inferred meanings that reflect back on each partner. As the object starts to carry meaning within the play, so the game play can extend and become more imaginative and interesting. We see just an example of this if I jump ahead briefly to the theatre project for under threes which I describe later, in which the actor wove non-verbal, mimed events around simple objects using gesture and facial expression to convey meaning. The actor found a banana under a bowl, ceremoniously holding it up, bringing finger and thumb close to imply peeling, looking at the children to convey expectation, looking back at the banana with fingers a little closer, giving the peel one little tug and looking back, eyes wide, at the children again. In this way the actor animated and organised the time-space and intensity relationships around a simple object which became the central focus of attention between herself and a group of rapt children, who, with prior knowledge of bananas, could interpret the gestures and anticipate the next moves. Adults working with young children in arts activities need to be the most flexible and responsive partner, sympathetically attuned to the children's contributions and making minute adjustments to what they sense is happening with the children. This is just the same responsiveness as mothers with infants or educators with the very young. However, as children gain in experience, we would expect them to become more able to adjust their own timings and 'vitality contours' in order to be empathetic to others. Empathetic adjustment to others may be an important goal of education, particularly in a world of increasing diversity.

Diversity

At this point in the chapter, I take a short, but important detour to draw attention to the fact that these studies of adult–infant interaction and all its ramifications have mostly been carried out with small samples of middle-class mothers from Western European and North American societies, and they have been carried out in the contrived conditions of laboratories. Cross-cultural research into different parenting styles suggest that these will be mothers who prize animated face-to-face interaction, who believe that it is important and worthwhile to talk to their babies as if they are equal partners in a dialogue, and who have time, energy and the conviction to play with them (e.g. Lancy 2008). Dissanayake (2000, 2001), writing from an anthropological perspective on the arts, has studied adult–child interaction and then applied these theoretical ideas to more diverse community groups and to art-making from a pan-cultural perspective. Dissanayake's attention to intimacy as the origin of arts is illuminating and very valuable. For me there is one proviso, however, that we need to be wary of taking a cross-cultural position and applying intimacy as enacted through face-to-face adult–infant interaction cast in a western model as if it were universal. Anthropologists, realising that babies and child-rearing have been neglected areas of much anthropological endeavour – or have been subject only to cross-cultural studies based on 'western' developmental norms – are beginning to explore patterns of parenting and interaction from within-culture perspectives, revealing differentiated patterns of interaction. When babies show no objection to being handed around from adult to adult in some communities (Gottlieb 2004), or spend most of the day strapped on backs, watching the world around them but receiving little direct interaction, there needs to be caution in setting up a model derived from minority, middle-class communities in so-called industrialised countries as a universal. Indeed, this cautionary point can be extended to apply generally to conceptualisations of children's creativity. They can tend to derive from images of childhood resting on white, western middle-class constructions, underpinned by desires for an ideal childhood of innocence and spontaneous freedom (Burman 2008). Towards the end of the chapter I will take up these important ideas again in describing a project that worked with majority Muslim communities in English children's centres. For now we return to the third example, which continues the themes and expands their scope.

Making theatre

Much arts work for young children in the United Kingdom is increasingly provided by arts companies, rather than educators. Some children's theatre companies, both in the United Kingdom and across Europe, have been breaking new ground in designing and presenting theatre pieces for babies and very young children. Their innovatory work has challenged the creative theatre teams to reconsider the basic elements of their art form. Using detailed, structured observation, video recording with analysis and formative discussion, studies, particularly the most recent with the Edinburgh-based Starcatchers project team, have revealed how the actors, dancers, musicians and designers working within the theatre pieces arrive at certain elements or principles (Young 2004; Young and Powers 2009). Key among these principles is that the children are not sitting as passive and silent watchers to theatre performed by adults, not an 'audience' in the conventional sense, but are taking a more active, participatory role. Thus by participating, the children's engagement feeds into the making of the theatre pieces. The pieces have a worked-out framework but are semi-improvised and thus flexible to the children's contributions (Young 2004). It is a risky process for their theatre-making may equally well be disrupted by outright, noisy rejection on the part of the very young children.

Recent developments in children's theatre to some extent mirror developments across all artistic fields. Here I am referring to artistic work intended for adults as well as work for children. Innovative artwork is increasingly being created from mixed forms of representation where the visual, auditory and kinaesthetic combine to create new art forms (Young and Powers 2009). In recent years there has been a significant shift from works of art to be contemplated by a detached 'audience' of onlookers, to works of art as generated within a social context. It is interesting to note a broad groundswell of thinking around similar ideas of integrative sensory experience, of interest in dissolving formal boundaries and replacing them with more fluid forms of relating that threads through research with babies and the very young, that threads through contemporary arts practice and its theorising, and here I am weaving into theoretical versions of creativity with children.

Conventional theatre separates performers from audience; the one gazes on the other. Contemporary performance art is increasingly designed around the idea of 'interactive installations' in which the conventional separation of performers from audience is dissolved. The 'viewer' is replaced by a 'participant' in a relationship with the artists and art works. For participants, this introduces an emphasis on sensory immediacy, on physical participation and on heightened awareness of others who are present, and who become part of the piece. In the Starcatchers' theatre piece, spaces where the audience might settle, mainly the adults who are always part of an audience for young children, are implied by cushions and grassy banks, but not designated. The children meanwhile are free to roam and move around the space in which items and objects are set out, partly as a kind of set, and partly to stimulate exploratory play.

The overall structure of the theatre piece moves between freedom for the children to play with the objects, constructions and space, which we described as 'interactive engagement', and times to watch some short performed elements, described as 'absorbed engagement' (Young and Powers 2009). The action in *Peep*, Starcatcher's final piece, was pre-designed to offer a number of small structured events around a narrative sequence that had beginning, development, climax and resolution. Our analysis of children's engagement and ongoing feedback to the team as part of our research role had suggested that these small events, based on structures of interactive games would engage and draw in the children. Some were minimally verbal, more vocalizations than verbal, being made up of simple trilling bird sounds or single words. The bird character, for example, takes a wash with a pretend bowl of water, rhythmically calling and repeating the rhythmic phrase 'splash!' ... 'splash, splash, splash', and matches these words with small flicking hand gestures of exact dynamic feeling form. These narrative sequences often focus on an object – a banana, a toy, some keys, a bowl of water – familiar, simple objects with which a kind of invitation to imagine joining in, not actual joining in, is offered. It is an extension of joint engagement between one adult actor, many children and the focal object. The performer looks up at the children, invitingly, at key moments, setting up inferred meanings woven around the objects. Donald (1991) describes mimesis as involving the 'invention of intentional representation'.

During the performed elements of the theatre pieces, the children are absorbed, watching and enacting, imaginatively projecting themselves into the action but having no direct hands-on experience; they are just watching the objects being played with by the actor, not playing with them directly. The young children's ability to grasp meaning arises from their ability to project themselves into the observed experience. The theory of mirror-neurons, mentioned earlier in the chapter, offers one explanation for how absorbed engagement may be operating. For Rogoff, from her studies of children's learning in South American communities (1997, 2003), peripheral participation, the close observation and projection of oneself into an activity without directly participating, is an important component of learning that is neglected in 'western' views of learning. Drawing this idea across into creative education, there is often the assumption that being creative is synonymous with concrete, hands-on experience. The absorbed engagement we theorised from the theatre project suggests that providing opportunities to watch, listen and 'participate peripherally' in artistic performances is also an important dimension for fostering creative thinking. The parameters of one kind of freedom on the part of the children may be confined in such theatre pieces, but I suggest that the thoughtfully pre-designed, developmentally appropriate opportunities for absorbed engagement on the part of the children can stimulate high levels of imaginative thinking.

Diversity again

This final reference to a fourth research project which explored approaches to creative play in children's centres serving majority Muslim communities, takes up the caution expressed earlier of not adopting models derived from minority parenting practices and applying them as if applicable to all families and at all times. It also, in my view, points importantly to the new frontiers for research and practice in early childhood creativity, and where we may wish to use critical analysis to reveal how one view may become privileged to the disadvantage of others. Socio-cultural theory, generally understood in terms of its emphasis on the social dimension of learning, is often co-opted to theorise the small-scale interactions, the micro-social context of adult with child. The macro-social context – the wider social, cultural, economic, racial, religious contexts – is less considered. While creative practice and research tend to focus on the moments of making, the intimacy of adult and child interaction – exactly as I have done in this chapter – we need also to understand creative process in wider socio-cultural context. In what Marsh (2003) has called 'one-way traffic' interest in children's home background and heritage tends to consist merely of what can be taken from the educational context back to the home, rather than vice versa. Moreover, reverse traffic should be more profound than simply bringing something from home, or the multi-cultural approach of 'festivals and celebrations' which many have criticised as tokenistic and superficial. It implies a deeper-level attempt to understand social and cultural mores, with an empathetic receptivity. I launched this chapter with mention of the deep-level anthropological interest in sensory orientations and cultural variation. Similarly, studies with culturally diverse mothers have discovered variations in core timing determined by the cultural environment of the mothers (Gratier 1999; Powers and Trevarthen 2008), mentioned earlier in the section on timing.

The Time to Play project sought to develop approaches to creative play in children's centres serving majority Muslim communities in four cities across South and Central England (Young and Street 2010). Through action research we increasingly realised the need to focus not only on the micro-interactions of child with art process, but on the macro-context of community and culture, and alongside this to question, reflexively, our own position. The project increasingly found that story, song, improvised music-making and game playing, such as games with stones, could offer media with which to engage the mothers and their children. The non-verbal media of creative play employed by the musicians, theatre practitioners and artists on the project offered alternative means of communication to overcome language barriers, particularly among young children only as yet speaking their home language, or mothers who were newly arrived.

The work raised certain key challenges, which will be represented by two examples. For those mothers following more devout doctrines of the Muslim faith, there were religiously based tensions around certain forms of freedom to dance and to make music, which were also transferred onto restrictions around their children's activity, particularly girls. At least, we, the project team, experienced them as tensions and restrictions to the type and style of embodied creativity and expressiveness that we considered beneficial to children. Therein lies a need, yet again, to re-examine the taken-for-granted conceptions of children's development, creativity and childhood that circulate and inform our practice. Conceptions of creativity may need to shift to incorporate the perspectives of communities for whom the perpetuation of traditions and collective responsibility, transmitted in more restrained use of body and voice, is valued above change and independence. As a second example, gender-differentiated upbringing we found to be more marked than might be the case in some other communities. Boisterous freedoms often accorded to sons contrasted with the emphasis on modesty and shyness encouraged among daughters. We found that ideas of creativity as generated from animated interpersonal exchanges, particularly using talk, needed to be revised when working with young girls who were enculturated into behaviours of bodily self-restraint and silence. This sent us back to theories of gender-differentiated practice and also raised for us the value of thinking in terms of practice as engendering 'absorbed engagement' and opportunities for peripheral participation in which imaginative and creative thinking is stimulated through observation and mirrored action.

Brief mention of these challenges at the very conclusion of the chapter risks setting 'new hares running' that are left under-discussed when I should be drawing the threads of the chapter to a tidy conclusion. My purpose in mentioning them is to acknowledge that although some theories and explanations of children's creativity in time-based arts are accumulating, they remain partial and incomplete and need to be continually and reflexively revised in the light of new challenges. The descriptions of practice, the ideas and theories presented in this chapter seek to destabilise much of what is taken for granted in conceptions of children's creativity and offer pathways to alternatives, some more clearly mapped out than others. In this chapter I have described some of the basic-level ideas in the human need for sociability that appear to be common to all, but at the same time are articulated through cultural experience so that they are endlessly varied. I have explained the processes of communication that are given meaningful form through rhythm, timing, phrase, narrative, dynamic contour and kinetic energy, and proposed that these provide generative sources for children's creative activity in the temporal arts.

References

Berrol, C. (2006) 'Neuroscience meets dance/movement therapy: mirror neurons, the therapeutic process and empathy', *The Arts in Psychotherapy*, **33**(4), pp. 302–15.

Blacking, J. (1989) *A Commonsense View of All Music: Reflections on Percy Grainger's contribution to ethnomusicology and music education*, Cambridge: Cambridge University Press.

Bresler, L. (ed.), (2004) *Knowing Bodies: Moving minds*, The Hague, Netherlands: Kluwer Academic.

Bruner, J. S. (1983) *Child's Talk: Learning to use language*, Oxford: Oxford University Press.

Bruner, J. S. (1990) *Acts of Meaning*, Cambridge, Mass.: Harvard University Press.

Burman, E. (2008) *Developments: Child, image, nations*, London: Routledge.

Clark, A. & Moss, P. (2001) *Listening to Young Children: The Mosaic approach*, London: National Children's Bureau for the Joseph Rowntree Foundation.

Classen, C. (1993) *Worlds of Sense: Exploring the senses in history and across cultures*, London: Routledge .

Condon, W. S. & Sander, L. S. (1974) 'Neonate movement is synchronised with adult speech', *Science*, **183**, pp. 99–101.

Cytowic, R. (1989) *Synaesthesia: A union of the senses*, New York: Springer-Verlag.

Dissanayake, E. (2000) 'Antecedents of the temporal arts in early mother–infant interaction', in N. W. Wallin, B. Merker and S. Brown (eds), *The Origins of Music*, Cambridge, Mass.: MIT Press.

Dissanayake, E. (2001) 'Becoming homo aestheticus: sources of aesthetic imagination in mother–infant interactions', *SubStance*, **94/95**, pp. 85–103.

Donald, M. (1991) *Origins of the Modern Mind*, Cambridge, Mass./London: Harvard University Press.

Egan, K. (1997) *The Educated Mind: How cognitive tools shape our understanding*, Chicago: University of Chicago Press.

Egan, K. (2003) 'The cognitive tools of children's imagination', pp. 27–38 in B. van Oers (ed.), *Narratives of Childhood: Theoretical and practical explorations for the innovation of early childhood education*, Amsterdam: VU University Press.

Fogel, A. (1977) 'Temporal organisations in mother–infant face-to-face interaction', in H. D. Schaffer (ed.), *Studies in Mother–Infant Interaction*, New York: Academic Press.

Fogel, A. (1993) *Developing Through Relationships: Origins of communication, self and culture*, New York/London: Harvester, Wheatsheaf.

Gallese, V., Keysers, C. and Rizzollatti, G. (2002) 'A universal view of the basis of social cognition', *Trends in Cognitive Sciences*, **8**(9), pp. 396–403.

Geurts, K. L. (2003) *Culture and the Senses: Bodily ways of knowing in an African community*, Berkeley, Calif.: University of California Press .

Gottlieb, A. (2004) *The Afterlife is Where we Come From: The culture of infancy in West Africa*, Chicago, Ill.: University of Chicago Press .

Gratier, M. (1999) 'Expressions of belonging: the effect of acculturation on the rhythm and harmony of mother–infant vocal interaction', *Musicae Scientiae*, Special Issue 1999–2000, pp. 93–122.

Johnson, M. (1987) *The Body in the Mind: The bodily basis of meaning, imagination and reason*, Chicago, Ill.: University of Chicago Press.

Lancy, D. (2008) *The Anthropology of Childhood: Cherubs, chattel, changelings*, Cambridge: Cambridge University Press .

Malloch, S. (2000) 'Mothers and infants and communicative musicality', *Musicae Scientiae* Special Issue 1999–2000, pp. 29–57.

Marsh, J. (2003) 'One-way traffic? Connections between literacy practices at home and in the nursery', *British Educational Research Journal*, **39**(3), pp. 369–82.

Meltzoff, A. N. (1986) 'Imitation, intermodal representation, and the origins of mind', in B. Lindblom and R. Zetterstrom (eds), *Precursors of Early Speech: Proceedings of an International Symposium held at the Wenner-Gren Center, Stockholm, 1984*, New York: Stockton Press.

Meltzoff, A. N. and Moore, M. K. (1985) 'Cognitive foundations and social functions of imitation and intermodal representation in infancy', in J. Mehler and R. Fox (eds), *Neonate Cognition: Beyond the blooming buzzing confusion*, Hillsdale, N.J.: Lawrence Erlbaum Associates.

Moore, C. & Dunham, P. J. (eds), (1995) *Joint Attention: Its origins and role in development*, Hillsdale, N.J.: Lawrence Erlbaum.

Pavlicevic, M. (1997) *Music Therapy in Context: Music, meaning and relationship*, London: Jessica Kingsley.

Piaget, J. (1953) *The Origin of Intelligence in the Child*, trans. M. Cook, London: Routledge & Kegan Paul.

Pink, S. (2006) *The Future of Visual Anthropology: Engaging the senses*, Abingdon, Oxon: Routledge.

Powers, N. and Trevarthen, C. (2008) 'Voices of shared emotion and meaning: young infants and their mothers in Scotland and Japan', in S. Malloch and C. Trevarthen (eds), *Communicative Musicality: Exploring the basis of human companionship*, Oxford: Oxford University Press.

Rogoff, B. (1997) 'Evaluating development in the process or participation: theory, methods, and practice building on each other', pp. 265–85 in E. Amsel and K. A. Renninger (eds), *Change and Development: Issues of theory, method and application*, London: Erlbaum.

Rogoff, B. (2003) *The Cultural Nature of Human Development*, Oxford: Oxford University Press .

Sawyer, K. (2006) *Explaining Creativity: The science of human innovation*, Oxford: Oxford University Press.

Seitz, J. A. (1997) 'The development of metaphoric understanding: implications for a theory of creativity', *Creativity Research Journal*, **10**(4), pp. 347–53.

Shore, B. (1996) *Culture in Mind: Cognition, culture and the problem of meaning*, Oxford: Oxford University Press.

Spelke, E. (1976) 'Infants' intermodal perception of events', *Cognitive Psychology*, **8**, pp. 553–60.

Stern, D. (1985) *The Interpersonal World of the Infant*, New York: Basic Books.

Stern, D. (1993) 'The role of feelings for an interpersonal self', in U. Neisser (ed.), *The Perceived Self: Ecological and interpersonal sources of self knowledge*, Cambridge: Cambridge University Press.

Trevarthen, C. (1977) 'Descriptive Analyses of infant communication behaviour', in H. R. Schaffer (ed.), *Studies in Mother–Infant Interaction*, London: Academic Press.

Tronick, E. (ed.) (1982) *Social Interchange in Infancy: Affect, cognition and communication*, Baltimore, Md.: University Park Press.

Young, S. (1996) 'Contributions to an understanding of the music and movement connection', *Early Child Development and Care*, **115**, pp. 1–6.

Young, S. (2000) *Young Children's Spontaneous Play with Instruments*, unpublished Ph.D. thesis, University of Surrey.

Young, S. (2003a) *Music with the Under Fours*, London: RoutledgeFalmer.

Young, S. (2003b) 'The interpersonal dimension: a potential source of creativity for young children?', *Musicae Scientiae* Special Issue 1999–2000, pp. 165–79.

Young, S. (2004) 'It's a bit like flying: participatory theatre with the under twos: a case study of Oily Cart', *Research in Drama Education*, **9**(1), pp. 13–28.

Young, S. (2005a) 'Musical communication between adults and young children', pp. 281–99 in D. Miell, R. MacDonald and D. Hargreaves (eds), *Musical Communication*, Oxford: Oxford University Press.

Young, S. (2005b) 'Changing tune: reconceptualising music with the under-threes', *International Journal of Early Years Education*, **13**(3), pp. 289–303.

Young, S. (2008) 'Collaboration between three- and four-year-olds in self-initiated play with instruments', *International Journal of Educational Research*, **47**(1), pp. 3–10.

Young, S. and Gillen, J. (2010) 'Musicality', in J. Gillen and C. A. Cameron (eds), *International Perspectives on Early Childhood Research: A day in the life*, Basingstoke: Palgrave Macmillan.

Young, S. and Powers, N. (2009) *Starcatchers: Research report*, Edinburgh: Imaginate. Available at: http://www.imaginate.org.uk (accessed 2 November 2009).

Young, S. and Street, A. (2010) *Time to Play: Final report*, Oxford: Peers Early Education Partnership. Available at: http://www.peep.org.uk (accessed 9 January 2010).

Zeedyk, M. S. (2006) 'From intersubjectivity to subjectivity: the transformative roles of emotional intimacy and imitation', *Infant and Child Development*, **15**, pp. 321–44.

Chapter 10

A generative framework for creativity: encouraging creative collaboration in children's music composition

Sylvia M. Truman

Introduction

A question that is of widespread interest in education today is 'How can learning tasks be structured to encourage creative thinking in the classroom?' Recent advances in music education research have focused on using technology to assist schoolchildren to learn how to create music. This chapter describes SoundScape, a music composition environment designed to facilitate children's collaborative creativity. The development of SoundScape has been influenced by psychological accounts of creativity, socio-constructivist accounts of learning and accounts of the development of musical expression. Traditionally, music education software has focused upon the use of staff notation whereby students manipulate musical notes to construct their compositions. However, the extensive and sustained research effort into musical representations over the last decade has produced studies reporting music notation as an inhibitor of musical creativity (Walker 1992; Auh 2000), owing to difficulties in mapping the sound properties of music to the visual specification of staff notation. Furthermore, adherence to the traditional notation system excludes those with little to no formal music training.

Although it is a requirement that staff notation should be taught in school, as part of the National Curriculum for England, Wales and Northern Ireland and the 5–14 Curriculum for Scotland, in this chapter I argue that it need not be the only mechanism by which practice in musical composition is taught. This is because it is widely accepted that music notation is difficult to learn for some students. The abstract representation of traditional notation holds little meaning for younger students and those not technically trained in playing a musical instrument.

Research within the field of music education suggests that if the traditional notation system is prescribed for classroom-based composition activities, then those without knowledge of music technicalities may lack confidence in their abilities when approaching a music composition task (Seddon 2002). Furthermore, studies into children's music composition also emphasize that alternative graphical representations of music allow children to explore musical sounds and structures for themselves unconstrained by the formal notation system (Pond 1981; Levi 1986). An example of this is the Jungulator Prototype, a digital tool that allows learners to play and develop ideas for music composition through visual images and sound (Dillon 2005). In this chapter I argue that the use of imagery to represent musical sounds can assist with enhancing the creative experience for the student, as visual imagery is widely accepted to be a crucial element of creative thinking (Gruber and Wallace 1999). Creative thinking is also facilitated by metaphorical and analogical thinking (Weisberg 1993). The use of analogy and metaphor is guided by a direct similarity between the elements involved (Holyoak and Thagard 1996). Therefore, I suggest that if music is represented through a metaphorical, real-world representation, then unlike traditional staff notation, this would allow the visual parameters of the metaphor to directly relate to the sound properties of the music (Walker 1978). Furthermore, real-world representations would also allow the sound properties to relate directly to an analogous action (such as the purr of a cat). In this way, the representation would be more meaningful to the student, situating the task of composition in an appropriate context.

Contemporary accounts of learning suggests that effective learning occurs through the active construction of meaning and the social interactions that take place during the learning process, and also that learning is situated and integrated with activity (Von Glaserfeld 1995; Vygotsky 1978; Brown, Collins and Duguid 1989). Many scholars suggest that similar processes also hold true for creativity (Csikszentmihalyi 1993). While few have suggested there exists an inherent relationship between creativity and learning, the similarities between the two are evidently striking (Karnes et al. 1961; Torrance 1981; Guilford 1950). In this chapter, I argue that theories advocating learning as a socially constructive process may provide insights into creative phenomena such as music composition. In the next section, salient aspects of theories of learning and creativity will be used to explain a generative framework of learning and creativity using music composition as an example of how the framework can be instantiated. Following this, a music composition program, SoundScape, will be presented. This has been designed in accordance with the generative framework. SoundScape is aimed at school children around the age of eleven years.

Theories of learning and creativity: implications for learning and technology

Theories of learning

In traditional models of pedagogy, learning is characterized as the passive absorption of knowledge, which is later tested in exam-based scenarios. The underlying assumption of this approach places expectations upon the student to learn and effectively recall knowledge that is delivered by way of authoritarian, didactic teaching methods (Jarvinen 1998). Consequently, students may respond in ways that meet what they perceive to be the teacher's expectations (Edwards and Mercer 1987). Also, this tradition isolates the learner from social interaction as it centers on a one-to-one relationship between the learner and material to be learned. Thus, although students may be able to recall the information during exams, they may encounter difficulty when attempting to apply the knowledge in authentic contexts (Baccarini 2004).

Drawing on Piaget's (1954, 1955) theories of cognitive development, constructivist theories suggest that learning occurs through active exploration and interaction with the environment. This provides the individual student with opportunities to construct knowledge and form their own understanding of the world (Raskin 2005; Von Glaserfeld and Steffe 1991; Ernest 1995). According to the constructivist approach, the important features of learning are as follows. First, learning is contextual (Schank 1995). That is, it is not possible to assimilate new knowledge without having an already existing knowledge structure. Second, one needs this knowledge structure to learn. Students learn by constructing meaning for themselves through active participation within various knowledge domains. Third, learning is a self-regulated process (Bandura 1986) where each individual learns at a different rate depending on their prior knowledge and experience.

Finally, drawing on the social constructivist and socio-cultural accounts of Dewey (1916), Vygotsky (1978), and Rogoff (1990), many theorists view learning as a social activity that takes place through interactions with others and the external environment (e.g. Frank 2005). This approach has a number of advantages. For example, by discussing their experiences with others, children develop shared understandings (Stager 2005). This is especially advantageous in collaborative settings. Many have argued that social interaction is of paramount importance to cognitive development: as learning takes place first on the 'intermental' plane through interacting with others, and second, on the 'intramental' plane, when newly acquired concepts are integrated into the mental structures of the individual (Derry 1999; McMahon 1997; Vygotsky 1978).

Examples of practice that draws on all three types of learning theory can be observed in current educational contexts including e-learning contexts. With the growing advancements in technology, educational software has become a pervasive element of education today (Frank 2005). This technology, however, is often framed or characterized as a conduit for disseminating knowledge to students. This relegates the learner's role to that of a passive receiver of knowledge. By contrast, many educators and educational software designers utilize technology as a 'virtual space' that offers students the freedom to explore concepts for themselves (Stager 2005). These people maintain that to maximize productive learning and exploration, it is important to design educational software that is appropriate for the context of use (Johnson and Dyer 2005; Bruckman 1998), and that it is important to perceive students as active learners rather than passive recipients of electronic content. This growing concern is pressed by the evolution of the internet and ideals of collaboration and lifelong learning (Johnson and Dyer 2005), which have heralded a shift away from passive learning to learning of a more participative nature.

This has led to more contextualized approaches towards learning such as constructivist and constructionist learning perspectives. Students may come to rely upon particular features of the classroom context in which a learning task is embedded so that, in their minds, the task becomes a disembedded rather than an authentic activity (Brown et al. 1989). Therefore, for any given learning task, setting the appropriate context is of paramount importance. Constructionism is an educational method based upon constructivist learning theory (Papert 1993). Whereas constructivism advocates that knowledge is constructed in the mind of the individual, constructionism extends this, suggesting that an effective way to learn is to build something tangible that exists in the real world. This enhances the overall learning experience, making it more meaningful to the student. The emphasis of constructionism, therefore, is on the importance of allowing students to be actively engaged in personally creating a product that is meaningful to themselves and to others (Papert 1993, 1999). Finally, social constructivist theories imply that educational technologists should design tasks and environments that facilitate active collaboration between pairs or groups of children, (e.g. McMahon 1997).

Theories of creativity

Recent years have seen a huge increase in research on creativity, and this has led to a number of new theories and explanations (e.g. Amabile 1996; Csíkszentmihályi 1993; Runco 1996). Here, however, I outline a particular account of the creative process first developed by Wallas (1926). Creativity research originally focused upon stage models of the creative process, starting with the work of Poincaré (1913). Poincaré describes the creative process as commencing with conscious thought, followed by unconscious work that eventually resulted in 'inspiration.' Based on Poincaré's account of the creative process, Wallas (1926) formalized a four-stage model of creativity. He defined creativity as a process whereby individuals progressed through four stages: preparation, incubation, illumination, and verification (see Figure 10.1). Preparation concerns immersing oneself in a domain, and developing a curiosity about a particular problem (Getzels 1964). During this stage, knowledge is consciously accumulated and influences are

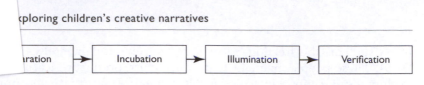

Figure 10.1 Wallas's four-stage model of creativity

drawn from previous experience. During the incubation stage, conscious thought pertaining to the problem is rested and left to the unconscious mind to process (Claxton 1998). Illumination is said to occur when the individual experiences a sudden flash of insight (Wallas 1926) or sudden inspiration results from this unconscious processing (Poincaré 1913). Finally, verification concerns forming judgments pertaining to the value or worth of the resulting creative idea or creative artifact.

Although there have been many debates and redefinitions of the stages of creativity said to lead to creative acts and outcomes, certain points gain widespread agreement (Osborn 1953; Taylor 1959). First, there is the need for preparation. Preparation is multifaceted, and involves accumulating existing facts and resources and preparing mentally for the creative process. Second, time is required for the incubation of ideas if illumination is to occur. Finally, the verification of creative ideas and novel products has both a personal and social element. The new idea or product must satisfy the aims of the individual and be able to stand up to evaluation by the wider community.

It is widely accepted that creativity is not a phenomenon that exists in isolation. Any creative idea or artefact evolves from the relationship between the individual creator and their interactions with others and their environment (Fischer 2000). This is especially true regarding the phenomena of group creativity, where group interaction and collaboration assists the creative process (Hennessey 2004). Recent studies suggest that the environment in which one is situated can invoke creativity by igniting an idea (Fasko 2001; Sternberg and Lubart 1991; Torrance 1981). In terms of education, it is widely accepted that the creative development of students is largely dependent upon the nature of the learning environment (Runco and Johnson 2002). As Fasko (2001) points out, students' overall motivation and educational experience are enhanced when they are situated in environments where the follow-up of creative ideas is encouraged and rewarded by active evaluation and feedback.

The relationship between learning and creativity

Houtz and Krug (1995) argue that constructivist and social constructivist theories of learning and theories of creativity share a number of similarities. First, learning is social in nature, and takes place through constant interaction with other people and with the environment (Vygotsky 1978). Vosniadou (1996) describes learning as the outcome of interactions between social agents and their environment. Second, students construct their own meanings through actively participating within a domain (Forrester and Jantzie 2001; Honebein, Duffy, and Fishburn 1996). Similarly, creativity is social in nature, and it is widely accepted that creative ideas and artefacts can arise from the relationship between an individual creator, other people, and the environment (Hennessey 2004; Fasko 2001; Sternberg and Lubart 1991; Torrance 1981). Third, for both individuals and groups, both learning and creativity are situated within the wider socio-cultural context. This means that as people acquire new knowledge (learning), or come up with novel thoughts and ideas, they will inevitably be influenced by the prevailing knowledge and socio-cultural traditions of their society (e.g. Csikzentmihalyi 1988; Rogoff 2003).

Two other important influences on learning and creative processes are time and previous experience. Learning is not an instantaneous process; it takes time. Time is required for students to revisit, reflect on, and consolidate new knowledge and ideas. In addition, when they are allowed time for reflection, students can generate different perspectives on a problem or idea. This may be assisted partly by analogical and metaphorical thinking. Time is also important to creativity owing to the need for subconscious processing during the incubation stage (Claxton 1998). Like learning, creativity involves using metaphor and analogy to compare alternative perspectives and ways of thinking in order to develop new ideas or approaches to a problem situation (Runco 1996; Guilford 1967). This implies that creative ideas are inspired by previous situations and experiences. Similarly, learning occurs when the student is able to relate new concepts to previous situations and experiences (Schank 1995, 1999). According to the theory of creativity developed by Vygotsky in the 1930s (as discussed in Moran and John-Steiner 2003: 64), there are key differences between learning and creativity. In the initial stages, creative processes are internal to the individual, although eventually these usually result in the externalization of a novel idea or concept. By contrast, learning is initially an external process, as both children and adults learn by developing knowledge and shared understanding through collaboration and social interaction, and it is only later that the individual internalizes this knowledge. Many creative processes, however, take place when pairs or groups of people come together, as for example, to make music. As Hennessey (2004) points out, creative activity of this kind highlights the important role that group interaction and group composition play in the creative process. The generative framework of creativity described below has been developed to accommodate both the internal, personal processes and the social, external processes that take place when pairs or groups of children undertake musical composition tasks. The next section discusses the influences of different representational systems on the expression of children's musical composition.

Representations for musical expression

A central concern of creativity researchers working in the domain of music is how to develop methods of enhancing creativity in music composition, and in particular, how to identify factors that influence creativity in the classroom (Swanwick and Tillman 1986; Levi 1986; Kratus 1991). Literature within the field suggests that musical creativity can be affected by formal music training (FMT) in how to play an instrument and/or how to use musical notation. Several research studies have reported that musical creativity is affected by the visual representation used to express music, and that children's musical creativity is inhibited if they have to use conventional, abstract music notation (Walker 1992; Auh 2000). This is because they have difficulty mapping the sound properties of music to the visual specification of the staff notation. In the traditional notation system, the visual parameters of the notes do not directly relate to the sound itself. For example, a crotchet note is represented by a black circle with a vertical line. It is not instantly apparent that this means a sound that lasts for one beat, except to those trained in music fundamentals. Unless the individual student knows this, they will be unable to derive the meaning from the symbol. As a result, when approaching a music composition task, if children are required to adhere to the traditional notation system, those without knowledge of music fundamentals may well lack confidence in their abilities (Seddon 2002).

A number of scholars have suggested that alternative forms of graphical notation might prove more effective, for example, where the symbols used visually reflect the properties of musical sounds (e.g. Dillon 2005, Walker 1978). Symbol systems used in this way do not rely upon retrieval of previously learned meanings, as visual elements are matched to auditory elements through readily identifiable representations. In addition, this means that musical tones can be represented cross-modally. For example, sounds can be described as 'bright,' 'dark,' 'harsh,' 'soft,' and so on. As outlined above, salient aspects of learning and creativity are active exploration and the consideration of alternative meanings and perspectives. It can be argued that alternative forms of graphical representation have two advantages. First, these encourage students to use their own graphical representations to specify the properties of musical sounds using visual metaphors. This allows them to apply their own meanings to these visual symbols unconstrained by musical technicalities. Second, through constructing their own symbol systems of meaning, students are more likely to explore musical sounds and structures independently (Pugh 1980).

Auh and Walker (1999) report that when compared with the use of traditional staff notation, the use of graphic notations in children's music composition is associated with an increase in diverse compositional strategies. Further support for this arises from literature concerning the shift from childhood to adult cognitive modes in music that takes place during the teenage years. Around this time, self-criticism is likely to exceed musical competence (Zimmerman 1993). For example, Seddon (2002) reported that children without FMT appeared to lack confidence in composition tasks, and frequently attributed this to a lack of formal training. By contrast, children with FMT display much higher levels of perceived confidence (Seddon and O'Neill 2001; Folkestad, Hargreaves, and Lindström 1998). In terms of their compositional works, the above studies concluded that students with FMT had a greater preference for displaying their musical expertise (such as the use of musical structure) within their compositions. Students without FMT, on the other hand, preferred to display more originality and exploration (Seddon 2002; Sloboda 1985; Webster, Yale, and Haefner 1988). Seddon also reported that those with little to no FMT exhibited higher levels of exploration in the compositional strategies used. The findings from other studies suggest that musical pieces composed by formally trained musicians may be less original than pieces composed by people without formal training (Webster et al. 1988).

The difference in students' preferred approaches towards music composition associated with FMT might exert a causal effect on the different styles of thinking involved in composition and the acquisition of skill. Webster (1996) associates the compositional process with divergent thinking and skill acquisition with convergent thinking. This is in accordance with theories that suggest that creativity is concerned with breaking away from established patterns of thinking (De Bono 1967). This is usually attributed to divergent thinking (Baer 1993; Vosburg 1998). Because of their expectations and previous experiences, however, students are likely to approach the compositional task with differing perspectives (Chase and Simon 1973; Schank 1999). The compositions of those previously educated in the playing of an instrument and traditional notation are more likely to conform to prescribed music notation and the technical demands of their instrument. Those without prior training will have more creative and compositional freedom due to the absence of such constraints.

This is not to suggest, however, that the use of staff notation should be entirely removed in music education, rather it should not be perceived as a prerequisite to compositional tasks. The music curriculum adhered to by secondary schools within the United Kingdom requires that children develop an appreciation for staff notation in their music learning. Therefore, although staff notation and music fundamentals must be taught at some point, many music educators argue that initially music composition should be introduced in a way that does not stifle creativity. For example, creative alternatives towards music that allow children to explore musical sounds and structures should be seen as a prerequisite to the introduction of formal notation systems (Pond 1981; Levi 1986). The next section presents a framework designed to support these alternatives.

A generative framework of learning and creativity

The generative framework of creativity attempts to explain the concepts and processes involved in creativity. As illustrated in the framework (see Figure 10.2), the creative learning process begins with social and individual preparation, and ends with social and individual evaluation. It is characterized by three main processes: preparation, generation, and evaluation. The framework acknowledges social and individual elements within the creative process. Additionally, the framework does not commit to a strict linear route. The framework adopts the position that the creative process is cyclic in nature, and that it may go through several iterations (see also Amabile 1996).

The generative framework draws on the theories of learning and creativity discussed above, focuses on education, and is intended as a support tool to assist the development of lesson support materials and the design of educational technologies. The framework assists the design of creative educational experiences for the classroom by ensuring that support materials are scaffolded to six components. These are represented as white boxes (see Figure 10.2). Wallas's four-stage model has been adapted as the fundamental basis for this generative framework. The processes of preparation, generation, and evaluation are represented laterally across the framework. The vertical dimensions reflect the individual (denoted here as personal) and social components of creativity. The 'social' level refers to others, peers, and society. The 'personal' levels reflect explicit and tacit levels of thinking.

The lateral and vertical phases and sub-components of the generative framework are described next.

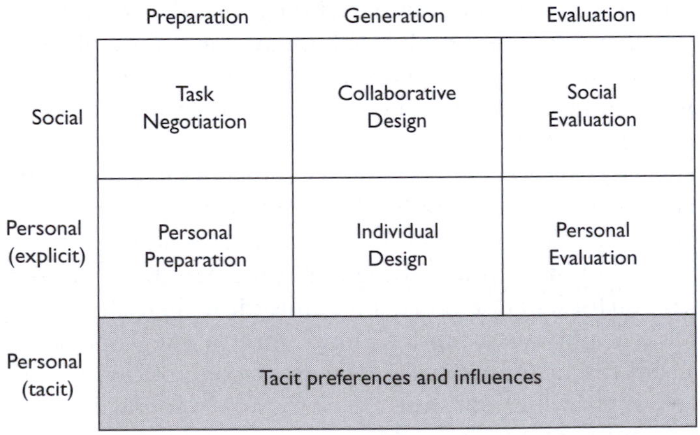

	Preparation	Generation	Evaluation
Social	Task Negotiation	Collaborative Design	Social Evaluation
Personal (explicit)	Personal Preparation	Individual Design	Personal Evaluation
Personal (tacit)	Tacit preferences and influences		

Figure 10.2 A generative framework for creativity

Lateral process: the preparation process

During the preparation process, at the personal level, an individual will develop a curiosity or a desire to create. Once this desire or need has been established, information is consciously accumulated from the external environment, and thoughts may be discussed with others on a 'social' level, which the individual can reflect upon on a 'personal' level (Getzels 1964). If working in a collaborative setting, group-wide negotiations of the task will also take place. Inevitably, the way in which an individual prepares for the task will be influenced by past experiences which may be explicit or tacit (Schank 1995).

Lateral process: the generation process

The generation process of the framework encompasses social and personal design. Within this process ideas are generated, which can involve interactions and negotiation between the individual and peers in their environment. Additionally, idea generation is assisted partly by a continuous interaction occurring between levels of explicit and tacit thinking (Claxton 1998). The creativity literature refers to these subconscious processes as incubation and illumination. 'Incubation' takes place when conscious thought pertaining to a problem or idea is rested or suspended, and subconscious processes take over. 'Illumination' happens after a period of incubation at the point when creative ideas are consciously realized. A number of scholars suggest that external environmental influences at a 'social' level can trigger the process where, at a 'personal' level, creative ideas progress from tacit to more explicit thoughts (Claxton 1998, Csikszentmihalyi and Sawyer 1995). The generative framework acknowledges the importance of environmental factors upon the creative process, and the importance of allowing time for creative ideas to evolve.

Lateral process: the evaluation process

The evaluation process is concerned with the review of creative ideas at all stages from their early inception through to the creation of a final solution or artefact. Individuals can conduct this at a personal level, or the wider community can carry it out at a later stage. A wide body of literature also supports these two evaluative dimensions (Amabile 1983; Csikszentmihalyi 1988, 1999; Martindale 1990). Although not all creative acts culminate in historically significant acts (Briskman 1980), the creative individual may wish to verify their work with others residing within the community. When this evaluative process does not lead to individual or societal acceptance of the creative artefact, an individual may revisit earlier stages of the framework, for example for the refinement of an idea (Amabile 1996). Additionally, evaluation may also involve an implicit or tacit emotional response. If an individual feels 'uncomfortable' about the final product, they might revert to earlier processes such as preparation or incubation (Schon 1983). Similarly, if an individual feels 'satisfied' with their work they might evaluate it at the conscious level. It is suggested that in terms of personal evaluation, a natural dialogue takes place between explicit and tacit levels of thinking.

It is only when this evaluation process has been reached that it is possible to revisit earlier stages if further generation or preparation is deemed necessary. This cyclic nature of the framework permits iteration and reiteration until a positive evaluation has been attained and the individual is satisfied with their creative idea or artefact produced.

Vertical dimensions: the roles of social, personal explicit, and personal tacit levels of the framework

The vertical dimensions of the framework capture the personal and social components of creativity. This encompasses interactions and discourse with others, and influences drawn from the environment. The personal levels, which are exclusive to the individual, encompass explicit and implicit levels of thinking. At the explicit level, an individual consciously prepares for the task, generates ideas, and reviews them. At the tacit level, 'ideation' may occur (Sanders 2001). 'Ideation' refers to the formation of thoughts and ideas that initially defy expression in language. Root-Bernstein and Root-Bernstein (1999) maintain that creative thinking occurs pre-verbally, manifesting itself via emotions, images, and intuition. When thoughts cross the boundary between implicit and explicit ways of knowing, illumination may occur, and lead to the generation of new ideas or the reorganization of existing ways of understanding (Rothenberg 1979; Barsalou 1983). Previous

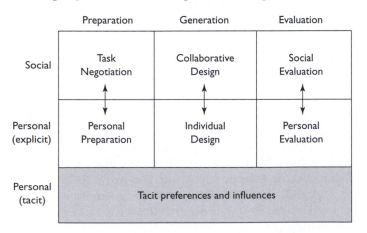

Figure 10.3 Vertical interactions occurring within the framework

studies suggest that a number of creative thinking approaches can assist these processes, such as metaphorical and analogical concepts (Harrington 1981; Ainsworth-Land 1982). When illumination occurs, the individual may evaluate their ideas tacitly or explicitly, and/or they might seek further evaluation from the wider community.

Figure 10.3 illustrates interactions between the vertical levels of the framework. Interactions between social and personal levels take place continuously, and are influenced by environmental and cultural factors. As discussed above, interactions between personal (explicit) and personal (tacit) levels also occur continuously throughout the creative process.

Instantiating the framework: a music composition example

The generative framework proposed here offers many advantages in terms of facilitating creative thinking and learning within the classroom context. Teachers and designers of educational technology can use it to develop lesson plans that provide the time and resources necessary to ensure that all aspects of the creative process are considered. The framework has been designed so that it can be applied to any domain. Here, the framework is instantiated through a music composition example where students are set the task of composing music in pairs. This instantiation is illustrated in Figure 10.4.

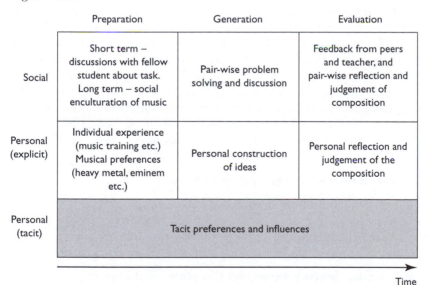

	Preparation	Generation	Evaluation
Social	Short term – discussions with fellow student about task. Long term – social enculturation of music	Pair-wise problem solving and discussion	Feedback from peers and teacher, and pair-wise reflection and judgement of composition
Personal (explicit)	Individual experience (music training etc.) Musical preferences (heavy metal, eminem etc.)	Personal construction of ideas	Personal reflection and judgement of the composition
Personal (tacit)	Tacit preferences and influences		

Time

Figure 10.4 Instantiation of the framework – a music composition example

The implicit and explicit personal dimensions identified in Figure 10.4 attempt to capture the fact that over the long term, students acquire a great deal of knowledge about music and the kinds of musical styles dominant in their culture. In the short term, during the preparation stage of musical composition, students work in pairs and jointly negotiate how to carry out the task. Each member of the pair brings unique experiences to the task in terms of any musical instrument training and personal musical preferences. Coordination of their different perspectives may generate new musical insights, at which point the framing for the composition is recognized, discussed, and acted upon during the evaluation phase. If the pair dismiss the idea, or they are not satisfied, they may return to earlier phases to seek further refinement or further verification. This evaluation occurs at both a personal level, when each individual in the pair reflects upon their composition, and at a social level, when they evaluate it as a pair. In addition they may seek evaluation from their teacher and the wider student group through discussions that encourage others to comment on the compositional piece.

SoundScape: a creative–collaborative music composition environment

SoundScape is a music composition environment that has been designed as a vehicle to demonstrate how the generative framework can be applied in practice. This approach is intended to set compositional tasks in an interesting and appropriate context in the hope that the overall learning experience will prove more meaningful to the student. The SoundScape software has been specifically designed for school-aged children, and allows them to work collaboratively and creatively to construct a piece of music.[1] It does this by replacing traditional musical notation with cartoon-style 'themes' and 'objects.' It can be used by those with little to no formal music training as well as by children who are experienced musicians. The cartoon-style design of the program seeks to situate music education in an appropriate and entertaining context for children.

The 'visual metaphor' SoundScape prototype

SoundScape allows children to work in pairs or groups of three to compose a piece of music. Upon entry to the program, students enter the 'system mode' of the program and enter their names (see Plate 23).

The preparation process: setting up templates and objects

Students are set the task of selecting one of four themes as the metaphorical context for their composition. These themes include a street, a jungle, an ocean, and a space theme (see Plate 24).

Plate 23 illustrates the name given to the program, as 'SoundScape' involves the creation of musical landscapes. Auh (2000) has suggested that a way forward for research into children's creative music composition is to use 'sound scapes' to open up their understanding of the nature of musical composition by introducing the notion that this involves the collection and organization of interesting sounds. To date, very little research has been conducted on this. Previous studies have focused upon encouraging children to draw their own graphical notations and symbol systems to represent music rather than employing visual representations that act as metaphors for sounds. SoundScape allows students to relate new musical concepts to what they already know by using pictures of real-world objects as visual metaphors that can be used to specify the sound properties of music.

During the theme selection stage, students enter the preparation stage of the generative framework discussed above. Here, students can be expected to discuss the task to be completed, and negotiate which theme to select from the possible choices. By requiring students to justify their learning choices to each other, SoundScape seeks to offer reflexivity and a more meaningful approach towards compositional activities by encouraging students to think on a deeper level, For example, following theme selection, students are asked to explain why they have selected a particular theme in which to set their musical work (see Plate 25).

With regard to Plate 25, the SoundScape system stores students' responses. Their teacher, using the appropriate system mode, can view these responses later. Depending upon the theme selected, students are presented with ten cartoon objects associated with that theme. For example, if the 'jungle' theme is selected, students are presented with cartoon objects such as a tiger, a monkey, and a giraffe. Students are also presented with fourteen pre-recorded music samples (see Plate 26) and are set the task of associating the visual cartoon objects with the musical sounds on the basis of those attributes they perceive the pictures and sounds to share. Visual and sound objects are selected from lists displayed at the interface as shown in Plate 26.

If students wish to associate a visual object with a musical object, they select the 'link image and sound' button. This presents a prompt that asks students to enter a reason for their association. The inclusion of the prompt is intended to elicit information that will allow tones within the music to be represented cross-modally. For example, a sound that is perceived as 'soft' or 'harsh' by the student might be associated with a pictured object with similar qualities. The teacher, prior to the task, determines the minimum number of objects that are to be associated with the sounds. When the required number of objects and sounds has been chosen, the 'create SoundScape' button appears. This allows students to progress to the compositional environment.

The importance of allowing time for preparation: alignment with the creative process

SoundScape places a great deal of emphasis upon the preparation process of creativity, and allows plenty of time for students to make learning choices concerning their theme and object selections. It is this particular focus upon the preparation stage that sets SoundScape apart from other music composition programs aimed at children. When students have worked through this preparatory stage they then progress on to generating and evaluating their ideas both individually and collaboratively.

The generation process: working within the composition environment

When the 'create SoundScape' button is selected on the object selection screen, the program then moves to the composition screen. It is at this point that students enter the generation process. The focus here is on sharing and generating musical ideas through collaborative discussion. As can be seen from Plate 27, the interface relays the theme the pair have selected by setting this as the background. The associated objects are presented in colored boxes at the bottom of the screen. The lines running from top to the bottom of the composition screen represent musical bar lines. These make it easy to depict images that are associated with longer or shorter sound durations. The students simply drag the objects from the colored boxes and structure or arrange them on the composition background as they wish. They can also remove objects from the composition by dragging them off the background. Additionally, when placed in the composition, objects can be moved to another location on the background at any time.

By using visual objects to structure a visual pattern at the interface, a relationship is formed which directly corresponds to the musical pattern made by the sounds the objects represent. This allows the structure to be represented cross-modally. The composition interface also features 'play,' 'rewind,' and 'stop' buttons which allow students to play back their work and restructure the objects at any time. When the 'play' button is selected, a red play line travels from left to right of the environment to indicate which objects are being played.

The evaluation process: reviewing the composition

In terms of the evaluation process, the context of SoundScape has been designed so that once they have created a composition, students can judge its merits both individually and collaboratively. SoundScape also allows students to move in and out of the generation and evaluation process to refine their composition. This cyclic iteration continues until the students are satisfied with their composition, at which point they might seek wider evaluation from their teacher and peers. Using SoundScape, students can listen to each other's compositions and can print out pictorial representations of their music. These can be exhibited in the classroom to encourage peer-wide evaluation.

The 'abstract representation' SoundScape prototype

An alternative SoundScape prototype was also built as a comparator to the version that allowed children to use visual metaphors to specify their music. This prototype used abstract representations to specify music, similar to those used in commercial programs such as the E-Jay range.[2] E-Jay-type representations depict musical sounds via blocks that show only the sample names of sounds and instruments. These blocks can be arranged on bar lines to compose a sequence of musical sounds. This prototype was developed in order to compare the effect of the two differing representations on children's perceptions of musical composition and the compositions themselves. The E-Jay-type composition interface is illustrated in Plate 28.

With regard to Plate 28, the abstract representation prototype possessed the exact same system functionality as the visual metaphor SoundScape prototype. Before they accessed the composition interface, students were presented with a list of sounds that they could listen to by selecting an item on the list. Students were able to assign sounds to composition objects by selecting the 'save' button. Once the required number of sounds had been selected, the 'Create SoundScape' button appeared and students were able to progress to the composition environment. The sample selection interface is illustrated in Plate 29.

A research study was designed to evaluate the impact of the two prototypes (visual representation and abstract representation) on children's experience of composing their own music during a collaborative composition task. The next section describes this evaluation and its outcomes.

Using SoundScape to evaluate the effectiveness of visual metaphors to specify music composition

The research study sought to evaluate whether using visual metaphors as opposed to abstract musical representation to specify music would be a more meaningful activity for primary school children. It was also designed to evaluate whether using visual metaphors would lead to greater depth of engagement and enjoyment in musical composition. The research was carried out with 48 children aged eleven to twelve years at a middle school in Milton Keynes, England. Twenty-four participants were allocated to one of two experimental conditions: Group A used concrete visual metaphors with SoundScape to specify their music; Group B used abstract visual representations with SoundScape. There were four male–male pairs, four female–female pairs and four female–male pairs in each group. Both groups contained equal numbers of low and high-ability students as matched by class teachers at the school. The classroom used for this study was a small music room which contained a laptop loaded with the appropriate SoundScape software. Working in pairs, students were instructed to create a piece of music using SoundScape. They were told, 'There is no right or wrong way of carrying out this task. Spend as long as necessary until you feel you have completed the task.'

Analyzing the depth of engagement with the music composition task

During the students' interaction with SoundScape, points of discussion between pair members were recorded for later analysis. The length of time pairs took to complete the task was also recorded. In addition, after they completed the SoundScape task, each pair of students was interviewed informally. Results from the study indicated that students from Group A (the visual metaphor group) were more engaged with the music composition task than students from Group B (who used abstract representations). Depth of engagement was measured by comparing:

- the time spent creating the composition
- the number of composition objects used
- the number of composition objects moved during engagement with the task
- the number of musical bars completed during engagement
- the number of individual sounds played during engagement
- the nature and type of comments students made during engagement.

Results were then compared across Groups A and B to ascertain differences existing within the depth of engagement. On all of these measures, statistical analyses revealed significant differences between pairs in Group A and the pairs in Group B that indicated greater depth and complexity of engagement for students in Group A, in terms of the time they spent on their compositions and the range and number of compositional devices they employed. Full details of these findings are reported in Truman (2008). There were also differences between the groups in terms of the comments they made when interviewed afterwards.

The comments students made while engaged on the task were of two distinct types: comments about individual sounds, pictures, or symbols, and mapping comments (that is, comments on the relationship between the representational symbols and the sounds these represented). Findings here indicated that students in Group B, who used abstract musical representations, made significantly more comments about individual sounds than those in Group A. By contrast, students in Group A made significantly more mapping comments. This type of comment frequently referred to the visual and auditory associations of a composition object, for example, 'I think we should put a line of cars there so it looks like a traffic jam and all the horns will be playing.' In addition, 100 percent of students in Group A commented that their music told a 'story.' During the interviews that followed the SoundScape session students were asked to elaborate on these stories. Examples of comments made by students are given in Box 10.1.

Box 10.1 Student comments on their composition 'stories'

Oysters were sitting down at the start looking around and the angel fish were swimming on by. Dolphins were moving along with the waves following each other. Sharks were trying to catch each others' tails. Scuba divers were kicking each other and the jelly fish were chilling at the end, and the sea horses were looking at everyone thinking they were loopy.

Katherine and Gemma, Group A

Our music told a little story about a shark trying to get the red fish.

Louise and Ashleigh, Group A

A cat and dog were out and when it started to thunder a boy came out and then a man went to work.

Dennis and Sam, Group A

Was a story about a house with a letter box and cars. The suns were rising and setting and there was a man walking along the road. Although we had to change it when we listened to it (composition) as what looked good didn't sound good because of the gaps in the middle (space between objects).

George and Thomas, Group A

Analyzing the depth of enjoyment with the music composition task

Students' depth of enjoyment with the composition task was measured by responses collected during their interview. They were asked what they liked about using SoundScape. Their responses could be grouped into the following five categories:

- I can make music without having to play an instrument.
- I liked the sound samples.
- I like the way music was made.
- Using SoundScape was fun.
- SoundScape was easy to use.

In Group A (visual metaphors), 58 per cent of students commented that they found using SoundScape fun, 50 per cent stated that SoundScape was easy to use, and 41 per cent stated that they liked the sounds available within SoundScape. None of the students from the pairs in Group A commented on the importance of being able to use SoundScape without being able to play an instrument. Nor did they discuss how the program actually created music. In Group B, only 8 per cent of students commented that they found SoundScape was fun to use, although 50 per cent stated that they found it easy to use. In addition, 33 per cent stated that they liked the way they could make music, 50 per cent liked the sounds available, and 16 per cent commented that they liked being able to create music without playing an instrument. These findings illustrate that students using the visual metaphor prototype commented more on the 'fun' aspect of SoundScape, whereas students using the abstract representation prototype commented more on its ease of use and the range of sounds available.

Analyzing the depth of 'meaning' within the music composition

The 'depth of meaning' evident in the compositions was measured by looking at how students placed the musical objects in the two SoundScape environments, and by discussing with them how they perceived their compositions. This showed that students perceived the compositions either as musical pieces or as music that relayed a story. Here there were very clear differences between the two groups. None of the participants in Group B commented that their composition reflected a story, whereas 100 per cent of participants in Group A did so. When the pictorial representations created by students in Group A were studied, it was found that in 75 per cent of cases composition objects were placed in their real-world locations. For example, in some compositions objects such as cars, post boxes, and people were placed within the 'ground' area of the composition, while sun and cloud objects were placed in the 'sky.' This indicated that many pairs used the composition objects in a literal sense to create both a meaningful, real-world visual narrative and a meaningful soundscape. As discussed earlier, these students also produced compositions that were more structurally complex and which employed a greater variety and number of composition objects than the students who used the abstract representational system.

Conclusions

In the United Kingdom composition is regarded as integral to music learning (Berkley 2004). It is included in music curricula, and since the 1980s it has been a requirement of the award of the General Certificate of Secondary Education (GCSE) in music. The importance of creativity to this process, however, is often overlooked and appears to be undervalued. Within the curriculum, there is an emphasis on the 'structure' and 'form' of musical composition. The findings of the study reported above suggest that this does not reflect the natural process of children's compositional strategies, particularly in the primary school. Paynter (2000) draws a similar conclusion. For many children, participation in music education and composition is largely an imaginative and intuitive process unconstrained by technicalities such as 'musical structure' and 'form,' and instead relies upon an imaginative response to a stimulus. As previous studies of children's informal music-making indicate, during the compositional process, children explore and discover musical sounds, forming patterns that may represent real-world situations, animals, and so forth. As the discussions presented in this chapter suggest, the provision of real-world metaphors to specify music in a composition task may assist with leveraging creative thinking in children's music composition.

There are several possible interpretations of why this may be the case. First, the generative framework used to inform the design of SoundScape draws on theories of creativity and learning. This means that time was built into its design for preparation, generation, and evaluation, which are key processes involved in creative thinking and meaning making. Second, SoundScape encourages children to think about the metaphorical relationship between sounds and the visual objects used to represent these sounds. This is likely to deepen their understanding of the qualities of those sounds. Third, SoundScape allows children to draw on both visual and auditory perceptual modalities to acquire cross-modal, internal representations of the sounds. Finally, replacing traditional notation with cartoon-style 'themes' and 'objects,' allows children to create narrative structures that situate the task of composition in a more meaningful context.

This chapter has also discussed an approach towards advancing music composition through technology by considering the creative process and processes related to collaborative learning. In particular, this chapter has focused upon a generative framework that offers a design support tool for educators, teachers, and designers of educational technologies to facilitate the preparation and design of learning material. This chapter has identified the motivation behind the framework, demonstrated how it can be instantiated, and discussed how it applies in practice. The evaluation of the two prototypes provides compelling evidence that when pairs of children use visual metaphors to represent sounds in the SoundScape environment, they experience a greater depth of engagement and enjoyment in their music-making.

Acknowledgment

The author acknowledges and extends appreciation to Ben Hawkridge (Knowledge Media Institute, The Open University) for his assistance with developing the SoundScape program.

Notes

1   Details of how to obtain a copy of the SoundScape software are available from dr_truman@hotmail.co.uk
2   Details of E-jay software can be accessed at http://www.ejay-store.co.uk/index.html

References:

Ainsworth-Land, V. (1982) 'Imagining and creativity: an integrating perspective,' *Journal of Creative Behaviour*, **16**, pp. 5–28.

Amabile, T. M. (1983) 'The psychology of creativity: a componential conceptualization,' *Journal of Personality and Social Psychology*, **45**, pp. 357–76.

Amabile, T. M. (1996) *Creativity in Context*, Boulder, Colo.: Westview.

Auh, M. (2000) 'Effects of using graphic notations on creativity in composing music by Australian secondary school students,' *Proceedings of the Australian Association for Research in Education Conference*, Australia 2000.

Auh, M. and Walker, K. (1999) 'Compositional strategies and musical creativity when composing staff notation versus graphic notation among Korean students,' *Bulletin of the Council for Research in Music Education*, Special issue 141, pp. 2–9.

Baccarini, D. (2004) 'The implementation of authentic activities for learning: a case study,' *Proceedings of the 13th Annual Teaching Learning Forum, Perth: Murdoch University, Australia, 9–10 February*.

Baer, J. (1993) *Creativity and Divergent Thinking: A task-specific approach*, N.J.: Erlbaum Associates.

Bandura, A. (1986) *Social Foundations of Thought and Action: A social cognitive theory*, Englewood Cliffs, N.J.: Prentice Hall.

Barsalou, L. W. (1983) 'Adhoc categories,' *Memory and Cognition*, 11, pp. 211–27.

Berkley, R. (2004) 'Teaching composing as creative problem solving: conceptualising composing pedagogy,' *British Journal of Music Education*, **21**(13), pp. 239–63.

Briskman, L. (1980) 'Creative product and creative process in science and art,' *Inquiry*, **23**, pp. 83–106.

Brown, J. S., Collins, A. and Duguid, P. (1989) 'Situated cognition and the culture of learning,' *Educational Researcher*, Jan.–Feb., pp. 32–43.

Bruckman, A. (1998) 'Community support for constructionist learning,' *Computer Supported Co-operative Work*, **7**, pp. 47–86.

Chase, W. G. and Simon, H. A. (1973) 'The mind's eye in chess,' in W. G. Chase (ed.), *Visual Information Processing*, New York: Academic Press.

Claxton, G. (1998) *Hare Brain Tortoise Mind: Why intelligence increases when you think less*, London; Fourth Estate.

Csikszentmihalyi, M. (1988) 'Society, culture and person: a systems view of creativity,' pp. 325–39 in R. J. Sternberg (ed.), *The Nature of Creativity*, Cambridge: Cambridge University Press.

Csikszentmihalyi, M. (1993) *The Evolving Self: A psychology for the third millennium*, New York: Harper Collins.

Csikszentmihalyi, M. (1999) 'Implications of a systems perspective for the study of creativity,' pp. 313–35 in R. J. Sternberg (ed.), *Handbook of Creativity*, Cambridge: Cambridge University Press.

Csikszentmihalyi, M. and Sawyer, K. (1995) 'Creative insight: the social dimension of a solitary movement,' in R. J. Sternberg and J. E. Davidson (eds.), *The Nature of Insight*, Cambridge, Mass.: MIT Press.

De Bono, E. (1967) *New Think: The use of lateral thinking in the generation of new ideas*, New York: Basic Books.

Derry, S. J. (1999) 'A fish called peer learning: searching for common themes,' in A. M. O'Donnell and A. King (eds.), *Cognitive Perspectives on Peer Learning*, Mahwah, N.J.: Lawrence Erlbaum Associates.

Dewey, J. (1916) *Democracy and Education*, New York: Macmillan.

Dillon, T. (2005) 'Jungulator: Research report,' Bristol: Futurelab Available at: http://www.futurelab.org/projects/jungulator (accessed February 2010).

Edwards, D. and Mercer, N. (1987) *Common Knowledge: The development of understanding in the classroom*, London: Methuen.

Ernest, P. (1995) *The One and the Many: Constructivism in education*, N.J.: Lawrence Erlbaum Associates.

Fasko, D. (2001) 'Education and creativity,' *Creativity Research Journal*, **13**(3 and 4), pp. 317–27.

Fischer, G. (2000) 'Symmetry of ignorance, social creativity and meta-design,' *Knowledge Based Systems*, **13**, pp. 527–37.

Folkestad, G., Hargreaves, D. J., and Lindström, B. (1998) 'Compositional strategies in computer-based music making,' *British Journal of Music Education*, **15**(1), pp. 83–97.

Forrester, D. and Jantzie, N. (2001) 'Learning theories' available at: http://www.ucalgary.ca/~gnjantzi/learning_theories.htm (accessed January 2002).

Frank, C. (2005) 'Teaching and learning theory: who needs it?,' *College Quarterly*, **2**(8).

Getzels, J. W. (1964) 'Creative thinking, problem-solving, and instruction,' in E. R. Hilgard (ed.), *Theories of Learning and Instruction*, Chicago, Ill.: University of Chicago Press.

Gruber, H. E. and Wallace, D. B. (1999) 'The case study method and evolving systems approach for understanding unique creative people at work,' pp. 93–115 in R. J. Sternberg (ed.), *Handbook of Creativity*, Cambridge: Cambridge University Press.

Guilford, J. P. (1950) 'Creativity,' *American Psychologist*, **5**, pp. 444–54.

Guilford, J. P. (1967) 'Creativity: yesterday, today and tomorrow,' *Journal of Creative Behaviour*, **1**, pp. 3–14.

Harrington, D. M. (1981) 'Creativity, analogical thinking and muscular metaphors,' *Journal of Mental Imagery*, **6**, pp. 121–6.

Hennessey, B. A. (2004) 'Creativity, classrooms, culture, and communication,' , pp. 761–763 in J. Houtz (ed.), *Review of the Educational Psychology of Creativity, Contemporary Psychology: APA Review of Books*, Vol. 49.

Holyoak, K. J. and Thagard, P. (1996) *Mental Leaps: Analogy in creative thought*, Cambridge, Mass.: MIT Press.

Honebein, P. C., Duffy, T. M., and Fishman, B. J. (1996) 'Constructivism and the design of learning environments: context and authentic activities for learning,' in T. M. Duffy, J. Lowyck, and D. H.. Jonassen (eds.), *Designing Environments for Constructive Learning*, Berlin: Springer-Verlag.

Houtz, J. C. and Krug, D. (1995) 'Assessment of creativity: resolving a mid-life crisis,' *Educational Psychology Review*, **7**, pp. 269–300.

Jarvinen, E. M. (1998) 'The LEGO/LOGO learning environment in technology education: an experiment in a Finnish context,' *Journal of Technology Education*, **9**(2), pp. 47–59.

Johnson, J. and Dyer, J. (2005) 'User-defined content in a constructivist learning environment,' *Proceedings of M-ECITE 2005, 'Recent research developments in learning technologies.'*

Karnes, M. B., McCoy, G. F., Zehrbach, R. R., Wollersheim, J. P., Clarizio, H. F., Costin, L., and Stanley, L. S. (1961) *Factors Associated with Overachievement of Intellectually Gifted Children*, Ill.: Champaign.

Kratus, J. (1991) 'Characterisation of the compositional strategies used by children to compose a melody,' *Canadian Journal of Research in Music Education*, **33**, pp. 95–103.

Levi, R. (1986) 'Investigating the creativity process: the role of regular music composition experiences for the elementary child,' *Journal of Creative Behaviour*, **25**(2), pp. 123–36.

Martindale, C. (1990) *The Clockwork Muse*, New York: Basic Books.

McMahon, M. (1997) 'Social constructivism and the World Wide Web: a paradigm for learning,' *Proceedings of the ASCILITE Conference, Perth, Australia, December*.

Moran, S. and John-Steiner, V. (2003) 'Creativity in the making: Vygotsky's contribution to the dialectic of development and creativity,' in R. K. Sawyer, V. John-Steiner, S. Moran, et al. (eds.), *Creativity and Development*, Oxford: Oxford University Press.

Osborn, A. F. (1953) *Applied Imagination*, rev. edn, New York: Scribners.

Papert, S. (1993) *The Children's Machine: Rethinking school in the age of the computer*, New York: Basic Books.

Papert, S. (1999) 'The century's greatest minds: Papert on Piaget,' *Time*, 29 March, p. 105.

Paynter, J. (2000) 'Making progress with composing,' *British Journal of Music Education*, **17**(1), pp. 5–31.

Piaget, J. (1954) *The Construction of Reality in the Child*, New York: Basic Books.

Piaget, J. (1955) *The Language and Thought of the Child*, New York: Meridian Books.

Pond, D. (1981) 'A composer's study of young children's innate musicality,' *Bulletin of the Council of Research in Music Education*, **68**, pp. 1–12.

Poincaré, H. (1913) cited in G. Leytham (1990) *Managing Creativity*, Norfolk: Peter Francis.

Pugh, A. (1980) 'In defense of musical literacy,' *Cambridge Journal of Education*, **10**(1), pp. 29–34.

Raskin, J. D. (2005) 'Constructivism in psychology: personal construct psychology, radical constructivism and social constructivism,' *American Communication Journal*, **3**(5).

Rogoff, B. (1990) *Apprenticeship in Thinking: Cognitive development in social context*, New York: Oxford University Press.

Rogoff, B. (2003) *The Cultural Nature of Human Development*, Oxford: Oxford University Press.

Root-Berstein, R. and Root Berstein, M. (1999) *Sparks of Genius: The 13 thinking tools of the world's most creative people*, New York: Houghton-Mifflin.

Rothenberg, A. (1979) *The Emerging Goddess: The creative process in art, science and other fields*, Chicago, Ill.: University of Chicago Press.

Runco, M. A. (1996) 'Creativity from childhood through adulthood,' *New Directions for Child Development*, **72**, Summer.

Runco, M. A. and Johnson, D. J. (2002) 'Parent's and teacher's implicit theories of children's creativity: a cross cultural perspective,' *Creativity Research Journal*, **14**(3 and 4), pp. 427–38.

Sanders, E. B. (2001) 'Collective creativity,' *LOOP: AIGA Journal of Interaction Design Education*, **4**.

Schank, R. (1995) *What We Learn When We Learn by Doing*, Technical Report no. 60, Institute of Learning Sciences, Northwestern University, Illinois.

Schank, R. (1999) *Dynamic Memory Revisited*, Cambridge Mass.: Cambridge University Press.

Schon, D. (1983) *The Reflective Practitioner*, London: Harper Collins.

Seddon, F. A. (2002) 'The relationship between instrumental experience, adolescent self-perceived competence in computer-based music composition and teacher evaluation of composition,' in C. Stevens, D. Burnham, G. McPherson, E. Scubert, and J. Renwick (eds.), *Proceedings of the Seventh International Conference on Music Perception and Cognition, Sydney 2002*, Adelaide, Australia: Casual Productions.

Seddon, F. A. and O'Neill, S. A. (2001) 'Creative thinking processes in adolescent composition: an interpretation of composition strategies adopted during computer-based composition,' paper presented at the Second International Research in Music Education Conference, University of Exeter, April 2001.

Sloboda, J. A. (1985) *The Musical Mind: The cognitive psychology of music*, Oxford: Oxford University Press.

Stager, G. (2005) 'Towards a pedagogy of online constructionist learning,' *Proceedings of the 2005 World Conference on Computers in Education, Stellenbosch, South Africa*.

Sternberg, R. and Lubart, T. (1991) 'An investment theory of creativity and its development,' *Human Development*, **34**, pp. 1–31.

Swanwick, K. and Tillman, J. (1986) 'The sequence of music development: a study of children's composition,' *British Journal of Music Education*, **3**(3), pp. 305–39.

Taylor, A. (1959) 'The nature of creative process,' in P. Smith (ed.), *Creativity*, New York: Hastings House.

Torrance, E. P. (1981) 'Creative teaching makes a difference,' in J. C. Gowan, J. Khatena, and E. P. Torrance (eds.), *Creativity: Its educational implications*, Dubuque, Ind.: Kendall/Hunt.

Truman, S. (2008) *A Computer Supported Approach towards Collaborative and Creative Musicality in the Classroom: Study and Framework*, unpublished Ph.D. thesis, available at: http://ethos.bl.uk/

Von Glaserfeld, E. (1995) 'A constructivist approach to teaching,' pp. 3–15 in L. P. Steffe and J. Gale (eds.), *Constructivism in Education*. New Jersey, USA: Lawrence Erlbaum Associates.

Von Glaserfeld, E. and Steffe, L. (1991) 'Conceptual models in educational research and practice,' *Journal of Educational Thought*, **25**(2), pp. 91–103.

Vosburg, S. K. (1998) 'The effects of positive and negative mood on divergent-thinking performance,' *Creativity Research Journal*, **11**, pp. 165–72.

Vosniadou, S. (1996) 'Towards a revised cognitive psychology for new advances in learning and instruction,' *Learning and Instruction*, **26**, pp. 414–34.

Vygotsky, L. S. (1978) *Mind in Society: The development of higher psychological processes*, Cambridge, Mass.: Harvard University Press.

Walker, R. (1978) 'Perception and music notation,' *Psychology of Music*, **6**(1), pp. 21–46.

Walker, R. (1992) 'Auditory-visual perception and musical behaviour,' in R. Colwell (ed.), *Handbook of Research on Music Teaching and Learning*, New York: Schirmer Books.

Wallas, G. (1926) *The Art of Thought*, London: Jonathan Cape [republished in 1931].

Webster, P. (1996) 'Creativity as creative thinking,' in G. Spruce (ed.), *Teaching Music*, London: Routledge/Open University.

Webster, P., Yale, C. and Haefner, M. (1988) 'Test-retest reliability of measures of creative thinking in music for children with formal music training,' MENC National In-Service Meeting, Indianapolis, Indiana.

Weisberg, R. W. (1993) *Creativity: Beyond the myth of genius*, New York: Freeman.

Zimmerman, M. P. (1993) 'An overview of developmental research in music,' *Bulletin of the Council for Research in Music Education*, **116,** pp. 1–10.

Chapter 11

Inside – outside: exploring learning and creativity in early years dance education

Kerry Chappell and Susan Young

> Invite a child of two to move whole-heartedly and spontaneously with you and they will probably be happy to play. Make the same invitation to an eight year old and you will probably be met with embarrassment.
>
> (Greenland 2007)

Penny Greenland's words cannot fail to strike a chord with practitioners, parents and researchers alike. This shift in young children from being playful explorers to followers of the crowd has also been noticed in recent studies of creative learning (Craft et al. 2006) and creative dance for older students (Rolfe et al. in press). Greenland's philosophy places particular emphasis on 'everyday dancing', which she describes as the 'spontaneous, physical often playful response to everyday life'. By working with younger children in educational settings, experienced dance practitioners like Penny Greenland and her past collaborator Jasmine Pasch, provide important contexts of dance work from which to better understand children's creative processes and the expression of their creative imaginations. These understandings may then offer insight for children of all ages when eliciting more playful, exploratory responses to everyday life. As suggested by Greenland, these may have gone underground, smothered by embarrassment and the other inhibitions to embodied expression which seem to go hand-in-hand with enculturation in Western European and North American societies.

By the turn of the century opportunities for children to dance in English schools had been squeezed out by the policy drive to raise standards in the curriculum basics of literacy and numeracy, a situation that may have a familiar ring in many other countries. This policy drive created external pressures on schools and early years settings which persuaded them to focus on narrow academic achievement and cognitive experience. As a result, arts-based curriculum areas, and the creative, embodied and affective experience that they engender, have received less attention. A seminal report into creativity in English schools produced by the National Advisory Committee on Creative and Cultural Education (NACCCE) in 1999 drew attention to this curricular imbalance. By 2006/7, when this study took place the priorities of the curriculum had little changed.[1]

More recently, building on this acknowledgement of curricular imbalance, there has been recognition that the future will require people who not only have basic skills and knowledge but are also flexible, independent-minded and innovative. This has led to further emphasis on developing creativity as an educational aim (e.g. Craft 2000, in press). Prior to and alongside this, shifts in understandings of creativity as going beyond an individual experience to a more collaborative and communal undertaking have also come to the fore in research arenas – often drawing on expert practice (e.g. John-Steiner 2000; Sawyer 2003). In turn, this has led to fostering creativity in English educational settings through a number of national initiatives designed to place artists working in partnership with educators. It is just such an initiative that formed the basis of the research into young children's dancing described in this chapter. All too often creative arts-based activity is still being co-opted to serve the main curriculum drive, rather than being valued and recognised for its intrinsic benefits. It could be argued that current curriculum policy has yet to catch up with the full implications of a shift to a curriculum that aims to develop both collaborative creativity and independent thinking. From the research community's perspective, there is a responsibility to help make this shift by providing argument rooted in prior research and contemporary evidence.

The Zest project

The research was embedded in a project called 'Zest', based in South-West England and managed by a regional arts organisation called Take Art[2] working in partnership with the local authority education support service. Two professional dance artists, Annabelle and Anna, led the movement aspect of the project. With experience of community arts work, particularly of working with children in educational settings, they were placed in two rural schools, Cranborn School and Highton School,[3] to work with children aged four to five years, once a week, over a twelve-week period. The aim of the project was to introduce creative dance into the curriculum experiences of the children. The dance practitioners were familiar with working in an approach framed by the principles of education developed in the Reggio Emilia nurseries of Northern Italy. Accordingly, they introduced certain initiating stimuli, or 'provocations' to use the Reggio Emilia term, designed to encourage spontaneous, imaginative bodily activity on the part of the children. These starting points might be physical – making a circle and dancing together to lively music – or material objects – such as large cardboard boxes or a piece of stretchy Lycra fabric. As ideas emerged from the children's responses to these starting points, the adults took up those ideas which had potential for development and extended them by collaborating with the children. This extension would continue within a session and then extend week by week.

In addition to their knowledge of 'Reggio', the dance practitioners had also trained in the Jabadao approach to early years creative movement. Jabadao is a development agency based in the United Kingdom, directed by Penny Greenland, which promotes awareness of the importance of movement for learning and wellbeing. It has developed the concept and practice of 'body intelligence and movement play'. This approach emphasises providing an environment within which children can contribute and explore their own movements, thus being certain that the activities as they evolve are developmentally appropriate. The principles of Jabadao thus sit comfortably with the Reggio Emilia approach.

In addition to the two dance artists, the project included additional artists, Richard at Cranborn School, specialising in film-making and Rod at Highton, specialising in clay work. These two artists worked alongside the dance artists, sometimes in separate time periods and sometimes in an integrated way. The film-maker's art form meant that he preferred to work mainly with the children during the dance activity, often using simultaneous film and projection techniques to enable the children to dance with their own digital images. The clay worker tended to initiate separate activities which could then be transferred into dance. Small movements shaping the clay with hands could become whole body movements in dance, or modelled shapes, such as eggs, were taken up as a theme for dance. The interaction of the two media and how they could combine and converge to support certain directions in the children's imaginative ideas is an interesting dimension of this project which will become apparent later when we discuss our findings. Our focus will be on the children's dispositions and their creative dance movement, but this aspect of the interaction of media in generating creative thinking and drawing it into certain directions is worthy of further consideration.

The project funders hoped that creative dance activity, by liberating the children's own ideas, would not only foster the children's imaginative and creative thinking but also spill over into their overall participation in school, and might then translate into better learning. Both schools served populations of pupils disadvantaged by rural poverty who, it was thought, might have most to gain from such enrichment. It is indicative of the times and the current educational climate that dance education was seen not as valuable for dance alone, but for how it could serve the wider demands of an English National Curriculum focused heavily on learning the 'basics'. As commissioned researchers, we had to understand this context, and how it shaped the project and the research we were being asked to carry out.

There was a tension, we discovered, between the project initiators' wish to explore the possible impact of dance education on the children's wider learning, and our own recognition that this is not only methodologically difficult, if not impossible, but also unwise, rooted as it is in value assumptions about the nature of learning. Increasingly, since the turn of the century, there has been recognition that the sole use of experimental pre- and post-test designs to investigate arts interventions is problematic (e.g. Fisk 2000). Biesta (2007) argues that there is an increasing trend within government approaches to educational research, particularly noticeable in the United Kingdom and United States, towards evidence-based practice. By this he refers to practice which is developed using the results of experimental impact studies of 'what works' as the basis for designing, and indeed resourcing, future developments in practice. This trend goes against the ideas of researchers such as Ridgway, Zawojewski and Hoover (2000), who argue against such narrow impact-based educational research particularly within arts education. The opponents of evidence-based education, according to Biesta, have queried the positivist assumptions underlying such approaches to educational development. Biesta argues convincingly that educational research must pay attention to the importance of teachers' and practitioners' professional action, based on judgments of what is educationally desirable in their own situations.

In the light of these arguments, we turned away from attempting any kind of impact-based approach and adopted qualitative methods to explore the experiences of the young children, practitioners and artists in the process of taking part in the work, rather than merely assessing at its conclusion. We adopted a broad notion of 'engagement', on the premise that first and foremost we needed to understand whether the dance activities, particularly since they were designed around principles of child-initiated work, were motivating and engaging to the children. For this purpose we adopted Laevers' work on involvement, and adapted its five-point levels of involvement to indicators most relevant to dance movement (1994, 2005).

Mindful, however, of the educational context and the need to serve wider issues of educational underachievement we extended the focus on 'engagement' to include 'learning dispositions'. Carr and Claxton (2002) developed a theory of 'learning dispositions' which was sufficiently generous to embrace the kinds of qualities of experiences we anticipated were most likely to evolve in the creative dance sessions. At the same time, it would provide information about the generic qualities that might underpin children's learning across all domains. We hypothesised that we could identify changes to the children's approach to participating in the creative dance sessions. Having identified any changes, we might then propose that these would persist into their approach to learning in other areas of their school life. There was then, a pragmatic reason to adopt a theoretical frame rooted in the notion of 'learning dispositions'; this was, after all, applied research commissioned to serve a purpose and not a 'pure' research design. We argue that it is no less valuable for that reason, and that the tensions drew us to consider important aspects of dance education in schools in its real-life situation. As an aside, we would argue that educational research cannot remain esoteric in ivory towers, but must work adaptively in real-world contexts, heeding Biesta's words that research should pay attention to teachers' and practitioners' professional action and the constraints of the situations they work in.

The focus on dispositions for learning drew on Claxton and Carr's (2002, 2004) work both theoretically and methodologically. The study began with their description of dispositions as being ready, willing and able to learn, and their suggestion that these dispositions are learned responses that become habitual. In other words, a conducive environment, such as a creative dance session, could engender dispositions. Three key learning dispositions were selected from Claxton and Carr's work which were felt to be appropriate to the dance education context that we were studying. They were resilience, playfulness and reciprocity. Resilience is defined as the inclination to take on learning challenges where the outcome is uncertain, to persist with learning despite temporary frustration. Playfulness means being willing and able to construct variations on learning situations and to be more creative in interpreting and reacting to problems. Particularly pertinent for this study is the inclusion of imagination and experimentation in their definition of playfulness. Reciprocity is about the confidence and inclination to give opinions and ideas, both verbally and non-verbally: that is, to learn 'in relationship'.

Laevers' (1994) work on 'involvement' in early years settings was also felt to resonate strongly with the 'dispositions for learning' focus. Laevers' use and definition of the term 'involvement' has much in common with Carr and Claxton's definitions of resilience and playfulness. Laevers (1994) defines involvement as recognisable by a child's concentration and persistence, characterized by motivation, fascination and an openness to stimuli and determined by an exploratory drive. The Zest research therefore proceeded with an understanding of the term 'disposition for learning' that encompassed notions of resilience, playfulness, reciprocity, motivation and fascination. Since we were applying these dispositions to dance movement, we considered that there would be evidence to support their presence in children's behaviours that was both physical and cognitive. There might, for example, be instances where the children were moving with an intensity and energy that was identifiable through careful observation of bodily movement – both visually and sympathetically perceived – that conveyed a level of engagement

One of the advantages of research that is process-oriented and designed qualitatively is that unanticipated findings can emerge during its course. As the practical work with the children progressed, we identified recurrent ideas and themes that resonated with recent socio-culturally grounded theorising of creativity in dance education as individual, collaborative and communal (Chappell 2006, 2008). This chapter will consider the detail of how creative movement helped children develop their dispositions for learning in the Somerset sites, and how these dispositions might provide the foundations for the children to engage in creative processes that go beyond the individual.

The sites

The first school, Cranborn School,[4] was a large primary school of 400 pupils (aged four to eleven years), and the other, Highton School, was a small village primary of thirty-seven pupils. Cranborn School is located in a small market town in a rural region of South West England and serves a rural working-class population. The two classes taking part in the project included a few new arrivals from Eastern Europe, but all other children and their families were local to the town. The school occupies a large Victorian building, recently extended with the new rooms including a hall with wooden floor ideal for dance. This was still not sufficient accommodation, however, and classes were also housed in temporary buildings erected in the playground. Some of the dance work took place in one of these hutted classrooms, once classroom furniture was pushed aside, and some took place in the hall. By contrast, Highton School was located on the very border of its administrative region, had experienced frequent changes of staffing, and the number of pupils had diminished as parents with cars opted to drive children to neighbouring village schools. All these factors added to an air of neglect. Sited in open, windswept agricultural landscape, it too was housed in an old Victorian village-school building with additional temporary huts outside. A proportion of the school population were from traveller/gypsy[5] families who had settled in the village in local authority housing. The children attended regularly but nevertheless the staff reported that their parents retained some of the ambivalence towards school-based learning that the traveller/gypsy community can hold, which then communicates to their children (Levinson 2007).

Methods

We focused the research on children aged four to five years. At Highton School there were only six children in this age phase, so we randomly selected the same number of children from Cranborn School. Individually we made five visits to each school at regular intervals through the duration of the twelve-week project. One of us also visited both schools in order to gain an overview.

We used a combination of data collection methods that included observations with researchers' field notes, photographs and video clips taken directly from the dance sessions. To these were added notes from the reflective post-session discussions, artists' and teachers' observation and planning notebooks, an informal interview with teachers and informal interviews with selected children. We therefore accumulated information from a number of different sources, thus strengthening the research process and its findings.

The observations of children were the central plank of our methods. These were structured to encourage systematic and detailed focus on the children's participation. Sample observations of each of the six children at the two schools were made at regular intervals (of ten minutes) throughout the hour-long sessions. A brief description of the children's participation in an activity was noted, together with an assessment of their level of engagement. The levels of engagement were based on the Leuven Involvement Scale for Young Children (Laevers 1994) with some observable indicators adapted for the children's involvement in movement activity. Table 11.1 shows the involvement levels.

In addition to the structured observations, we kept a running flow of field notes in which we not only kept an overall record of the kinds of activities that were developing but also noted anything pertinent to the notion of learning dispositions and its various dimensions. These were interspersed with photographs.

Following the session of working with the children, the dance artists and teachers met for reflective discussions about the work and the children's responses, referring to observation notes and sometimes video recording that had been made during the period of practical work. These processes of recording the children's responses and reflective discussion were in keeping

Table 11.1 Involvement level

Involvement	Indicators
L1 Low Activity	Simple stereotypic, repetitive, and passive. Child absent + displays no energy. May stare into space (but may be a sign of inner concentration)
L2 Frequently interrupted activity	Engaged in activity but half of observed period includes moments of non-activity/staring into space. Frequent interruptions to concentration
L3 Mainly continuous activity	Child is busy at an activity but at a routine level + real involvement missing. Some progress, but energy lacking + conc is routine, also easily distracted
L4 Continuous Activity with Intense moments (immersion)	Activity has intense moments where L3 activity can have special meaning. L4 is for kind of activity seen in some intense moments – Stimuli from enviro cannot seduce child from activity
L5 Sustained Intense Activity	Continuous + intense activity = greatest involvement. In observed period not all involvement signals need to be there, but essential ones must be present for almost all the obs period

with the principles of the Reggio Emilia approach. This approach advocates documentation of the children's responses and dialogue to develop understanding of their participation and learning in order to plan ahead, building on what has taken and held the children's interest. We both attended some of these discussion sessions, and they provided another source of valuable information.

Findings

In this chapter we have chosen to focus on detailed observations of a single child, Nancy, to show how her learning dispositions developed and changed as a result of her creative engagement with dance through the Zest project. The full study report included consideration of the results from the observation scale, case studies of two children from each school, and detail of the emerging themes.[6] Nancy's case study details her developing learning dispositions, offers examples and insights concerning key themes that emerged from the larger study, and describes how these might relate to the notion of creativity as individual, collaborative and communal.

The case study has been drawn from written descriptions of Nancy's activity identified from the observational schedules, combined with photos, video clips, observation notes made by school staff and artists, the artists' notebooks and conversations with the children. It plots and illustrates the child's unfolding experiences through the development of the project. These begin to reveal the texture and complexity of experience and the interdependent nature of setting, events, media and adult interventions with the child's responses and actions. Through this process the case study draws attention to any changes in the child's participation and to the kinds of situations which lead to the development of positive dispositions for learning.

Nancy's story

Nancy was four years old at the time of the study; she had done a small amount of dancing out of school, and was described by her teacher as quite timid. Nancy reinforced this when asked about some photos of her moving in the Zest project, she said that her favourite part of the session was 'being still' because 'I might get shy.' She was quite short for her age compared with her classmates.

The first observation of Nancy was in the second week of the project when she averaged a 3 on the involvement scale. This indicated that she was mainly, but not always continuously, engaged. Two of her observed episodes were marked as 3–4, which indicated that she had some intense moments of activity; one of these sees her 'immersed in rolling, she has sparkling eyes and looks like she is thoroughly enjoying the activity'. In terms of the dispositions for learning, alongside this level of involvement, there is evidence from this session's field notes that Nancy is 'motivated to be engaged,[7] she 'holds hands ready for the friendship dance' (the notes indicate that there was also 'excitement' for the three girls doing this and this action is not necessarily about pleasing the teachers by being ready).

There is also evidence from the data in this session that Nancy was *fascinated,* and demonstrated *persistence* and *reciprocity* in a movement exploration. This was within an activity which involved drawing round your partner's body and seeing how you physically fitted into it: 'drawing round her partner with great concentration', 'Nancy tries to fit in Jane's. Jane comments that she's not at the end … Nancy has a conversation with Anna [dance teacher] re fitting in. Anna suggests that they both try fitting into Anna's shape, they both manage it.'

The drawing and fitting activity provided Nancy with an opportunity to ask questions and explore both with her partner and the teacher to satisfy her curiosity about not fitting into her partner's shape and fitting into the teacher's shape, the latter part of the exploration prompted by Nancy herself. It should be noted that Nancy showed *persistence* rather than *resilience* here as there was no major challenge to her exploration, thus demonstrating only one dimension of the resilience disposition for learning. Regarding *reciprocity*, Nancy certainly demonstrated the confidence and inclination to give an opinion both to Jane and Anna about not fitting into Jane's shape, with the reciprocal exploration continuing both verbally and non-verbally.

The creative movement session certainly provided the space for Nancy to demonstrate the learning dispositions under scrutiny. But how did they develop across the project? For the next three observations Nancy's numerical scores only averaged 1.7. Photographic evidence from observed session 3 (12 February 2007: see Plate 30) showed Nancy sitting to the left of the picture, seemingly reticent about getting involved. The sessions had developed by this point to include creating and playing with movements in and around cardboard boxes, objects of which Nancy seemed uncertain and slightly afraid, despite her positive disposition to engage in creative movement learning in earlier sessions. In interview, her classroom teacher had described her as not wanting to try things that she thought 'I can't do'. Indeed, when interviewed about a similar image of herself from a previous session, Nancy explained 'I might get scared.' Her lack of involvement therefore made it difficult to display any of the dispositions for learning being studied. This non-involvement was not helped by a change of dance teacher to someone whom Nancy did not know, because of maternity cover a little later in the project, which seemed to add to her uncertainty.

Interestingly, during the final observation of the project Anna (the first dance teacher) dropped in to watch. Working closely near Anna initially, and with no cardboard boxes used in this session, Nancy quickly became engaged in the creative movement, even reaching a 5 (intense activity/ greatest involvement) described in the fieldnotes as:

she is happily smiling and experimenting with her body parts in front of the projector. She moves her hand. Then stands up and lifts her leg up and down from the knee, then sits on bottom and kicks legs up and down as shadow. She watches the next person intently and laughs as they do different shapes.

Plate 31 also shows her, on the far left, engaged at level 4 (continuous/intense activity): 'she freezes v well when Claire gives "freeze". She says "I'm a frog." She jumps up and down like a frog.'

Returning to the learning dispositions under scrutiny, *resilience* is not a disposition engendered for this child within the creative movement sessions, as it was acceptable to the dance teachers for any of the children, including Nancy, to not join in and persist with a particular activity if they chose not to, and for some time Nancy chose not to. However, when engaged, the last observation shows Nancy again exploring *playfully*, both in terms of her 'as if' behaviour of the frog, and also in terms of her extended movement explorations with body parts regarding how she can make shadows in front of the projector. *Motivation* and *fascination* are both also evident within this last observation, as the exploration was extended rather than momentary, and it might be suggested that because of her fascination with this process her involvement reached a classification of level 5. *Reciprocity* is harder to attribute during this episode as she is exploring on her own, but she engages with laughter at the next child's exploration, and offers an interpretation of herself out loud as a 'frog', which indicates that when she chooses to engage she does so with a reciprocal approach.

Nancy's case study was certainly not typical of the four children that the study focused on. For example, Brian, the other case study child in her class, was more persistent than Nancy. Brian persisted with a long imaginary journey with his friends, moving with a cardboard box as though he was driving a racing car, which found him then not engaging with the following exploratory activity that the dance artist instigated. However his explorations were often very playful and full-bodied, suggesting an immersion in the dance activity which was above the average for the children in the sessions. A particular episode saw Brian engaging in moving *playfully* with his shadow, seeing how its size and shape changed as he experimented with different distances from a projector, and when he turned his body into different configurations, concentrating on being upside down with his feet against the wall in a handstand position. He described it in interview as 'we liked doing it ... making it bigger'. He was, it seems, very *motivated* and *fascinated* by this experimentation, and perhaps by exploring the feeling of exhilarating movement itself.

Nancy also showed herself to be consistently more *playful* than a little boy called Leo in the other school site. Early on, Leo had a tendency to copy others and therefore was slightly behind in activities. However as the sessions went on he began to exhibit his own original movement ideas for pretend play. Although present at the first clay-making session he was absent for the first couple of weeks of creative movement sessions and so missed the settling-in period. He often gave the impression of being detached from the creative movement sessions and slightly bemused. When it came to activity, the field notes indicated that that 'L. is relying on visual cues and imitation to find his way.' However, during a later session a change occurred. The theme of running up and down pathways mapped out in the space of the room which evolved in later sessions had given rise to the idea of moving as animals. For this activity Leo crawled up and down, not a movement he had imitated from any other children. We later learned that Leo's home life is woven in with a family history of keeping horses and working with horses. His desire to be a horse and to imitate the horses in movement, such as crawling, suddenly made sense, and was subsequently endorsed by staff.

What is important here is that all the children went on a journey of some description, which saw them all develop in at least two of the dispositions for learning under scrutiny during their dance and movement sessions.

Emergent themes

This section draws themes from across the individual case studies and offers a broader analysis based on comparisons between the different nature of the activities that took place in the two schools. Carr and Claxton (2002) draw attention to what they term the 'dispositional milieu', meaning the extent to which an activity has the potential to encourage dispositions. It is clearly relevant, therefore, to examine the themes that evolved during the work and were 'co-constructed' in a two-way process between children's and artists' creative inputs, and to identify how these themes enabled the children to develop positive 'dispositions' for learning and become creatively involved.

Internal, external and self

Our analysis suggested that within the creative movement sessions there was a constant interplay and tension between movement experienced internally and movement/objects (both real and imaginary)/others perceived externally. This interplay is inherent within creative movement and dance as young children are encouraged to move and create, as well as share their creations and watch those of other children. Here, the children's developing sense of internal and external bodily (or physical) self emerged in relation to their own movements and in relation to other embodied beings and objects.

In particular, the children experienced the internal/external interplay through their work inside and outside of the cardboard boxes (see Plate

30), physically exploring body parts, relationships and sensations. In particular Brian revelled in rocking his weight in the cardboard boxes and running backwards and forwards in front of a light box to make his shadow grow and shrink on the wall in front of him. Movement dynamics were explored by the children within and outside the box shape and its enclosing or excluding framework. This was alongside other examples of their work on internal/external: for example, that seen above in Nancy's case study involving drawing around your partner and investigating your relationship with the ensuing outline.

In this project this dynamic was magnified again because of the inclusion of film and shadow work. For example, in one post-session discussion Richard (the film-maker collaborating with the dance artist) commented on how the children had 'enjoyed identifying themselves on film' (when they watched the play back) – that is, perceiving themselves and others from the outside. In the field notes one of the researchers also noted that the children were 'very engaged …. Richard is playing with the fact that he's on playback and sitting talking to them. He says "How can that be?"' (Richard played back an image of himself from seconds before, and then appeared from behind the screen to stand next to the playback image of himself.) Here the children were perceiving Richard experiencing being himself as well as perceiving an image of himself. The children and teachers were creating, presenting and watching images of themselves and others in a variety of real-time and virtual set-ups. This magnified the normal interplay in a creative movement session between internal and external, and triggered the children to experience and think about, if not to understand, how this might all be possible.

In discussing the children's experiences with the boxes, Anna, the dance teacher, commented on how one of the children had managed to cover herself entirely with a box, and another child commented, 'She's disappeared!' Anna wanted to pick up on 'this theme, keep using it, watching and looking at disappearing'. She also commented on how 'when children become informed about their own bodies, they are more able to take their own risks, through understanding their ego and social relationships, it's about knowing yourself'. The connection between internal/external and the development of some kind of self-concept working in relationship with others emerged as a strong theme in the work. This will be discussed further in the next section.

Being inside and being the outside

A similar – but differing in important respects – theme of internal/external arose from the way activity evolved at Highton School. Here working with clay gave rise to more concrete imagery from the solid material moulded into shapes and objects, which then fed into imaginative transformations in bodily movement. Thus interesting differences become apparent when the possibilities afforded by the film medium in interaction with creative movement are contrasted with the clay plus creative movement. The clay engendered two types of movement activity, the one referential, as in the case of 'being an egg', and the other of movement vocabulary; as in moving the clay as medium. To explain the second in more detail, an activity of lobbing quite large lumps of clay in the playground led to qualities of movement focused on weight and lifting. Another activity of rolling out very fine 'snakes' of clay with the hands and laying them lengthways to form lines became a stimulus for rolling movements and enacting pencil-thin lines with the body.

At Highton School a theme of eggs arose from the first week of working with the clay. The theme was continued into the creative movement sessions and evolved into a number of interesting directions. The children shaped themselves into eggs, crawled into egg shapes, either under one another or under a gym podium, and the whole group clustered, enclosed inside a stretch-Lycra 'shell'. Imaginary creatures lived in these eggs – chicks and dinosaurs mainly – and hatched out.

In her notebook Annabelle wrote that she intuitively thought the egg theme was an important one to develop with the children. Her notes (see Figure 11.1 and Plate 32) provide illustration of how the children could find ideas to elaborate around the egg theme based on their own experience, and introduce humorous ideas – playful ideas – such as being a hard-boiled egg or having laid an egg.

Notes from Annabelles's notebook

Session 1: (clay) C. rolling a smooth ball, 'it's a dinosaur egg'. 'This egg is huge!' Lots of talk with C and B about eggs and what could come out of them. B. has a TRex dinosaur egg. L. talks about Godzilla, he's bigger than TRex. C.'s egg finally breaks open and King Kong comes out.

Planning for session 2: Elements from observation to take into working: Making eggs and creatures coming out.

Session 2: Group 1 – Children rolling into a ball now. We remind children of eggs with clay – what is inside your egg? 'Baby chick, TRex, Elephant, ostrich.' Children make sharp movements and use different body parts spontaneously to push out of egg. Creatures move in different ways. J. is a 'hard boiled egg'! Some running up and down, lots of excitement. Some go back to the egg and do it again.

Group 2 – suggestion to make 'one big egg and creature all together emerges'. All together and moving and then a few break off and make own eggs. O. pretends to sit on R. – 'I've laid an egg' – and laughs. Now children make eggs in twos and threes. Now I am the egg, kneeling and R and F are under me in the egg. The two settle and are very still, espec. R. They want to stay there for a long time, very still.

Session 4: 'what shall we do to finish? Children ask to make eggs. Some choose to use the material and others want to be human eggs. C and R in golden egg, Ch, B and K use other fabric as an egg, some do egg cracking routine, C. flies as a bird, some run out, J. makes fabric into wings.'

Figure 11.1 Notes from Annabelle's notebook

The moulding of clay also gave rise to constructions of walls and doorways, which was again taken up in movement and extended into houses, castles and igloos. Thus the inside and outside theme re-emerged in another form.

Pathways

The theme of lines and running along the lines as pathways again arose from the first week of clay-working when the children created long strips of clay across the playground and ran up and down them. The pathways were transformed into masking-tape lines on the carpet floor of the hall, and on one occasion a path made of paper. The main school hall where the movement work took place offered a long open space. The children enjoyed the physical freedom and sense of energy in running up and down. Visible mappings on the floor assisted the children in learning how to manage their own movements in relation to others within the space. In later sessions pathways extended into journeys further afield, as these two notebook entries from Rod illustrate:

> The whole class had visited the Yeovil main post office and had seen how the post is sorted. They followed the journey of a letter which was posted locally and went to Edinburgh. It went by foot, bicycle, van, truck, train, airplane. So we made the journey in clay.. Some children wanted to continue working through their break time.
>
> (Rod – notebook entry, 21 March 2007)

> We continued with the idea of a journey, travelling from home to a place of their choice. Some of the children worked together in groups, going for a sleepover, to the bicycle racing track, or to the swimming pool. Another group went to the fairground. There is much more 'creative' bashing of the clay into a road, the sea, a wall, a mountain, rather than just 'bashing' the clay for the sake of it.
>
> (Rod – notebook entry, 28 March 2007)

Discussion

As this was a small-scale piece of research we would not want to make grand claims as to the applicability of its findings beyond these specific contexts. The strength of this research, however, is that it provides detailed, and in our view insightful, description of the children's experiences and the processes that took place. It is rare in an early years education arts project for two experienced researchers to be able to focus on a small number of children in frequent visits, carrying out detailed observation over the duration of the project. The intense and collaborative nature of the research supports our claim for its value and rigour. The challenge with research such as this into children's creativity is that it is dealing with things that do not lend themselves to being pinned down – but these are the essential and meaningful aspects of the children's experience for research endeavours, in our view, to attempt to understand.

What follows is a discussion which treads cautiously in considering the contribution of this project to these children's dispositions for learning and their creativity. As stated earlier, we were less interested in impact than in looking at process, and in understanding the 'how' of process, which we would argue is ultimately more useful.

Relating to the dispositions for learning

The fundamental principle upon which the project was founded was that the children's movement should be self-initiated, generated from their own imagery and movement vocabulary. The artists' role was to provide a context which would encourage the children to contribute ideas, one where their ideas would be received positively, and one that provided input to support, extend and develop those ideas. Thus the approach was dedicated to fostering creativity, imagination and playfulness. In its underlying principles, therefore, the project was already likely to offer the 'dispositional milieu' of which Carr and Claxton write. However, the project was short-term: it only lasted for twelve weeks, and so any changes that we observed were likely to be in their early stages.

Resilience, motivation and fascination

An important aspect, one that can easily be overlooked, is how much the children enjoyed the physical movement, the manipulation of the clay and the visual tricks of digital filming. It is easy in school contexts focused on achievement in cognitive skills to neglect this simple fact. The analysis shows that no strategies were needed to persuade or coerce the children into participating; with enjoyment came self-motivation and fascination – an increased 'inclination to take on learning challenges'.

The open-ended nature of the activities in this project meant that risk of failure was reduced because success was not predefined. In one sense, therefore, as suggested in the literature review, the opportunity provided by the arts activities to meet with challenges and to test out 'persistence' may actually be reduced in comparison with other more goal-directed activities. Equally, it can be argued that the movement activities provided a context for children to set their own challenges for exploration and risk-taking, thus enabling the children to develop confidence and positive self-concepts. To take part in the movement sessions, for some children, required a bold step to launch themselves into the group, or the space, and a willingness to take the risk. There were unfamiliar adults presenting a new activity in which the children had to commit themselves 'whole-bodily'. With freedom to move how you choose comes opportunities to exercise autonomy. But freedom of choice can also mean confusion and uncertainty. In the view of Carr and Claxton, 'persistence' is not something a child acquires. What might be seen are changes in the way children respond to what they perceive as challenging activities. For example, as the sessions progressed, there were some observable changes in how Nancy participated. Initially, when the teacher changed she withdrew from participating almost completely. As time went on this became more about holding back to find points of entry, and she then ultimately stepped into these and took part again.

Nevertheless, there were instances noted by both researchers of children being able to 'take time out' from activities and withdraw themselves voluntarily with no expectation that they should re-enter the activity until they were ready to by their own decision. Children would opt out, often for emotional or physical reasons, if the ongoing activity somehow overwhelmed them. A tendency to give up in the face of frustration or confusion could be interpreted as having low persistence. But learning to recover from such moments, and to do so of your own volition, could be a sign of increasing 'resilience', as evidenced by Nancy's case study.

Playfulness

The moving body can transform itself. It can become an egg and then change to become something inside the egg, as at Highton School, or represent an octopus and equally quickly change to a fish, as with the filmed movement work at Cranborn School. This requires not only a trickier imaginative projection – how to move and shape body parts to represent something – but also shifts of imaginative perspective. The transformation of movement and perceptions of self-image were considerably expanded by the possibilities afforded by the integration of digital imaging in the work at Cranborn School. The case studies demonstrated that the project sessions were high in potential for the children to exercise playfulness, imagination and experimentation.

According to constructivist views of learning, the child's mind does not simply store and copy impressions from the world, but is constantly constructing and reconstructing highly individual conceptions and representations of the world. Thus the abilities to imaginatively transform ideas, make novel connections and think analogically, for example, are key tools that assist children to develop flexible, productive learning.

Reciprocity

Importantly, reciprocity according to Carr and Claxton is about using others as a valuable learning resource, being able to both express and receive ideas. Most of the group sessions provided discussion times when children were invited to express ideas in response to open-ended questions. In terms of this project, reciprocity refers to contributing ideas not only verbally but also non-verbally. Thus creative movement provides opportunities for children to communicate and contribute non-verbally. A prime example is detailed above in Nancy's case study. It is important also to consider how the sessions supported a climate of trust – which is central to reciprocity. Working as a group, needing to be more aware of one another as they moved in and around, in contact with or in interaction with others, helped the children to build interpersonal skills and develop forms of trust. The children were trusted and then started to feel trusted. Nancy was trusted to take her time to access what the new teacher had to offer, and when she was ready she was welcomed into the activity; trust led to feeling trusted and to children's exploratory playful movement activity.

The 'dispositional milieu'

The above discussion demonstrates how the case studies exemplify resilience, motivation, fascination, playfulness and reciprocity. As well as attempting to demonstrate these influences, this small piece of research is also looking to offer understanding of process rather than purely impact.

Our analysis suggested that the dispositional milieu in the creative movement sessions included the constant interplay between movement experienced internally (inside) and movement/objects (both real and imaginary)/others perceived externally (outside). It emerged strongly as understood in relation to the children's developing sense of self. Supporting Greenland's (2001) writing about the Jabadao approach, observations within this research demonstrated children seemingly experimenting bodily with ideas of self, self-image and other – particularly through the creative movement/film work – integrated with their demonstration of learning dispositions.

To extend the connections to existing literature further, there are also strong resonances with the work of one of us, Chappell, whose recent socio-culturally grounded theorising of creativity in dance education sees it as individual, collaborative and communal (Chappell 2006, 2008). In particular there are strong parallels between the outcomes of the Zest research and an emphasis in this research on understanding the relationship between personal and shared responsibility for individual and collaborative creativity, and providing space for teacher and child creativity.

Focused on older primary children in England, Chappell's empirical study investigated three expert specialist dance teachers' conceptions of and approaches to creativity. These specialists were working in a variety of educational settings and had extensive experience as dance educators, with some degree of experience, past or present, of creating and/or performing as dance artists. The study was carried out in order to increase understanding of specialist dance teachers' conceptions and creative practice, and how these relate to theories of creativity and teaching for creativity within dance education and wider relevant education literature, particularly in light of the turn of the century creativity agenda.

The study evidenced the importance of a number of core foundations in engendering creativity. These were motivation, tenacity, an attitude which valued dance, openness to the unusual, acknowledgement of an embodied way of knowing, and reciprocity. When these are compared with the developing dispositions for learning evidenced within the Zest study, the importance of motivation, openness and reciprocity are similar, with the emphasis on embodied knowing, an additional feature of the Zest activities alongside the learning dispositions under scrutiny. Interestingly, perhaps because of the older age focus of Chappell's (2006) study, the ideas of valuing dance and tenacity are less evident; this relates to the discussion above of the young children not exhibiting resilience to challenges, only persistence. However with the importance of motivation, openness and reciprocity in common with Chappell's earlier work, when the kinds of creative process in the two studies are compared there are further similarities.

Chappell's work acknowledges the importance of understanding individual creativity but emphasises that in order to fully understand creative activity in these kinds of contexts, the collaborative and communal aspects of the process are also vital. At the heart of this theorising is the interrelationship of individual and collaborative creativity: self-responsibility in developing dance and movement ideas being brought from individual creative endeavours to inform collaborative creative activities, and outcomes of collaborative interactions being used to fuel individual creativity. Collaborative creativity is argued to involve 'shared purpose' and 'shared responsibility' for joint creative outcomes, where imagination, energy and ownership ignite the social activity, watching, responding and sharing responsibility for new ideas. Chappell also found that the integration of teacher and child creativity was vitally important to engendering collaborative and communal creative processes.

When this framework is considered in terms of the Zest research findings there are important common ideas, particularly regarding the Zest emergent themes. The focus on internal, external and self, the constant interplay between movement experienced internally and movement/objects/others perceived externally, and understood in relation to the children's developing sense of self, perhaps indicates a kind of preparation for more formal collaborative creativity when the children are older. In the Zest practice we see a focus on encouraging the children to explore the boundaries between themselves and others and to understand, albeit in a fledgling way, how their self might relate to and reciprocate with others during creative activities. The Zest themes of being inside and being the outside, and pathways also demonstrated how opportunities can be created for children to share responsibility for undertaking collaborative imaginary adventures. These were realised, for example through their play with the egg theme and the shared imaginary journeys they undertook, which were then captured in both movement and clay.

Interestingly there is less resonance between the Zest findings and the evidence provided in the previous study of communal creativity. In the research with older children this was characterised by an almost guaranteed stress on individual and collaborative outcomes wound together cumulatively into whole group dance outcomes across which children and teacher experienced shared ownership, a higher-order whole group collaboration. This was rooted in shared group movement identities developed through teachers and children cross-fertilising their ideas, and often led to children communicating ideas with and interacting with wider circles of community such as other classes in their school or their parents. Within the Zest practice there was almost no time spent on these more communally oriented, more performance-focused kinds of creative movement activity; rather the emphasis was on individual and collaborative processes. It seems most likely that this is because of the introduction of more formalised dance vocabulary and performance opportunities in older children's dance, reflecting a stronger primary school dance balance towards educating in, as well as through, dance.

This difference is important in recognising the value of exploring creating in early years settings in both practice and research. Chappell's work draws on Vera John-Steiner's (2000) theorising of creative collaboration amongst exceptional creative collaborators, developing that theorising within the context of the everyday creativity of primary school children dancing. Contexts like the early years Zest project provide an opportunity to further develop our understanding of the nuances of individual, collaborative and communal creativity. In particular, the Zest research shows how to create a particular dispositional milieu and open-ended spaces for individual and collaborative creative exploration which differ from the make-up of the dispositional milieux and kinds of spaces created in primary contexts. It is impossible to comment on the potential preparatory nature of this early years work for later collaborative and communal creativity from such a small scale study, disconnected as it is from Chappell's original empirical work. But the Zest research certainly demonstrates a more exploratory, collaborative (but not communal) process-focused approach to creativity in the early years setting.

It is also worthy of comment that the thinking underpinning all of this work is grounded in a socially distributed, relationship-oriented view of knowledge and development, critical of the notion of the solitary thinker. This is a view that often still appeals to those moulded by a western belief in individualism, and which still permeates school-based assessment systems, even those related to creativity in an educational context. This belief can lead to a view of creativity in education as marketised and over-individualised (Craft 2005), which can overpower the time and space for creativity as a group, collaborative or communal endeavour. Although a small-scale study, the findings here offer insight into what developments can occur creatively and in terms of the related learning dispositions when more collaboratively oriented creative practice is encouraged. We see evidence of the development of reciprocity and shared playfulness embedded amongst and fuelled by the other learning dispositions, contributing to the children's developing sense of internal and external physical self in relation to their own movements and to other embodied beings and objects. With such evidence we can surely strengthen the argument for considering more collaborative conceptualisations, teaching and assessment of creativity in our education systems.

Conclusion

We return to our opening Penny Greenland quotation which highlights the potential spontaneity, playfulness and openness of the two year old, compared with the eight year old. These are dispositions that the four and five year olds in this study could be halfway to losing. And yet the movement and dance activity explored in the practice and research seems to have provided the opportunity to nurture playfulness, reciprocity and fascination to varying degrees for all the case study children. Not only that, but the milieu within which this occurred seemed to provide the opportunity for inter-relating individual and collaborative creativity. This kept alive the children's explorations of themselves, others and the world around them.

A key aspect in encouraging resilience was enjoyment, and its relationship to motivation and fascination. Also, we saw that the open-ended nature of the dance activities appeared to encourage persistence rather than resilience. On occasion the open-ended nature of the activities could lead to some uncertainty and children therefore were holding back. However, because of the open-ended nature of the activities over time, the children were afforded an opportunity to build on their confidence when persisting. We therefore suggest that the question of how creative movement develops autonomy in an embodied way is worthy of further investigation. In the long term this kind of autonomy may support a more deep-rooted resilience than externally sourced motivators such as teacher approval.

The project sessions were high in potential for the children to exercise playfulness, imagination and experimentation. This is demonstrated developing over time in Nancy's story. The imaginative transformation of movement and perceptions of self-image were considerably expanded by the integration of digital imaging. Most of the group sessions provided discussion times when children were invited to express ideas in response to open-ended questions; verbal and non-verbal reciprocity was clearly in evidence (both expressing and receiving ideas). The climate of trust within the creative movement sessions was felt to be central to supporting reciprocity.

These findings indicate that this kind of creative movement work which enables children to contribute their own ideas and develop from these as starting points can provide an environment that is conducive to children developing dispositions for learning. It seems likely that those children who have most to gain from the work may need longer to arrive at a point where they can begin to show benefits. Therefore, future learning dispositions projects and accompanying research would benefit from taking place over an extended period of a year or more. The findings also demonstrate that understanding process, and including practitioners' professional knowledge and reflections in this activity, is potentially more informative to practice than research that focuses only on outcomes.

Moving on from this context, one of the challenges facing practice in the current climate is how to keep alight for older children the spirit of exploration evident in this kind of collaboratively focused early years creative practice. This is all the more important when Chappell's (2008) work on the humanising capacity of individual, collaborative and communal creativity is considered. She has argued that amongst other aspects, this humanising capacity emerges from the embodied, 'bottom-up' way of knowing prioritised within dance education, the inclusion of conflict and controversy as a live creative dynamic, and the way in which children are encouraged to interact with new cultures and subcultures as they create and share with other children and visiting adult professionals. Despite resonating with aspects of individual and collaborative creativity, this small-scale study was not able to touch on these humanising concepts in great depth, although this is not to say that the project was not tapping into them. We would like to suggest that there is certainly a case for further exploring from a very early age the contribution that dance and movement have to make to a holistic, collaborative and humanising approach to creativity in education as a balance to more individualised, over-marketised notions.

Acknowledgements

The authors would like to thank Dr Shirley Larkin, University of Exeter for her contribution to the literature review, as well as the teachers, artists, managers and children for the contribution of their perspectives to the research. The research was supported by grants from Somerset County Council and Sport England.

Notes

1 The balance may begin to be readdressed by very recent changes to the English secondary (http://curriculum.qca.org.uk/key-stages-3-and-4/skills/plts/index.aspx) and primary (http://www.dcsf.gov.uk/newprimarycurriculum/) curricula across 2009 to 2011, which for example in the secondary curriculum refocus learning on to personal learning and thinking skills, but at the time of writing it is too early to tell.
2 More information about Take Art's aims and activities can be found on their website: http://www.takeart.org.
3 The names of the schools have been changed and also the names of the children. The artists asked for their real names to be used.
4 The research was conducted within the University of Exeter's ethical guidelines for research which included parental permission.
5 We were advised in the use of these terms by Levinson (e-mail 19 March 2010), who referred us to Levinson (2007) which includes this footnote: 'My decision (re choice of terms) is determined to a large degree by participants' choices; although these varied, many preferred the term "Gypsy", often on the grounds that it distinguished them from "New Age" or "New Travellers" .... Children in schools quite often continued to state a preference for "Traveller", as the word was not associated with abuse to the same degree as "Gypsy".'
6 The report is available to download at: http://takeart.org/projects/entry/the-zest-project/start-research
7 Italicisation is used where one of the learning dispositions under scrutiny is discussed.

References

Biesta, G. (2007) 'Why "what works" won't work: evidence-based practice and the democratic deficit in educational research', *Educational Theory*, **57**(1), pp. 1–22.

Carr, M. and Claxton, G. (2002) 'Tracking the development of learning dispositions', *Assessment in Education*, **9**(1), pp. 9–37.

Chappell, K. (2006) *Creativity within Late Primary Age Dance Education: Unlocking expert specialist dance teachers conceptions and approaches*, Ph.D. thesis, London: Laban. Available at: http://kn.open.ac.uk/public/document.cfm?documentid=8627 (accessed 19 March 2010).

Chappell, K. (2008) 'Towards humanising creativity', *UNESCO Observatory E-Journal*, Special issue on creativity, policy and practice discourses: productive tensions in the new millennium, **1**(3).

Claxton, G. and Carr, M. (2004) 'A framework for teaching learning: the dynamics of disposition', *Early Years*, **24**(1), pp. 87–96.

Craft, A. (2000) *Creativity across the Primary Curriculum: Framing and developing practice*, London: Routledge.

Craft, A. (2005) *Creativity in Schools: Tensions and dilemmas*, Oxon: Routledge.

Craft, A. (forthcoming) *Creativity and Education Futures*, Stoke on Trent: Trentham Books.

Craft, A., Burnard, P., Grainger, T. and Chappell, K. (2006) *Progression in Creative Learning: Final report.* Available at: http://www.creativitycultureeducation.org/research-impact/thematic-research/ (accessed 19 March 2010).

Fisk, E. (ed.) (2000) *Champions of Change: The impact of the arts on learning,* Washington: Arts Education Partnership.

Greenland, P. (2001) *Movement Play,* Leeds: Jabadao Centre for Movement Studies.

Greenland, P. (2007) Jabadao website: http://www.jabadao.org/programmes_children_young.php (accessed 19 March 2010).

John-Steiner, V. (2000) *Creative Collaboration,* Oxford: Oxford University Press.

Laevers, F. (1994) *The Leuven Involvement Scale for Young Children (LIS-YC) Manual,* Experiential Education Series No 1, Leuven: Centre for Experiential Education.

Laevers, F. (ed.) (2005) *Sics(ziko): Well-being and Involvement in Care: A process-oriented self-evaluation instrument for care settings,* Kind and Gezin, and Research Centre for Experiential Education. Available at: http://www.kindengezin.be/Images/ZikohandleidingENG_tcm149-50761.pdf (accessed 15 November 2010).

Levinson, M. P. (2007) 'Literacy in gypsy communities: cultural capital manifested as negative assets', *American Educational Research Journal,* **44**(1), pp. 1–35.

National Advisory Committee on Creative and Cultural Education (NACCCE) (1999) *All our Futures: Creative and culture and education,* London: Department for Education and Employment.

Ridgway, J., Zawojewski, J. and Hoover, M. (2000) 'Problematising evidence-based policy and practice', *Evaluation and Research in Education,* **14**(3/4), pp. 181–92.

Rolfe, L., Platt, M. and Jobbins, V. with Craft, A., Chappell, K. and Wright, H. (in press) *Co-Participative Research in Dance-Education Partnership: Nurturing critical pedagogy and social constructivism,* Conference proceedings of the CORD Conference 2009, Leicester, UK.

Sawyer, R. K. (2003) *Group Creativity: Music, theatre, collaboration,* Mahwah, N.J.: Lawrence Erlbaum Associates.

Chapter 12

Epilogue

Dorothy Faulkner and Elizabeth Coates

The initial inspiration for this collection came from a three-day workshop on creativity and cultural education that took place during the Fifth Warwick International Early Years Conference (2005). During this workshop, delegates from around the world drew on their various national and international perspectives to discuss and debate how best to understand children's creativity. Although there was substantial agreement that existing theoretical accounts and explanations were profoundly unsatisfactory, at the end of the workshop, delegates were left with more questions than answers:

- What is the relationship between the development of thinking and the development of creativity?
- How should we accept that children's play is synonymous with creativity, and if not, how should be understand the relationship between the two?
- What is the role of adults, the environment, culture and education?
- Do we need a new theoretical framework or frameworks to explain creativity, or is it sufficient to define creative thinking in terms of existing theories of children's cognition?

Workshop delegates returned to their universities and research programmes with these questions in mind. Four to five years later, many of them responded to our invitation to contribute to this new collection and to share the theoretical, methodological and practical insights that have emerged from these research programmes. As a result, we can now go some way towards developing some answers and solutions to these questions.

While we freely acknowledge that the collection does not offer definitive answers to these questions and that it has limitations (for example, it does not address diversity specifically, nor does it address the expectations and educational practices of non-western cultures), we believe that the contributions to this edited collection are topical and timely. The authors offer new insights and discuss novel interdisciplinary theoretical and analytical frameworks. We hope that readers will be inspired by these and draw on them to inform their own theoretical and interpretive explorations of children's creative narratives. This collection highlights the importance of narrative and narrativity as explanatory concepts for understanding imaginary play, collaborative improvisation, the conversations children have about their artistic productions and the stories they create through dance, theatre and music. Contributors also draw attention to the fact that thinking about the development of creative processes in domain-specific terms is unlikely to bear fruit. Instead, they argue that theoretical frameworks must accommodate new thinking about the embodied, situated and distributed nature of cognition, the nature of multimodal representation and the role of affect. In addition, they draw attention to the need to understand the pervasive, mimetic influence of popular culture and new technologies on children's sense of identity and the ways in which they think about real and imaginary worlds. These insights raise important questions about teachers' training and continuing professional development and about school curricula, as it is clear that, in the past, these have not necessarily favoured an open-minded approach to understanding and evaluating children's creative work. It is clear that there is much that we still need to explore about what teachers and creative professionals can learn from each other, but we hope that reading about projects where this collaboration has been successful will inspire further development in this area. Finally, many authors shed considerable light on the conditions and contexts that motivate children to invest physically, emotionally, intellectually and collectively in the work of developing creative narratives both with their peers and with adults in mutually supportive and intimate play partnerships. As editors, we have found the preparation of this collection intellectually challenging and deeply rewarding. We hope that it inspires a similar response in other readers.

Index

Please note that page references to non-textual content such as illustrations will be in *italics*, while the letter 'n' will follow references to Notes.